Women as Unseen Characters

Social Anthropology in Oceania

Michele Dominy, Series Editor

A complete list of books in this series is available from the publisher.

Women as Unseen Characters

Male Ritual in Papua New Guinea

Edited by Pascale Bonnemère

PENN

University of Pennsylvania Press

Philadelphia

9 8 7 6 5 4 3 2 1

Published by
University of Pennsylvania Press
Philadelphia, Pennsylvania 19104-4011

Library of Congress Cataloging-in-Publication Data
    Women as unseen characters : male ritual in Papua New Guinea / edited by Pascale
Bonnemère.
        p. cm.
    ISBN 0-8122-3789-7 (cloth : alk. paper)
    Includes bibliographical references and index.
    1. Sambia (Papua New Guinea people)—Rites and ceremonies. 2. Kukukuku (Papua New
Guinea people)—Rites and ceremonies. 3. Women, Sambia—Social conditions. 4. Women,
Sambia—Attitudes. 5. Women, Kukukuku—Social conditions. 6. Women, Kukukuku—
Attitudes. 7. Initiation rites—Papua New Guinea—Eastern Highlands Province. 8. Puberty
rites—Papua New Guinea—Eastern Highlands Province. 9. Secret societies—Papua New
Guinea—Eastern Highlands Province. 10. Eastern Highlands Province (Papua New Guinea)—
Social life and customs. I. Bonnemère, Pascale. II. Series.
DU740.42 .W65   2004
390'.09953—dc22   2004041298

Contents

                                                          ·

Note for Readers

Throughout the book, terms given in Melanesian Tok Pisin are underlined, while those given in vernacular languages are placed in italics.

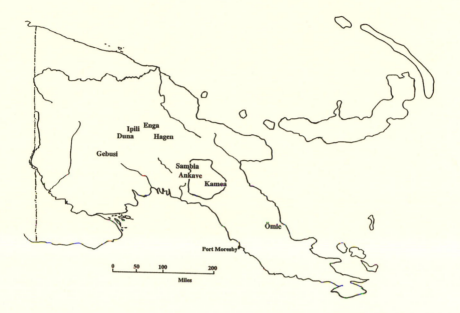

Location of case studies.

Introduction
The Presence of Women in New Guinea Secret Male Rituals: From Ritual Space to Ritual Process

During the fall of 1994, while I was in the New Guinea Highlands, male initiations were held in an Ankave valley. There I saw that, while the male novices stayed in the forest, their mothers and elder sisters were secluded together inside a vast house built of branches erected on the outskirts of the village. For the duration of the ceremonies, they left this house only in order to execute certain rigidly codified ritual gestures, and they respected a number of dietary and behavioral taboos similar to those imposed on the young boys. The presence of these close female relatives of the novices was, the Ankave told me, an absolute condition for the initiations. And it had always been this way.

This ethnographic situation did not quite match up with what I had read about the male rituals of the region. Regarded both as the place where maturation of the boys takes place and as the instrument for reproducing and legitimizing the domination of men over women, male initiations were analyzed as an exclusively masculine area founded on secrecy and on the exclusion of women (Read 1952: 5; Herdt 1987b: 72; Langness 1999: 98). Because women were effectively denied access to the male ritual *space* where the small boys lived with adult men, it was somewhat hastily deduced that they were consequently excluded from the ritual *process* itself.

Clearly the commonplace that male rituals are an exclusively male affair did not tally with the Ankave ethnographic reality. Ankave ritual practices and what men and women alike said about them drove me to broaden my focus to embrace a larger ritual "space," one that was not confined to the forest, where novices and adult men stayed during the rituals, but took in another space, located at the edge of the hamlet, where the novices' mothers were secluded. This "female" ritual space was by no means less marked by codified and imposed gestures and behaviors than the male space in the forest.

Insofar as the presence of women during male rituals had been established in other parts of the world, such as Africa, Amazonia, and Australia, it seemed unlikely that the Ankave situation, in which mothers and sisters are part of the rituals, was unique in Papua New Guinea. Although in anthropological literature in general, participation of women in such rituals has not been the object of the detailed descriptions accorded to men's acts and gestures,[1] there was enough evidence to show that male rituals concern women as well as men.

This conviction was the original stimulus for the Association for Social Anthropology in Oceania (ASAO) symposium that led to the present book. And because the island of New Guinea is home to many populations that until recently performed various collective male rituals, it seemed legitimate to center our discussion on this country, even though the aim was to raise questions of a broader nature. Moreover, thinking about the conditions in which the early fieldwork had been done in New Guinea and about the gender relations prevailing in the societies studied, it seemed to me that several factors may have combined to mask the presence of women in male rituals, and that this combination may well be peculiar to the area.

In the present introduction, I will try to clarify why analyses of male rituals in New Guinea have not regarded women as potential participants and to evaluate the implications of considering female participation for analytical models and theorizing. In other words, should we simply abandon earlier styles of analyses and develop more recent ones (e.g., Marilyn Strathern's) so as to integrate heretofore neglected ethnographical data or should we try to combine both approaches by considering them to be complementary rather than exclusive? Finally, I will develop a few relevant analytical points and illustrate them with examples taken from contributions to the present volume.

Explaining the Invisibility of Women in Analyses of New Guinea Male Rituals

The first anthropologists to work in the Highlands of what is now Papua New Guinea were men, and, given the strict compartmentalization of the male and female spheres of activity, most of their informants were also men. Their only access to the female world was therefore provided by male informants whose discourse was characterized by systematic denigration of female practices and an emphasis on the danger of too much contact with women. Under such conditions, how could these pioneers have heard of roles played by women in rituals performed for boys and organized by men? As Henrietta Moore said, writing on the representation of women in anthropological writing, the so-called male bias is "one inherent in the society being studied. Women are considered as subordinate to men in many societies, and this view of gender relations is likely to be the one communicated to the enquiring anthropologist"

(1988: 2). As a result, male anthropologists went to the forest with men under the assumption that women were doing nothing of importance in the meantime.[2] No more was needed for an important ethnographic reality to go unnoticed; and for "women's analytical 'invisibility'" (Moore 1988: 3) in anthropological accounts to continue.[3]

It is more difficult to explain why the women anthropologists who worked in Papua New Guinea did not question the purportedly all-male character of these male-organized rites. Their highly critical attitude toward the "male bias" of their masculine colleagues (Milton 1979) does not seem to have extended to the sphere of secret male rituals. Perhaps this is because male initiations had largely been discontinued by the time anthropologists—women in the main—began their critical enquiries into the role of women in such male affairs as ceremonial exchanges (M. Strathern 1972; A. Weiner 1976; Josephides 1985; Lederman 1986; see also Feil 1984).

In a world focused on the actions and words of men, a few exceptions stand out, however. One is Arve Sørum, who reported ethnographic details of women's participation in the male rites of the Bedamini, on the Papuan Plateau in Papua New Guinea.[4] Another is Annette Weiner, who called attention to the need to include women in ethnographic analyses, stressing the theoretical implications of such an approach. Using Fitz Poole's ethnographic material on the Bimin-Kuskusmin to substantiate her views, she noted that older women act as ritual leaders during the male rituals, while young women attend in their role as sisters (Weiner 1982: 59; see also 1992: 115). For some reason, however, these authors did not pursue the subject, and the few lines that did appear in their articles found no echo.[5] The question of the presence of women in male rituals remained largely unasked by anthropologists working in Melanesia and, to my knowledge, by those working in Africa or Amazonia as well. Regarded as a peripheral phenomenon (Beidelman 1997: 143–45, 311), the role of women on these occasions has not been a focus of inquiry, even with the advent of feminist studies.

The converse examples found in research on Aboriginal peoples in Australia would tend to confirm that the preponderance of the sexual-antagonism model is to be blamed for this failure to investigate the possible presence of women during male rituals. Indeed, male domination is not a major theme in the ethnographic literature on Australia, and the participation of women in male rituals was remarked on much earlier. In a survey of initiation rites in several Aboriginal groups, Monica Engelhart reports that women's participation has been noted a number of times. From ritualized attacks on the men removing the novices to operations performed on their bodies, participation during the initiations by the boys' female kin or affines is fairly common (1998: 101–9).

Earlier Studies of Secret Male Rituals of the New Guinea Highlands

Until late into the 1960s, '70s, or even '80s depending on the location, male initiations were the main collective events for a large number of New Guinea Highlands peoples; their explicit purpose—according to men and women alike—was to make young boys into adult men and warriors capable of defending their tribes against enemy attacks. Before the colonial pacification campaigns in the mountainous interior, first undertaken by Australia in the 1920s or '30s, intertribal feuding was part of the daily life of the peoples of what is now Papua New Guinea. A man was supposed to be a strong, brave fighter; to get that way, he had to leave the world of women, and above all his mother, so as to mature and to be prepared physically and psychologically to control his fear in the face of the enemy. It took time to achieve this, and boys would often leave the village for several years to live in an all-male world.

During the months of seclusion deep in the forest or on the outskirts of the hamlet, and sometimes years of shared living in a ceremonial house, novices were subjected to painful physical and psychological ordeals designed to eliminate the harmful effects of their childhood years spent in close contact with their mothers. Maternal nurturance was considered indispensable until the age of three, but it prevented the male child from reaching full maturity. Mother's milk, although vital to their health, and the foods they ate as young children later became an obstacle to their development. It was therefore necessary for the men to take things in hand and to perform the rites that would enable the young boys to attain manhood, a state that, unlike womanhood, could not be achieved without outside intervention (Read 1952: 15; Herdt, this volume).

Groups practicing male initiations were characterized by highly antagonistic gender relations (Herdt and Poole 1982). The two sexes were believed to have opposite qualities and attributes, and their activities were clearly circumscribed and contrasted. Female genitals, because they are open, represented a source of danger for men and their activities (Godelier 1986: 59). Menstrual blood, in particular, was central to a set of representations that imputed destructive powers to women, but it was also the sign of a woman's fertility. It was to menstrual blood that the peoples of the region attributed the early and seemingly spontaneous maturation of girls. Accordingly, menstrual blood and femaleness in general were usually characterized by ambivalence.[6] Women's reproductive substances were dangerous, but children nevertheless come from female bodies and women's physiological functioning was generally considered far superior to that of men. The men's ritual gestures were intended to "make boys be born again outside the mother's belly, apart from the world of women, in the world of men and by their efforts alone" (Godelier 1986: 52), after having usurped women's powers. The theme of the appropriation of specific fe-male powers of fertility is a constant in the anthropology of this region (Lattas 1989); it refers both to men's ritual use of objects that once belonged to women (as we see in the secret myths) and to certain ritual gestures that act out female physiological events. The first anthropologists to work in the Highlands be-lieved that male feelings of inferiority lay behind the initiation machinery of these groups (Read 1952: 15).

But rather than attempting an in-depth analysis of the symbols manipulated in these male rituals that would offer an interpretation of their cultural mean-ing, the anthropologists working in New Guinea in the 1950s and 1960s strove primarily to discern the social context in which these rituals were imbedded (Langness 1967; Meggitt 1964). They came to realize that in the Eastern High-lands, where warfare with neighboring groups was frequent, women regarded as polluting, and gender relations marked by antagonism, male initiations were the principal collective event. Further west, in the world of "big men" and large-scale "economic" exchange networks, women seemed to enjoy higher status, partly because of their role in raising the pigs that were the primary medium of exchange and partly because of their position as link between the groups involved in these exchanges, who were related by affinity. Instead of ini-tiations in the strict sense of the word, these peoples organized rituals both for young unmarried men (bachelor cults) and for mature men to promote fertil-ity (female spirit cults). In each case, men would enter into contact with a fe-male spiritual being who would transform them physically and mentally and endow them with competence in matters of exchange. Among peoples cele-brating such cults, exchanges occupied a more important position than did war (Feil 1987: 64), and that is how anthropologists came to define the contrasting cultural configurations. On one side, intertribal warfare, strong male domina-tion, and initiations seemed to go together: this combination characterized what came to be known as "great men societies." On the other, large-scale cer-emonial exchanges, less opposition between the sexes, and male cults based on the intervention of a female spirit seemed to form a single social logic: that of the "big men societies."

Although early ethnographies revealed the openness of Melanesian cultures (see, e.g., Mead 1938: 165; Wagner 1972: 19–33), more recently an increasing number of studies have shown the extent to which mythological lore, exchange systems, and cults circulated (Wiessner, this volume). But while a fair amount of mutual borrowing, translation, and reinterpretation of ritual practices be-tween neighboring communities exists (Biersack 1995b; Wiessner and Tumu 1998; Ballard 1999; Strathern and Stewart 2000b), there are no examples of Western Highland groups having abandoned spirit cults for male initiations, or of Eastern Highland groups having abandoned male initiations for bachelor cults. Such a situation would seem to indicate that import and circulation of rituals occurs only when it fits into the cultural context.

Whether the early analyses were comparative (Allen 1967; Meggitt 1964; A. Strathern 1970b) or not (Read 1952; Langness 1967), they elucidated the over-all sociological contexts of the male initiations, on the one hand, and of the fe-male spirit cults, on the other. In contrast, the 1970s and 1980s produced numerous monographs featuring symbolic interpretations of male rituals.[7] While these studies did not mention participation of flesh-and-blood women, anthropologists had long remarked the presence of symbols associated with femaleness and had interpreted certain ritual scenes as enactments of epi-sodes of the female physiological cycle, such as menstruation (Hogbin 1970; Lewis 1980) or childbirth (Tuzin 1980).[8] Such interpretations confirmed that initiations in this part of the world indeed fit the general rites-of-passage model outlined by van Gennep at the beginning of the twentieth cen-tury. Yet no attempt had ever been made to identify and analyze the particu-lar forms of these general themes as they appeared in specific cultural or historical contexts.

More generally, as Bruce Knauft writes (this volume), until the start of the 1980s, anthropological research leaned toward a view of the construction of personhood that, in accordance with a system of ideas proper to the West, considers individuals independently of the relationships in which they live (see also LiPuma 1998: 53–54). Viewing male initiation as a ritual institution concerning the male individual alone fit in perfectly with this perspective. It was only when Marilyn Strathern published her work in the 1980s that the accent shifted to the relational dimension of personhood. As we know, she argued that, in Melanesia, persons are considered to be the sum of the relations from which they stem and which make them what they become (M. Strathern 1988: 92–93, 96). From individual, a person goes on to become "dividual" (13), that is, "defined by relationality rather than individuality" (Strathern and Stewart 2000a: 63).[9]

Although in the present case my questions emerge from my own fieldwork, there is no doubt that the reanalysis of ethnographic material on male initia-tions in the context of the relational personhood proposed here has the po-tential to yield valuable insights. It would complement the understanding derived from gender categories, oppositions, and relations of domination with analyses of moments when the person is the object of manipulations aimed at transforming the configuration of relationships of which he or she is the prod-uct. When women participate in the rituals, as Ankave mothers do, occupying a special collective ritual house at the edge of the hamlet while their sons stay in the forest, the relational configuration in which they are embedded auto-matically claims the anthropologist's attention.

Male and female ritual spaces may be distinct in a geographical or physical sense, but they are joined by an invisible thread running between the main characters occupying the spaces: the novices in the bush and their mothers near the hamlet. It is on this particular relationship that the so-called male ritual operates, transforming it into a relation of another kind. In effect, the two ritual spaces are two connected loci involved in a ritual process designed to transform certain relations. It is this whole process that calls for analysis, since dealing with only one of the ritual spaces, as has often been the case, tends to obliterate this processual and dynamic aspect of the ritual.

Thus, when one sees women as agents rather than subordinated persons in both ceremonial exchange and secret male rituals, it becomes clear that such rituals are not restricted to the male person, but that they also alter relations between the novices and a number of persons with whom they are connected. Initiation rituals manipulate first and foremost the relationship between the novices and their mothers, whereas female spirit cults reenact other connections between men and women, more along the lines of affinity.

What to Expect of a Focus on Women in Male Rituals?

The present volume is therefore intended first of all to remedy an undeniable gap in the ethnographies of New Guinea societies and in women's studies. Three main types of male ritual, which had customarily been considered separately,[10] are discussed in the present work. The *initiations* to which all boys of an age-grade are subjected, without exception, in order to grow to manhood are discussed by Sandra Bamford, Gilbert Herdt, Pierre Lemonnier, Marta Rohatynskyj, and myself. For the boys in all these groups, the presence of flesh-and-blood women is essential for the ritual process, although to varying degrees.

In *bachelor cults*, on the other hand, the young men are not obliged by older men to attend; however, virtually all of them participate in the hope of improving their physical appearance and mental and social competence, and thereby being judged to be ready for marriage. They usually go through the ritual several times, establishing a relationship akin to marriage with a female spirit who will, among other things, protect them from the dangers stemming from sexual relations with human wives. Aletta Biersack and Polly Wiessner analyze this relationship as it appears respectively among the Ipili and their eastern neighbors, the Enga.

Last, when celebrating *female spirit cults*, which are aimed at restoring the overall fertility of land and humans and assuring success in ceremonial exchange, male ritual experts enter into contact with a female spirit who will restore lost fertility if the proper ritual operations are performed. Although theirs is a comparative essay, Strathern and Stewart's analysis emphasizes female objects manipulated by men in spirit cults. Wiessner's contribution is largely devoted to the development, import, and export of Enga male rituals and to their impact on homogenizing values throughout Enga and on altering relationships between men and women as ceremonial exchange expanded.

Because most of the chapters presented here offer fresh data, they invite new ways of thinking about questions that specialists in ritual or gender anthropology have been asking from the start. They show that, by inquiring into the modalities of women's participation in male rituals, anthropologists stand to gain an altogether different perspective on the same phenomenon (A. Weiner 1982: 51).

But does the suggestion that male rituals transform certain relational configurations in the course of the life cycle of the two genders imply that the ideological dimension that has always been foregrounded in the analyses of these rituals must now be relegated to the background? In other words, can these rituals still be interpreted as an institution for maintaining and legitimizing male domination in the framework defining the Melanesian person as "dividual" or relational? Must our interpretive models be overhauled? Or might we not in the end attempt to combine both perspectives so as to encompass the multiple meanings and aims such a complex ritual institution is bound to have?

It would of course have been ideal to have the broadest range possible of ethnographic cases when approaching these questions. However, such scope cannot be achieved in a single volume. Important omissions include the Mountain Ok peoples, where the women watched the novices dance and the mothers and sisters of the initiates felt responsible for their appearance (Barth 1987: 39). The Sepik region, for which we also have detailed analyses of male rites (e.g., Lewis 1980; Roscoe 1990; Tuzin 1980), would also have its place in such a line of research, even though these studies stress the exclusion of women rather than their possible involvement.[11]

Furthermore, as Knauft writes in this volume, it is a pity that the question of the women's role in male rituals arises just when information on these ceremonies is becoming increasingly scarce as a result of their frequent abandonment.[12] From the outset, when in 1998 I began organizing a workshop in the context of the annual ASAO meeting, I realized that very few anthropologists had observed what women did during male rituals, and that any comparison would have to be based on information gathered in different times and settings.

Some groups, like the Ankave, still live far enough from established administrative posts and churches for their ritual practices not to have been too affected. My own chapter is thus based on information that Pierre Lemonnier and I collected in the 1990s. On the other hand, Marta Rohatynskyj had to base her analysis of the Ömie initiations, last held in the 1940s, on the memories of old men who were initiated as children. As she notes, this situation influences the content of the accounts and therefore the type of interpretation that can be carried out. Fortunately, however, while some information is inevitably lost in such a situation, the remembered experiences can also be considered to be those that participants felt were important for understanding the ritual as a whole.[13]

The Notion of Women's Participation

As the contributions to this volume show, the notion of women's participation can cover a variety of realities. If we consider, at least as a starting point, that the presence of flesh-and-blood women is only one way in which men manipulate female symbols, we must ask ourselves what this presence means. In other words, are the women participating in the ritual representing themselves, or do they represent other persons and thus act as proxies? Or are they symbols of a reality located somewhere outside themselves, of something that might have to do, for instance, with general fertility (see A. Weiner 1982: 59; Herdt, this volume)? This raises another important question: does the presence of flesh-and-blood women need to be analyzed in the same way as that of spiritual female characters or objects connected with femaleness? Does it have its own specificity?

The present volume grapples with these questions. Some of the contributors consider the participation of real women (Bamford, Bonnemère, Rohatynskyj, Lemonnier, Knauft), others focus on spirit women (Biersack, Wiessner), while still others consider both real women and spiritual female figures (Herdt) or both spirit women and objects symbolic of femaleness (Strathern and Stewart). It is only by analyzing all these situations that we will learn whether women's participation is to be taken as the sign of a literal presence, metaphorical presence, or both.

According to the authors of this volume, the notion of participation of flesh-and-blood women refers to different realities. For some, like Strathern and Stewart, this includes the tasks women perform in the context of ritual preparations, such as food collecting, and the taboos they obey as a group. For others, it refers to their presence alongside men at the collective dances that open or close the celebrations in the immediate vicinity of the hamlets (Bamford, this volume). For still others, it designates the ritual seclusion of the mothers while their sons are secluded in the forest (Bonnemère, this volume).

Would the variety of situations be better served by a graduated scale of female participation (Lemonnier, this volume)? Whereas Strathern and Stewart use a presence/absence model, others think that the forms of participation need to be differentiated according to their nature. In their search for a global heuristic model to replace and oppose what they call the "Male Exclusivity Model," which reigned supreme until lately, these two authors suggest the notion of "Collaborative Model." This model includes any intervention whatsoever on the part of women and gives equal importance to the participation of men and women (see Lemonnier, this volume, for a discussion of this point). The question is, then, whether it is valid to place attitudes imposed on all members of the community, at the time of rituals, on a par with restrictions to which only a highly circumscribed category of women (the novices' mothers or sisters in particular) are subjected.

It is precisely our task, I believe, to identify and interpret the female interventions that involve a very specific segment of the female population (novices'
mothers or sisters, for instance, or "female ritual guardians" among the Sambia). In placing such interventions on an equal footing with tasks incumbent on
all women at the time of any ritual, such as food preparation or abstinence
from sexual relations, there is the risk of obliterating distinctions that could
turn out to be significant (see Herdt, this volume) both for analyzing the presence of women in a particular male ritual and for comparing rituals in which
this presence is of a different nature. In all events, we should not prejudge the
relevance or the nonrelevance of paying attention to differences in detail, to
the nuances (Lemonnier, this volume) in the ways women participate in male
rituals, before having made the effort to distinguish between the identities and
activities of participating women. It seems to me that conducting a fine-
grained study of this sort is the only way to move the analysis forward and to
allow us to see women as potential agents in male ritual practices and to understand these practices as dealing with the relational configuration boys are
part of rather than as focusing only on their individual person.

A Palette of Forms of Female Participation

When women take part in male initiation ceremonies or in episodes of these
ceremonies, the entire female community or only a circumscribed category of
women, for instance the novices' mothers, may participate. In the two Southern Anga groups described here (Ankave and Kamea), the women are secluded for the duration of the rituals in a special house made of branches. As
Bamford writes, "throughout this time [the seclusion of the boys] the fates of
a mother and her son are completely intertwined" (this volume). The types of
behavior in general, and the food taboos in particular, that mothers and sons
must respect is an additional indication of this "symbiotic" or "fusional" relationship.

For Herdt, writing on the Sambia, the fact that "the mother is symbolically
identified with the boy to be initiated is perfectly obvious from many of the key
rites and processes set in motion" (Herdt, this volume). Above all, what the
mother does and what the novice undergoes have reciprocal effects. This may
also be exemplary of what M. Strathern called "the unitary identity between
mother and child" (1988: 321).

So it appears that, in order for male initiation to make young boys into adult
men and, formerly, into warriors capable of defending their community
against enemy attack, it must first alter the relationship between a mother and
her son. A confirmation that this is indeed the case can be found in the fact
that today the Kamea do not initiate boys who have lost their mothers, yet they
allow them to take part in the male cult. As Bamford says, in her own terms,
"the son has, by his mother's death, already been 'de-contained'" (this vol-

ume). But the staging of the separation between mother and son can take various forms. Among the Ankave, the presence of the "real" mothers is required and the process is gradual, manifested by food taboos and special behaviors that must be respected for weeks not only by the mothers but also by their sons; furthermore, the outcome of the ritual, the transformed mother-son relationship, is materialized by a gift of game presented to their mothers by the novices upon their return to the village. The former symbiotic relationship between a mother and her son has become an exchange relationship (M. Strathern 1988: 222), in which the boy can now be an agent and no longer simply the product of the actions of others, particularly his mother. Among the Sambia, things are different: the severance of the bond between the mothers and their sons, to whom they are allowed to give one last bit of food and affection before the long years of separation to come, is violently dramatized (see below).

In all cases, male initiations enact the separation between mothers and their sons, as studies influenced by developmental psychology suggested several decades ago (Whiting et al. 1961: 361).[14] Earlier analyses of Anga rituals (those of the Baruya and the Sambia) developed another perspective, however. Godelier, for the Baruya, and to a lesser extent, Herdt, for the Sambia, tended to place this transformation of the symbiotic character of the mother-son bond in the context of the distance that must be established with respect to the world of women in general. In fact, before the present volume, their work did not address the question of the part played in the ritual by the novices' mothers. Now, with Herdt's contribution and the references to information gathered from Baruya women in my own chapter, the gap is at least beginning to be filled.

By taking the participation of women (here the novices' mothers) as seriously as that of the boys, we can no longer simply say that, to become adult men, the boys must first be separated from their mothers and that this is this the only process the ritual is enacting. Although such a statement is surely true, it is not sufficient. What actually seems to be going on here is not only the boy's accession to the status of subject in his own right, but a redefinition of the whole relational configuration around him. As Marta Rohatynskyj writes of the Ömie, in addition to severing the nurturing bond, initiations also bring about the social transformation of the status of the mother and of her relationship to the land of her spouse (this volume).

In other words, male initiations do not concern exclusively boys or even men, as earlier works, whether they were psychologically oriented or used a male-domination model, tended to conclude. Although these two aspects (male ontology and reproduction of a power hierarchy between the genders) are present, they do not exhaust the subject. The special attitudes the other persons involved in the ritual process must adopt lead us back to the innovative analysis of Melanesian sociality that Marilyn Strathern proposed in *The Gender of the Gift*. In a word, she posited that, in Melanesia, the person "is a *microcosm of relations*" (1988: 131).[15] If we adopt such a view, to make a male person grow or to prepare him for marriage the ritual should bear on the relations of which he is composed. For a change in his person to occur, the relational system of which he is the product must somehow be reconfigured. And we can presume that, for the relational system to be successfully reorganized, the presence of both terms of the relation is necessary, which is precisely the case in some of the male rituals analyzed here.

Although the Sambia isolated several categories of women (mothers, female ritual guardians, but also the older sisters of the novices) and gave them specific parts to play, they also assigned the anonymous community of women an important role. Herdt calls these collective yet perfectly codified and predictable manifestations "women's rituals of resistance" (this volume). In them, the mothers, together with the other village women, would cling to their sons as they were torn from them and led away, thereby entering openly into conflict with the men's group. For Herdt, this collective manifestation signals negation of femininity in the rhetorical and symbolic structure of the ritual and in the subjectivity of the men (this volume). In the first phase of this sequence, the older women lectured, scolded, and physically harassed the boys so threateningly that the men, initially approving, felt compelled to come to the boys' rescue. The episode left the novices with the impression of a female authority that was moralizing, punitive, and generally negative. At the same time, the men had gradually taken on the protective roles ritually assigned to the female ritual guardians (Herdt, this volume).

Among the Sambia, the female ritual guardians had a key role, since they were the women who accompanied the novices during certain ordeals. They were also closely associated with their male counterparts, the male ritual guardians, metaphorical but rarely classificatory mother's brothers. Both were surrogates for the novice's mother, fulfilling the role of protector during the ordeals, of "partner in pain," and they too were required to respect the prohibitions on use of names and on sexual relations that applied to relations with kin. This ethnography clearly shows that, when dealing with female participation in male rituals, one cannot avoid the question of "human surrogates" for, in particular contexts, women connected with the novices, most often their mothers, are replaced by other women, or by men,[16] who take on their role. From this point of view, in Anga initiations, the maternal uncle present at the novice's side, who protects his sister's son,[17] takes some of the blows meant for him, and empathizes with him, no doubt displays the attitude and posture the boy's mother would have adopted had she been able to be there.

What does this tell us? First, that some categories of women are excluded from some ritual spaces. Among the Sambia, while we just saw that the mothers of the boys participate in the collective "rebellion" of the women, other women (the female ritual guardians, as Herdt calls them) take on the mothers' role during some of the ordeals undergone by the novices. This clearly indicates that presence of the mothers themselves in the "ordeal ritual space" is impossible.

Does this imply that they are also excluded from the ritual process? To try to answer this question, I will again take the Ankave case. As I have said, the Ankave male initiations involve two geographically distinct ritual spaces: one, the forest, is occupied exclusively by boys and men; the other, the collective female house on the edge of the hamlet, is occupied exclusively by their mothers.

These two spaces are closely interconnected, as the behaviors and taboos that must be respected by both parties indicate. What relates them is their inclusion as part of the same ritual process, a process that affects both parties and that in the end will result in the relationship between them having been transformed. Once the initiation rituals are concluded, the Ankave boys have unquestionably undergone a change: people even say that they look different. But the primary object of the ritualized transformation is their relation with their mothers, which can be seen as a necessary condition for the success of the boys' own transformation into adult men. What we have here is a transformational process that connects the two ritual spaces by a powerful but not geographically inscribed link. Clearly, the relevant parameter here is not so much the ritual space but the ritual process.

Returning now to the question of proxies, I am inclined to think that the presence of such a figure in a ritual may not have much to do with the ritual process itself: a proxy replaces a person in those spaces where the person's physical presence is forbidden, provided of course the proxy's own identity makes him or her locally a legitimate substitute. In other words, the ritual process is clearly operating, whether it is the "real person" or his or her proxy who is physically present.

In the context of the present volume, which also contains analyses of female spirit cults, yet another question springs to mind: can these female spiritual figures, who live in the high forest, which is a male ritual space, be regarded as proxies for real women?

Let us start by asking who this spirit is and what is the nature of the initiates' relationship with her. In Ipili as in Hagen origin myths, the female spirit is a virgin woman who sacrificed herself and who, instead of having children, gave birth to rituals for protecting men from women (A. Strathern 1970b: 578; Clark 1999: 13). Concretely she is also the source of material objects (mainly bamboo tubes, bog iris, and sacred stones) which, manipulated by men in the rituals, sometimes served as vehicles for their relationship with her. The specialists contributing to this volume have all interpreted this spirit, with whom young bachelors enter into contact during their stays in the upper forest, as a wife for young bachelors, but a virgin one with a closed vagina, who will protect them from the pollution of their human wife's menstrual flow and will bring health, prosperity, and fertility to the entire clan (Wiessner, this volume).

Is it then possible to consider this spiritual figure as a surrogate for fertile women (the bachelors' future spouses, for example) who cannot enter the ritual space,[18] thus following the same line of interpretation as in the case of the Sambia female ritual guardians, who are substitutes for the boys' own mothers in ritual spaces they cannot themselves enter? In his writings on the Sambia mythic female flute spirit, who is present in secret ritual contexts, Herdt proposed that this figure is hostile to other women (Herdt 1981: 283), and that the boys are as though "married" to her (Herdt 1989: 350). The flute spirit is a liminal figure, at once the secret side of the female ritual guardian, with no doubt her maternal attributes,[19] and the spiritual wife who ensures the transition from boyhood to husbandhood. Thus, the Sambia flute spirit is a sort of "double proxy," as it were, combining two aspects in her person, the first, maternal, which she shares with the female ritual guardian, and the second, conjugal, which anticipates the novice's future status.

The hypothesis that the female spirit encountered in bachelors' and female spirit cults is a surrogate for the real wife may well reveal a common structure between rituals that are usually considered separately because they are formally different.

Conclusion

One of the major contributions of this book is of course to shift the focus of the analysis of secret male rituals. In effect, in directing attention to women's participation in these events, we cease to see them as being focused exclusively on boys and come to consider instead that they bring about a transformation of the relationships that bind these boys to their kin. In considering different kinds of female involvement in so-called male rituals, we are brought to understand that, if the boys are transformed into adult men, it is not so much because their bodies and minds have been subject to ordeals as because the relations they were made of have been totally reconfigured. We could say the same for their mothers. At different points over the life cycle of persons of both sexes, such transformations in their relational identity occur. The best way to see this process at work during secret male rituals is to focus on the persons to whom novices are related rather than on the novices alone.

I would now like to come back to some of the analytical points raised in the course of this introduction. Would it be fruitful for example to articulate the discussion about the necessary distinction between "ritual space" and "ritual process" with the question of proxies and the issue of the relational configuration being changed through and by the ritual? We have already seen that the question of surrogates may have to do not so much with the ritual process itself as with a system of classification and ordering spaces and persons, a sort of cosmology that attributes or prohibits some spaces to some categories of persons (male/female, spiritual beings/human beings, etc.). Seen in this light, the presence of proxies, whatever their nature and whoever they may replace, would certainly say something—indeed much—about the cosmological system underlying the organization of ritual spaces but less perhaps about the ritual dynamics. Of course, when a proxy stands in for a mother, it says something different about the purpose of the ritual than when a proxy stands in for a future wife. But I suggest, admittedly as a slight provocation, that the presence of proxies may well be considered independently of the ritual itself, and that it would say more about the local cosmology than about the underlying ritual process. In other words, analyzing the proxies can lead to an explanation of the visible forms the ritual takes and offer a way to reveal the local representations concerning ritual spaces, secrecy, taboos, and so on, but it would not say much about the relation-transforming process that comes into view when one focuses not merely on the novices but on all participants in a ritual process.

Finally I would like to make it clear that my aim in inviting a number of specialists to discuss the potential implications of the presence of women in male rituals was not to dismiss earlier analyses of male rituals on the grounds that some crucial ethnographical data was lacking at the time. I hoped that this discussion would be far more productive than that: indeed, I hoped to show that male rituals are complex phenomena and as such need a multidimensional approach in order to be fully and adequately analyzed. In other words, there seems to me to be no reason to present analyses in terms of male domination as being opposed to those emphasizing the psychological dimensions of the constitution of the male subject, or to yet others proposing that the purpose of these rituals is to transform the relational system of the male person. It seems more reasonable to attempt to combine them, precisely because male rituals do—and are—all this at once. Of course, the fact that the women linked to the boys are included in the ritual process may favor the last interpretation, but this does not invalidate the idea that initiations are also an institution in which gender inequality is reproduced and as well a place where psychic life-conflicts are reenacted and resolved.

Translated by Nora Scott

Chapter 1
Sambia Women's Positionality and Men's Rituals

Gilbert Herdt

The interpretation of gender positionality and hegemony have long been de-
bated in the literature, with scholars differing on the degree to which material
or ideological factors, or religious and ritual factors, or both, are primary in
how men and women interact.[1] As the work of Kenneth Read (1952) hinted
and Donald Tuzin (1980) in particular has stressed in Melanesia, the relationship between positionality and domination in the domestic sphere can differ
greatly from or even contradict matters in ritual. Maurice Godelier's (1986)
critical work among the Baruya has generally opened up the richer complex of
material, ideological, and sexual factors on the subject of male domination of
women.[2] Pascale Bonnemère (1996) is a new notable study of gender relations
and symbolic elaboration among the Ankave, an Anga area people. She shows
clearly the complex of factors that create parallels in the experience of men
and women, with a variety of ritual practices, both secret and public, underlying women's positionality in Ankave society. My own work among the Sambia
of Papua New Guinea has focused upon how sexuality and secrecy are critical
to the formation of male subjectivity and desires: male/female relations in
general and the cultural reality and homosociality of the men's house in particular create gender hierarchies between older and younger males (Herdt
1992, 1999a, b).

The Sambia collective male initiations include the first-stage, second-
stage, and third-stage rites, that form the Sambia "Mokeiyu" cycle of collective practices, spatially centered around the raising of a great men's cult
house every three to four years. The positionality of women in these events
has remained incomplete in my own writing (Herdt 1981, 1987b, 1999b).
However, among the neighboring Baruya, as described by Godelier (1986),
women's knowledge of male ritual, as well as their positionality vis-à-vis
men, leads to the impression that women's presence was a vital and neces-

sary ingredient of the success of male ritual performance (Bateson 1958 [1936]; Schwimmer 1984).

Thus, among the Sambia as well as the Baruya, women are brought into the arena of men's ritual. The men understand this as symbolically necessary and vital to the cultural performance, but they complain about it and regard the women as polluting and a nuisance to manage. It is as if the men desire for the women to serve as their primary audience, as Gregory Bateson once observed for the Iatmul, even though they complain about it. Women's positions in these events suggest that the men are transforming the women in certain ways, or— to take Marilyn Strathern's felicitous phrase—that the men are "making complete" what is incomplete (especially the status and sexuality of the boy-initiates) through the material and/or symbolic presence of women (1988). This view is well established in the Melanesian literature now—the product of a new perspective from gender studies and feminism, again, substantiated in the work of Marilyn Strathern most famously, as well as in Annette Weiner, Gillian Gillison, and the recent collection of Nancy Lutkehaus and Paul Roscoe (1995). Bruce Knauft (1999), in his important review of this area, has critically contrasted Melanesia and Amazonia, questioning the stability of "social organization" and "warfare" in tradition, and the postcolonial positionality of men and women's identities and material status.

Among the historical Sambia, women are, by custom as well as by male belief, a necessary "audience" for certain ritual male performances. However, women may only be present materially in public, never in secret. Women are represented by men's praxis in secret by icons and symbols, or sometimes by the proxy of a male actor who "performs" as or "fills in the cultural space" of women. For example, cassowaries are typically represented as "women" in secret praxis, and men who impersonate the flute spirit are dressed and serve as the proxy for male ideas about women (Herdt 1981). Why must women be kept removed physically from the secret rites? We enter here into the fundamental issues of ritual rhetorics and schismogenesis (Bateson 1935); of structural gender relations, well studied by Schwimmer (1984); and of male ritual secrecy, a large topic that has been treated elsewhere (Herdt 2003). What is particular to the Sambia men's ideology is to regard women's bodily powers as polluting to boys and a general threat to the men's secret society. Thus, as I have suggested before, the absence of the women in secret contexts enables men to create and instill a hierarchy of homosociality among the newly initiated or recruited boys, recently taken from their mothers; the absence of women also enables the men to abrogate the generative powers of women (e.g., menstruation and parturition), and thus to permit the secret knowledge that the men alone give birth to boys, have the boys menstruate, and suckle them into manhood through insemination (Herdt 1981).

In this chapter I will describe and analyze the position of women in men's rituals and the "positional" relationship between women and men in Sambia men's rituals.[3] The concept of "positionality" indicates both the symbolic status of the structural position taken by a woman or women in a particular ritual and the meanings men attribute to this position. In the latter sense, the position of women in certain ritual events is signified by secret male representations or icons, or by the performances of male persons that express these meanings.[4]

Here, I highlight four distinctive forms of women's positionality in men's rituals. All these types occur in the Mokeiyu ritual cycle, performed every three or four years by the Sambia. First is the generative position of female bodies, their fluids and reproductive functions, which are drawn upon symbolically and materially in raising the men's ritual cult house. Second is the structural role of a woman who serves as the female ritual "guardian" mother (the counterpart of the male ritual guardian or "father") in public practices; she gives ornaments to decorate, and she is also protective of the boy in public beating rites, for which she must be repaid in prestations by the boy and his male kin. Third is the collective practice of women in certain rituals of rebellion, a form of positionality that is the most active "voice" in protecting and protesting the "theft" of boys as sons from women and the women's community. Fourth and last is the moral pedagogy of women in publicly teaching and scolding boys, assuming a moral authoritative "voice" rarely allowed by men, as the boys are treated situationally not as sons but as prospective husbands and sons-in-law by the aggressive women. This marks a shift in the subjectivity and moral careers of the boys vis-à-vis their relations to the world of women.

One issue that always complicates such an analysis should be highlighted for a moment: ritual secrecy. Due to the existence of ritual secrecy as a separate sign system, existing apart from public discourse in the political economy of the village, the meaning of any object is always contingent upon the setting and the type of linguistic praxis. Thus, again, to speak of cassowaries in public is to speak of the mysterious ostrich-like bird which prowls the forests and which men hunt; in secret, the cassowary is a primary signifier for women, its meat forbidden to boys and women, and the ornaments made from it a means of representing the flute spirits as well (Herdt 1981). Likewise, the rhetoric of men about women must be marked off in ritual by a careful delineation of which women the men are referring to on any occasion. That is, Sambia men's discursive use of "women" in ritual and in language depends upon categorical distinctions made (in the first- and second-stage ritual initiations) between the mothers of boys, the category of female ritual guardians, and marriageable women, over all other women who participate in the male ritual. Sambia men's discourses about women also cut along these lines: the distinction between women related by kinship, especially within the nuclear family, and women who are unrelated and may become the object of marriage pursuits or sexual interest. This difference parallels a public/secret distinction also: public discourse lumps all women together at the most inclusive level of rhetorical cultural representations, generally depicting women as polluting, depleting, and disloyal, whereas secret discourse splits the imagery of women between marriageable and kin-related.

Sambia Male Rituals

In the period of the mid-1970s when initial fieldwork was conducted, the Sambia numbered some 2,000 people living in extremely rugged, isolated mountain valleys of the Eastern Highlands of Papua New Guinea. Airstrips and roads were absent, and first contact had occurred within the previous decade. The Sambia hamlets were built atop steep ridges formerly barricaded against enemy assault. The harsh beauty of the land belied the fierce, endemic warfare that pervaded Sambia life before pacification in 1964. Descent was generally patrilineal and residence was patrilocal; hamlets were composed of tiny exogamous patriclans that facilitated both intra-hamlet marriage and male solidarity in times of war. All marriage was arranged between clans by elders; social relationships between the sexes were not only ritually polarized but often hostile at the interpersonal level, although this tended to change as the couple had children and aged. Like other Highlands societies, these segmentary descent groups were associated with a men's secret society that ideologically disparaged women as inferior, dangerous creatures who could pollute men and deplete them of their masculine substance.

Since warfare was endemic, nagging, and destructive, and pacification was a recent memory, the male cult remained of supreme importance in local cultural and social tradition. Village gender relations were still based on the need to create and support a force of warriors on whom community survival depended. That defensive warriorhood was guaranteed by collective ritual initiations connecting neighboring hamlets. Males became members of a politically volatile regional age-grade of co-initiates. Within a hamlet, this warriorhood was locally identified with the men's clubhouse, wherein all initiated bachelors resided. Married men also frequented the clubhouse constantly, and on occasion (during fight times, rituals, or their wives' menstrual periods) they slept there. But once married, men normally lived with their wives in separate "women's houses" elsewhere in the hamlet—an institutional arrangement that makes Sambia anomalous compared to most Highlands people's enforcement of separate residence for the sexes.

The male secret cult was organized through six initiation grades that early on removed boys from their mothers and natal households, conscripting them into an authoritarian, male hierarchical system. First-stage (for boys seven to ten years old), second-stage (ages eleven to thirteen), and third-stage (youths aged fourteen to sixteen) initiations are collectively performed on boys as age-sets every three or four years by the confederacy of neighboring hamlets. Initiates reside exclusively in the clubhouse and absolutely avoid all interaction with females, including their mothers, on pain of severe punishment, including death. Only at fourth-stage initiation—performed for youths sixteen years and older, depending on their being assigned a girl for marriage—the formal marriage ceremony, does this absolute female avoidance change. Minimal contact with females is thereafter permitted, but heterosexual coitus remains forbidden until the adolescent wife's menarche. Only then may the girl, who has stayed with her parents, begin cohabiting separately with her husband. For the young man, his wife's menarche is celebrated in fifth-stage initiation rites that secretly focus on a painful nosebleeding and other bodily purifications. Last, a year or so later, the birth of a child triggers sixth-stage initiation and accords the young father, especially after the birth of his second child, full adult status.

Ritualized boy-inseminating practices are the object of the most vital and secret ritual teachings in first-stage initiation, and they tend to take on the most dramatic focus in men's narratives and later depictions of the events. The novices are expected to be orally inseminated. Homoerotic relationships are rigidly structured: novices may only act as fellators in private, appropriate sexual contacts with older bachelors, who are seen as dominant and primarily in control of the same-sex contacts.[5] The adolescent youth is the erotically active party during fellatio, for his erection and ejaculation are necessary for intercourse, and a boy's oral insemination is the socially prescribed outcome of the encounter. These rules mean that boy-insemination—as well as heterosexual coupling—occurs mainly between males of hostile groups who sometimes warred. Ritual insemination of boys is hidden from women and children; it is purported to have nutritive functions in "growing" (masculinizing) boys. Puberty and third-stage initiation result in the psychosexual transition from fellator to sexually mature fellated. Following the marriage rite, which occurs before the betrothed woman achieves menarche, he should slow down his involvement in boy-inseminating practices; with the achievement of fatherhood, the vast number of Sambia men become exclusively heterosexual.

Sambia conceive of the development of maleness and femaleness as fundamentally different. Biological femaleness is considered "naturally" competent and innately complete; maleness, on the other hand, is considered more problematic, since males are believed incapable of achieving adult reproductive manliness without ritual treatment. All males have a semen organ (*keriku-keriku*), but in boys this remains immature and empty, while in girls it will not activate. The purpose of ritual insemination is to fill up the organ and hence to masculinize a boy's body, ultimately masculinizing his phallus.

By contrast to boys, girls do not have initiations until they are well into their adolescence, typically beginning with the girl's ceremonial marriage to a youth. This event, often between the ages of fourteen and seventeen, comes before menarche, which is late (on average, nineteen years). However, girls are believed to be born with female genitalia, a birth canal, a womb, and, behind that, a functional menstrual-blood organ or *tingu*. An infant girl's *tingu* is thought to contain a smear of her mother's menstrual blood transmitted while she is still in utero. Following birth, that blood increases, filling the *tingu*, activating somatic development, and hastening motor coordination, speech, and overall reproductive maturation. This endogenous operator of femaleness eventually stimulates the appearance of secondary sex traits—especially breast enlargement and the menses. Feminine behaviors like success in gardening and mothering are also by-products. As the *tingu* and womb become engorged with blood, puberty and menarche occur; the menses regularly follow, and they are linked with the women's childbearing capacities. This initiates the girl's second initiation ceremony, at menarche, around age nineteen. All a woman then needs is a penis (i.e., semen) to facilitate adult reproductive competence: childbirth. Birth initiates the final initiation. These female ritual events occur in the menstrual hut and are secret and forbidden to men.

In my own work on the Sambia of Papua New Guinea, I have had little to say until now about the series of ritual events and symbolic positions of the great collective Mokeiyu cycle that locates women within the arena of men's initiation rites. Particularly regarding the first-stage *moku* initiation of boys aged seven to ten, the role of their mothers, female ritual guardians, male ritual guardians, and symbolic proxies for women inside the men's house all raise critical questions: Are women themselves undergoing a "rite de passage" during the male initiations? If so, what is the purpose or ritual intention of such a symbolic positioning of the women? Should we regard the changes in women's rites and duties, along with changes in temporal and spatial movements, as indications of liminality in women? My answer in general is yes. However, before I enter into the reasons for this, it is important to outline the Sambia ritual system and the positionality of women within it, since a clear structural pattern emerges from the overview.

The Positionality of Women in the Ritual System

The Sambia Mokeiyu cycle, performed every three or four years, is a grand seasonal event that articulates gender relations and the larger cluster of political relationships between groups. With respect to the male initiations, the women's participation is greatest in the launching of the Mokeiyu cycle itself, which includes the raising of a great cult house, and involves men and women who are related to the boy to be initiated. The symbolism grounds the collective ethos of emotions, gender avoidance, ritual cooperation, and exchanges that will unfold over the months that follow. This set of opening events then folds into the ritual events of the first-stage *moku* initiation, wherein women play important rhetorical, and material roles, as discussed below. The second-stage initiation, performed two or three years later, also has women engaged, though not as much as in the first-stage initiation, since the ritual events are shorter and less elaborate. Following this, the role of women declines markedly, and while they play a role in the opening ceremonies of the third-stage initiation, especially night-time dancing and feasts, they are totally left out of the ritual events that follow. During that time, their role as audience emerges, and they continue to take this role, with a few minor exceptions played from time to time by senior women and great women. In short, the women's agency declines and all but falls off. What accounts for this change?

In the first-stage initiation, the mother of the boy-initiate plays a pivotal role in providing material resources for the events that follow, as well as in taking a position at key stages of the events. That the mother is symbolically identified with the boy to be initiated is perfectly obvious from many of the key rites and processes set in motion, such as the very idea that the boy must be "separated" from his mother to grow "big and strong" and move over to the men's house. A part of this rhetoric is the understanding that the treatment of the boy has an effect upon his mother and what the mother does has an effect upon the boy. The mother and father are thus enjoined to strict sexual abstinence during the time of the Mokeiyu. Should the parents (especially the mother) violate this taboo, it is strongly believed that the initiate will be weak or sick, that his face will turn black, or that he will revert to a baby-like appearance, become ugly and stunted, and prematurely die. The materiality of resource provision consists of feast-crops and gardens the mother must plant, tend, and harvest (tubers, greens, bananas, etc.). It also involves bringing in material for the cult house raising at the outset of the Mokeiyu cycle. The mother is also responsible for weaving a new grass sporran for her son. When the events begin, she is expected to play a role in the thrashing rites staged in public at the beginning of the initiation, primarily by following the boy, who is carried on the back of his male ritual guardian, between the two lines of men. The mother will also attend to her son on the final night before the ritual procession or parade, and in the moonlight she will feed smoked frog to her son—the last food from her hands to reach him. Finally, she will play a role of wailing for the boy and at other times become part of the audience of the men's rites.

The residential segregation and the reshuffling of the genders at the time of initiation, and throughout the Mokeiyu cycle, is genuinely impressive. During the weeks and months that bring on the rites, not only is sexual abstinence enjoined, but the couple often reside apart, particularly after the hunting parties (which include a team of men and women, fathers and mothers of the initiates-to-be, including the boys themselves) are over, the game having been procured for the *moku* feasts. The husbands go to live in the men's house or the cult house. The women are left with their children in their regular domiciles; during the rituals, they build lean-tos and live with other women on the fringes of the initiation cult-house dancegrounds. Sometimes there are scores of these little camps dotted all around the great cult house.

Through residential segregation and regrouping, then, Sambia communities as a whole undergo patterned liminal changes necessary to accomplish the vast change in social status positions of "les rites de passage" (Herdt 1987b). The mother (as well as the father) undergoes a temporary change in symbolic positionality, which factors into the role that women take as the Mokeiyu cult seasonal cycle progresses (see also van Baal 1966).

The Generative Positionality of Women at the Cult House Raising

The positionality of women in the cult-house construction is cosmic and generative, assuming the powers of what might be called a mythic woman, akin to the Cassowary female spirit well known from Sambia myth (see Herdt 1981, chap. 5). The women make their grand entrance to the cult-house raising ceremonies as the mothers of the boys, and the "female ritual guardians" of the initiates come bearing bundles of wild cane for the thatching. Other women are present to watch; many have children, including their soon-to-be initiated. Several older initiates are dispatched to the forest to collect the "male grass" necessary for completing the crown of the thatch, overlaid on the "weaker" female roofing to protect the male occupants. Inside the house, hidden within an inner "secret house," a group of four flute-players (younger bachelors and men) wind their instruments as plaintive melodies. The ritual specialist "sings out," and this signals to all the men—everyone except the aged—to mount the house and wait on its roof. The danceground is now cleared for the women to enter. Here the spatial symmetry of sexual separation is most clear: men on top, women on the ground.

The women then form a line and dance impressively—assembling as "cassowaries" who are wild and present the bounty and generativity of nature in its fullness. There are some forty of them, mostly the mothers or female ritual sponsors (*nenaanjiku*, mother's sister), though a few nubile maidens (older sisters of boys) are among them. Their impressiveness stems from their decorations as well as their numbers: new grass skirts are everywhere, the finest necklaces and amulets—feathers, cowry shells, possum and pig tails, rattan, and flowers—grace their necks. Red New Guinea impatiens highlight their hair and form garlands on their chests and skirts. They carry red cordylines and other red flowers in their hands and grass bundles. The thatching is bundled on their backs. Most of the women have yellow mud painted on their faces, limbs, and torsos as well.

These Cassowary women enter as a close-knit and well-practiced train of rhythmic bodies, a long snake of hissing and hopping figures. Their noise is strong and shrill; they are frightening to the boy-initiates. One can hear the men compare the hiss to the challenging cassowary, which aggressively charges humans when cornered.[6] For some time the women circle the house, raising a cloud of dust. Then they throw down their bundles and stand dead in their tracks. A ritual leader takes over, and the women are sought out from above by

particular men up on the roof, who are responsible for completing the thatching with the gifts brought by the women. They are the fathers, brothers, and
male ritual guardians of the boys. Each bundle of grass thatching is handed to
a man perched on a pole-ladder.

The women were symbolically "appointed" in the night by the *kowup'ndumdu*
flutes. This custom indicates, by a few stalks of cane grass placed on the
doorsteps of the women, that they must collect thatching for the cult-house
roof (*kowup'ndumbu: dumbu*, you bring it, *kowup'n*, kunai/ or grass) on the following day. Now they can expect remuneration for their work. The women
themselves have decided beforehand who will ask for and receive selected return gifts. For example, a woman who knows that a certain man (the boy's father or ritual sponsor) has bark capes to give will attach an old bark cape to her
grass bundle. Several prestations are possible.[7]

Meanwhile, inside the secret hiding house, the flutes continuously blow, a
background to the women's ceremony, but a perplexing combination of what
is hidden and revealed in such close quarters. This drama of what is revealed
and what is hidden to boys and women already presages the key role of women
being present but also hidden from the flute-players. One by one the women
advance to present their thatching. As a woman calls the name of a man atop,
she hands the bundle up to him and then steps back. He in turn inspects the
thatching to identify the giver and name the expected return prestation. He
then responds, "You (woman-donor's name) should go to an *aruku* reed garden."[8] This signifies that the woman has been appointed to complete the next
requirement of initiation preparations: the weaving of a new *kuwatni'u* grass
sporran for the boy-initiate. Later, while the men are possum-hunting, these
women complete the skirts, for which they are also remunerated. They will in
general receive gifts of smoked possum or other meats, as well as bits of ceremonial salt and trade goods.

The generative role of providing the thatching, and later the boys' new grass
skirts, indicates the lack of completeness of the initiates; their dependence
upon their "mothers" and female labor; and the symbolic vitality of female fe-
cundity, especially at the cosmic level of the Cassowary women. That only
women can perform this role and thus fill the cultural space necessary suggests
the interdependence of men and women in the cosmic scheme of ritual regeneration.

Female Guardians—Substitute Mothers

The appointment of these female guardians creates a new category of female
ritual participants, who are more directly involved in the organizational arrangements, primarily by being responsible for some of the material requirements of the boys who will complete the Mokeiyu cycle. Female guardians are
classed as *nenaanjiku*, which in this context is "mother's surrogate." The *nenaan-*

jiku assumes the same taboos as the boy's mother, being unable to eat or drink in front of the boy or to say the boy's baby name. Ultimately, however, the female guardian is quintessentially a liminal position, as the role has little influence past the first-stage initiation, since, ideologically, the boy should shed all remains of the women's world and influence in taking up his male ritual personhood in the men's house. This female ritual figure looms as a central icon for the boy's ritual treatment and pedagogy throughout the first-stage initiation, intruding the presence of intimate women constantly into the ritual process.

The counterpart of the female sponsor is the *nyetyangu*, "mother's brother," either metaphorical or more rarely classificatory, a position of greater import and more lasting influence for far longer in the boy-initiate's life cycle. Sometimes a husband and wife from another village will take the parallel parts of *ne-naanjiku* and *nyetyangu*. Generally, however, sponsors are distinct ritual players unrelated to one another. The male ritual sponsor's greater role stems from the fact that he not only protects the boy and provides some material support for his first-stage initiation, but is a mentor to the initiate in the strict sense of the term in all matters of ritual knowledge, including sexual pedagogy. Sambia metaphorically refer to the *nyetyangu* as a "male mother," whose symbolic properties are to nurture the boy—feeding him during the ritual ordeals—as well as to carry him through onerous ceremonies and be exposed to thrashings and other punishments in tandem with the boy, a "partner in pain." Sambia indeed think of this more in maternal terms by the expression, "we cried together," as a result of these ordeals and pain—this is something not said of the father of the boy, who is absent from many of the ordeals, or of the female ritual guardian.

Moreover, the taboos of the male initiate/ritual guardian relationship are marked and rigid, though the relationship between the pair is generally warm and affectionate. A boy may not ever say the name of his guardians, male or female, in public or private; the name avoidance is a mirror of the mother/son taboo, which in later life is most commonly mirrored in the husband/wife relationship. Thus, the boy is forbidden to eat or drink in the presence of his sponsors and must avoid shaming them in public. Furthermore, all sexual intercourse is forbidden with either guardian—a barrier that extends the incest taboo from mother and father to ritual guardian "mother and father." During the long years of the boy's ritual career, in which he generally avoids all sexual matters in the presence of his father, the initiate turns to his *nyetyangu* for guidance in sexual relations (though his father is critical in the supply of ritual knowledge to aid the boy in preserving his strength and purity).

One of the foremost tasks of the female guardian, in concert with the male guardian, is to help protect the boy's body from being harshly thrashed in public ceremonies. This is regarded as a painful burden, and the women complain about it. During the first-stage initiation, the boys are taken into a sequence of thrashing rites over a period of days. The structure is simple and always the same: two lines of men and older initiates stand opposite each other, and use sticks and bundles of sticks to beat the backs and sides of the boys who pass between them. During the public thrashing, the women take a dual position—protecting the boy, in tandem with his ritual guardian, on whose back the boy is carried through the lines of thrashers, as well as being audience to the events.

A woman stands behind each boy as he is prepared for being carried down the gauntlet and thrashed. Thus, the trio moves as a group—the male ritual sponsor, the boy on his back, and his female guardian or mother following behind. The role of the mother is to protect the boy's behind, which she tries to do by holding a bundle of leaves over his naked rear end as he is thrashed by males on both sides. As she walks behind the boy, she, like the initiate and his male guardian, is fair game to be thrashed as well, and it is a favorite game (particularly of the young bachelors) to see if they can swat the woman hard enough to force her down on her knees. Indeed, this happens, and the men are merciless in flogging women who slip and fall or succumb to the blows, until they get up and are able to resume the position of protecting the boy.

The woman has a moral and ritual responsibility to take the position of sharing in the pain of "changing the boy's skin" through the thrashing, which literally is believed to cast off the dead skin flakes and residue of mother and female contact. Hence, the trio, man, boy, and woman, are all subjected to the ordeal and pain, and all may "cry together," though the ritual idiom recognizes only the shared experience of male guardian and initiate.

The symbolic positions of the ritual guardians may then be summarized as follows. (1) The female guardian provides some of the material aspects needed for proper ceremonial initiation, especially the grass thatching for the cult-house roof, as well as a grass skirt and some foodstuffs. (2) The guardian must take a public role in helping to protect the boy from the flogging of painful thrashing ceremonies, thus exposing herself to thrashings as well. (3) Unlike the male guardian, a woman assumes the taboos of a boy's mother, in avoiding physical contact and all sexuality with the boy as he matures. (4) The invocation of taboos that typically surround the mother and husband/wife relationship with respect to the boy-initiate suggests that an imaginary presence is brought into the secret ritual initiations.

This final dimension of the female guardian draws upon the imagery of women kept removed from the ritual processes except in public events, whereas in secret the mythic female flute spirit is drawn upon as an idealized cultural form. While the metaphoric power of the female ritual guardian is kept in check by a variety of forces and other symbols, most importantly the affectionate bond with the male ritual guardian, her influence is limited in time and space. By contrast, the omnipresent influence—ideological/mythical and in practice—of the flute spirit is very wide, overlaps with certain functions of the guardians, and supersedes the male guardians' imaginal power in the way the flutes displace the actual men in the pedagogy of ritual insemination of the boys.

Women's Rituals of Resistance

Sambia women, often ideologically dominated by men, for a short time create a space for resistance during the Mokeiyu cycle. The symbolic valence of this practice is far more important in rhetoric than the actual experience, though the latter is something remarkable to observe. Only twice, and then only in the first-stage initiation, is a structural position provided for women to take on a "rebellious" role; it has the flavor provided by Read's (1965) classic account of Gahuku-Gama women attempting to taunt and momentarily challenge men in their *nama* cycle of initiations. I would guess that once upon a time, in pre-colonial social formations, this sort of liminal rebellion was far more common than today, in which the social memory is represented in many New Guinea societies as a set of mythical events (Gillison 1993).

The Sambia occasion of female ritual rebellion occurs during the first several days of activities, when the Mokeiyu has gotten underway. I am unsure of the composition of the women's "gang" of rebels, though they surely include some of the mothers and sisters of the boys and no doubt their female ritual guardians as well. The social time around the nose-bleeding rites, which I have described in previous publications, seems to set off a mood of rebellion and counter-reaction in the men, especially the elders (Herdt 1982, 1987b). Some of these women, mostly younger nubile females, form a "hunting" party outfitted with bows and arrows, which is remarkable because women are not allowed to hunt with bow and arrows. They disappear into the grassland bordering the forest into which the boys will be carried for the first secret rites, particularly the nose-bleeding. A slight danger lurks here; the women are of course forbidden to enter any of the surrounds of the forest when the men are lodging there and hosting secret rites. To be discovered might bring death, and the men are constantly threatened by this, though they also joke about the ridiculousness of such a possibility—a true liminal time. The female flute spirit also watches over the men's doings, and would strike out against any female interloper, it is believed; she is feared by men and women alike.

The women rebels assemble and, from a distance, throw sticks and stones, taunt, and vaguely threaten the men with their bow and arrows. They imply that the boy-initiates have been stolen from their mothers and should be returned. They ridicule the men with obscenities. Some of the women have taken their cue from the Cassowary women performers from the original cult-house raising ceremonies, and momentarily dance and make threatening gestures in the same manner. I observed this ritual drama on two occasions and was surprised at how seriously the men regarded the challenge. Some of the younger men were genuinely angry at the women, with the attitude, "How dare they insult us!" The men then began to shout obscenities back at them, threatening them with arrows and even mocking them for a bit. The women generally ran off and responded with jokes and humor, but they got themselves out of the vicinity to prevent the men from retaliating further.

The second occasion of rebellion occurs during the night-time singing and dancing fests surrounding the great bonfire of the cult-house danceground. Here, on the second or third evening of the ritual events, before it gets too late, the women will stage a last-ditch effort to take back their sons (see Herdt 1987b: 132–39). Here the actual mothers of the boys are prominent; they are joined by the female ritual guardians and sometimes the older sisters of the boys. The initiates are being moved around in the company of a great body of men, and are specifically being shouldered, in general by their male ritual guardians. Now the male guardian feels the burden of responsibility in "holding on" to the boy and keeping him from being "recaptured" by the women. Eventually the men and boys tire and the boy simply walks beside the older man, but the male guardian is typically careful to keep the face of the boy shrouded by a bark cape so as to elude observation by the crowd of women and children. This becomes a game, common to male initiation ceremonies, in which the audience tries to see through the facade and decorations of the male performers, in order to learn their "personal identities."

Eventually a moment will come in the night-time dancing and singing when the women mass and their courage emboldens them to try to locate their sons and steal them away for a time: a liminal process of flux and change, when the physical control of the boys is in doubt. The male guardians often put up quite a fight, but the women by custom prevail. The mothers may take back their sons and have a last time with them, talking and crying or feeding the boys. The men give up control of the boys to the women because they know that before dawn the women must surrender them again, according to custom, as the boys will be led into the meadows for a purification with the morning dew at dawn, and then into the forest for more severe ordeals. Meanwhile, women take the boys and lead them in dancing around the fire; at first boisterous and vigorous, there is a feeling of frolic about this interlude. The carnival atmosphere, the jokes and jostling, the sense of momentary truce in the "battle between the sexes," together with the bright fire and colorful garb, all lend a memorable epic sense of a struggle of wills between the genders—as distinct categories if not in fact groups. The scene will change shortly after the men resume control.

This ritual of rebellion has a final counterpart that must be mentioned here. The next night, the mothers and female guardians take on their last active role—intruding into the male hegemony of the night-time ceremonies and again taking physical control of the initiates. This is typically accomplished by the mother of the boy, unless she is absent, deceased, or otherwise unable to play her role, in which case the female ritual guardian fills in. For one last time the initiates can be with their mothers, eat food directly from their hands, and spend a few quiet moments alone talking and holding hands in the company of other mother/son couples in the vicinity of the danceground. The boys are fed a special food, smoked frog, which the mothers have hunted with traps, and the delicacy is savored by the boys. The mothers are all too aware that their sons are forbidden to speak or interact with them again, once the female-avoidance taboos are implemented, until they are grown up and married, at which time youths move out of the men's house. The context of this final occasion is dramatic and sad, and the sorrowful mood is highlighted by the words of the mother: "You must leave me now; can't see me anymore. You must go off to the men's house."[9] This event occurs close to dawn, when the boys are thrust into the ordeals of bloodletting rites and the penis and flute ceremony, with the result that anxiety grips the men and boys alike.

The men grow impatient after a while, perhaps an hour: they want the boys back, and a struggle with pushing and pulling ensues. Eventually the men prevail and they begin to lead the boys back into the dancing, which continues till dawn, whereupon they move off as a body to the forest. Only the following evening do the women surface again for their last significant ritual role.

The Moral Pedagogy of Women in Public Ceremonies

On the second or third night of dancing and circling the bonfire on the cult-house danceground, a special ceremony is held to conclude the festivities for that day. The leaders are senior women, some of the mothers of the boys, and whoever else volunteers to enter the circle of the fire. I have described this ceremony elsewhere (Herdt 1987b: 132–36). I think the report that follows is typical of many Eastern Highland societies that provided a similar structural role for women at some point in male initiation ceremonies (e.g., Hays and Hays 1982; see also Reay 1992).

This is to be the final public occasion on which the women and boys will ever interact in face-to-face relationships, and the mood is serious and accusatory. The main actors are the female elders, to some extent held at bay by the male elders—who, on this occasion, uniquely assume the position of actually protecting the boys from being unduly harassed verbally and flogged too hard by the women. These elders may incidentally include the mothers and female guardians of the boys.

After a significant bonfire is built, and women dance around it, creating a dramatic display for the huge audience assembled, the women proceed to line up and lecture the boys. The women exhort the initiates to do their work and be responsible in all the round of seasonal economic duties, especially hunting, and also the necessary chores of collecting firewood for their mothers and later their wives. The women constantly exhort the boys "to think of their mothers in coming years." The initiates are scolded and reprimanded for their "lazy" ways, for "sassing" and "talking back" to their mothers and female elders. The more the women talk, the more they egg each other on, becoming more excited and critical, and gradually encompassing the adult men in their general critique of how the boys ignore the needs and welfare of their mothers. At the end of the performance, the women take up firebrands and strike each of the boys on the chest. Then they proceed to stomp the fire out with their feet.

On the two occasions of this female rhetoric I witnessed, the women were very strong, forceful, and full of fire in their speeches. I was indeed impressed by how far the women would go in their stern, even stinging reprimands of their boys and their admonitions to the men to be more mindful of their obligations to women and families. The men observed this, mostly approvingly, until the end. But as the rhetoric peaked, and one woman grew increasingly high-minded in tone and speech, she drew reactions from the crowd of men. I noticed that the other women were confident and generally emotionally supportive of this moral attack on boys and men.

One of the men got angry at the women for chastising the boys too much and began to lecture the women back. Another male elder, feeling the sting of the women's words, took up a firebrand and waved it threateningly at the women, telling them to cease. One of the reasons this occasion is remarkable is because of the male belief that words of chastisement and criticism can physically harm children, especially boys. In fact, Sambia men strongly believe that women's negative words directed toward boys are a prime force in stunting boys' growth or even making them sick. (This is a key reason why boys must be nose-bled soon after— "to remove the bad words of the women lodged in their noses and insides"; see Herdt 1987b.)

Here, I want to underline the importance of the physical presence of women in an event, as I once did in analyzing the structure of nose-bleeding rites (Herdt 1982). There are two reasons for this stress. One is that Sambia ritual ideology and subjectivity always proceed from a negation of women and femininity to an affirmation of men and masculinity, in which the purging of some female aspect (such as menstrual blood supposedly lodged in the body of a male) is a necessary precondition to the ritual implantation of semen, male foods, and ritual leaves, that follows the purging. The presence of women, my thesis goes, is the signal for negation in the rhetorical and symbolic structure of the ritual and in the subjectivity of the men. Thus, women's presence instigates a process of substitution in which the "female" element is displaced by a "male" one (M. Strathern 1988).

The second reason is my view that Sambia culture idealizes the male object, as the primary object of desire and attraction—on all levels (Herdt 1999a, b). This suggests that the men, by introducing the physical presence of the women as highly critical and negative, even striking blows against the boys with their firebrands, leave an impression of female authority that is quite negative and punitive in the minds of the boy-initiates. Through this ritual process, the men are actually preparing the boys for the resocialization of their desires away from the women and toward the men.

Here, I mean by desires the desire for boy-insemination and the desire to create emotional bonds of a different kind with the boys, thus changing the conditions for sociality and agency in the boys after initiation, planting the seeds for a bisexual development in the long years of living in the men's house. A change in desires, then, consolidates a fundamental change in personhood in the boys, which is produced by the initiations.

This remarkable transformation in the subjectivity and moral careers of the boys, vis-à-vis their relations to the world of women, paves the way for the future of the initiates. Although the women and the female guardians begin their positionality as generators and protectors of the boys, the men gradually assume this role and supplant the women in it. Concomitantly, the women's latter moral probity and their scorn for the boys creates the effect of lumping all males together, splitting up the women's emotional alliances, and signaling an end to the primary bond of mother and child. In its place, the women's rhetoric recognizes the new alliance of men with boys and signals that the main role of the initiates in future is as prospective son-in-law and husband. The shift in the subjectivity of desires for the women thus parallels the change in the boys' desires: they socially desire to be men and for a time erotically bond with the older males, while the women divest themselves of emotional (erotic) relationship to their sons and pave the way for a new kind of relationship between the boys and the world of women. This final dimension of women's positionality is a matter of the political economy of Sambia society, as well as the necessary gender segregation that moves males into alliance with men and women into eventual marriages with men.

Conclusion

For the Sambia, as for other Papua New Guinea peoples, renewed appreciation for the symbolic placement of women in male ritual suggests that we rethink the deeper core of gender and sociality in the Melanesian world. At stake in the early critiques of these matters, such as in Lindenbaum (1972) and Feil (1987), were interpretations of male domination, of women's roles and of women's greater than appreciated control of production (see Herdt 1992). For Godelier (1986), the matter of male domination of women was certain, though he saw the men's uses of the ritual domain and symbolic hegemony equally as manipulation and moral responsibility. The women were coopted and made agreeable to being the "guilty parties" of the male imagination, in Godelier's (1986) sense, by the men, who lent them just enough but not too much power to take on moral and political authority in liminal periods. I have had a good deal to say about this in my earlier work and need not repeat myself here, other than to note that we still need much greater understanding of men's and women's subjectivities of these processes (Herdt 1999b; Herdt and Stoller 1990). Clearly, this is a complex topic, in precolonial society as well as today; for as Knauft (1999: 180) has noted, this constitutes an "articulation between indigenous and contemporary notions of power and stigma."

Godelier's ethnography on the male domination of women, which takes a male point of view of course, finds structural and symbolic parallels in many Sambia customs, but we must now see the issues differently in the light of the new work among the Ankave. The work of Pascale Bonnemère in a series of papers, together with the writings of Pierre Lemonnier, and then most recently Bonnemère's book, *Le pandanus rouge* (1996), all provide valuable insights in contrasting the Ankave people of the southern fringe with the more northern Anga peoples. Gender roles, male beliefs about substance, economic activities, kinship cycles, and family relations are highly reminiscent of but show discernible differences with the Baruya and Sambia peoples. The Ankave daily pattern of gender and ritual relations is more amicable and softer; there is greater fluidity in residential arrangements; and ritual seems to promote less domination and makes much less use of the threat of violence than either the Northern Anga societies or the Eastern Highland precolonial peoples more generally. Thus, I would not expect a dramatic transformation of women's positionality in Ankave male rituals such as I have suggested for the Sambia.

In the precolonial world of the Sambia (especially prior to 1960), the roles of men and women were highly polarized and politically in opposition, in the condition proverbially described in the research literature as "sexual antagonism" (Langness 1967). The women, who came from other villages, invariably hostile and sometimes enemies of war, were forever regarded as alien and were mistrusted. They could never completely escape the accusation of betrayal. The residential segregation of unmarried, vulnerable initiates living in the men's clubhouse, tabooed to the women and children living in the women's houses, symbolized this deep structure of perceived social and material difference in village life. The bond created between mothers and their children was one of intense and anxious attachment that is difficult for us to imagine in the contemporary world (Herdt 1981). I believe that this developmental condition was very special in its effects upon the inhibition of agency among boys and sexual subjectivity in the initiates. Likewise, as the above account tries to show, the women's attachment to their sons was so profound that it required a patterned sequence of de-ritualization, or de-individuation, for the women to assume a necessary larger perspective on their social rights and duties.

Sambia women had a structural position that created contradictions and opportunities for transformation at the time of the men's ritual cycle. Women were present as placeholders and symbolic voices and objects in male ritual at different junctures and situations among the Sambia in precolonial times. Women's positionality took four distinctive forms, as I have shown, each of which successively moved away from the generative and then the maternal role toward the procreative and political role of prospective moral accuser, in the body of sexual partner and wife. The liminal ways in which these forms of positionality were expressed, including the rebellious role and the scolding moral voice of the final phases, were distinctive of a world of divides between what was public and secret, intimate and intensely political. The sum of the parts, to take Marilyn Strathern's phrase, was to make complete for women what was incomplete—but not through their own rituals as much as through the ritual treatment of their own male flesh, their sons. Ultimately, then, women's positionality was a patterned construction of reaction to an intensely gendered social and political economy.

Chapter 2
Embodiments of Detachment: Engendering Agency in the Highlands of Papua New Guinea

Sandra C. Bamford

The societies of Papua New Guinea have long occupied a prominent place with respect to the development of anthropological ideas of gender. Throughout much of the country, males and females appear as polarized beings who are not only different, but anathema to one another. As many ethnographers have noted (see, e.g., Herdt 1981; Meigs 1984; Langness 1967; Read 1972; Herdt and Poole 1982; Lindenbaum 1984; Godelier 1986; Meggitt 1964), the distinct sexual substances of men and women are often seen to adversely affect members of the opposite sex. A pervasive gender dichotomy is also revealed in a strict division of labor, where males and females are not only assigned to different productive domains, but are believed to be incapable of carrying out the work of the other.

Most analyses of male initiation in Melanesia have taken the existence of this dichotomy as their underlying baseline and have attempted to chart how it comes to be reproduced through time. Here, the men's cult is seen as an important vehicle through which boys acquire a masculine identity (Herdt 1981, 1987) and learn what is expected of them as adult male members of the community. Initiation, we are told, teaches boys how to be men. Yet, more than the creation of a gendered being is at stake. In many anthropological accounts, the rituals of the men's cult also operate as a political weapon through which men instantiate and perpetuate their domination over women. Because men maintain exclusive control over the ritual process and the sacred cult objects, their ascendancy over the world of women comes to be stamped with cosmological significance (Langness 1967, 1974; Meggitt 1964; Read 1952; Godelier 1986). Initiation, thus, emerges as a war between the sexes: one that pits men against women and reproduces a system of unequal power relations.[1]

The Kamea of highland New Guinea, with whom I conducted ethnographic research, represent a particularly interesting case to consider in light of the aforementioned paradigm. In particular, I wish to draw attention to three features of their initiation system:

1. In contrast to what has commonly been reported in the ethnographic literature, Kamea women figure intimately in the proceedings of the men's cult.
2. One of the most important tasks assigned to women at initiation is to guard the bullroarers (*mautwa*)—a preeminent symbol of male cult life.
3. If a boy's mother dies before he enters the men's cult, his initiation is seen to be unnecessary. Motherless boys are free to participate in men's cult-house activities without having to undergo initiation themselves.

In what follows, I shall be concerned with interpreting these facts. I will argue that an adequate understanding of Kamea initiation is contingent upon treating gender as a nonessentialized state. Here, the world is not seen to rest upon a ready-made system of cultural distinctions in need of being perpetuated; *it is the act of constituting those distinctions in the first place which is the aim of social action* (see Wagner 1975, 1977; M. Strathern 1988). As I shall demonstrate, Kamea initiation operates as a process of "de-containment" whereby a composite social form—a mother-son dyad—is differentiated to yield two separate gendered identities. Men do not reproduce other men independently of women. Rather, both sexes engender the social world through their mutually elicitive actions (M. Strathern 1988, 1993; Wagner 1975, 1977). The end result of this process is not the reproduction of an enduring political hierarchy, but rather the ongoing elicitation of meaningful social identities.

Ethnographic Background

The Kamea are a highland people who number some 14,000 and occupy the heavily forested interior of Gulf Province, Papua New Guinea.[2] Linguistically and culturally they belong to the Angan ethnic group who are, perhaps, best known to anthropological audiences through the ethnographic writings of Maurice Godelier (1982, 1986) and Gilbert Herdt (1981, 1987b).[3] Like most of their neighbors, the Kamea derive a living from a combination of shifting horticulture and the raising of pigs. Their main agricultural crop is sweet potato, which is cultivated in family plots at elevations ranging from 2,000 to 6,000 feet. Hunting and gathering contribute minimally to the diet, but figure centrally within the context of social and ritual prestations (see Godelier 1986; Herdt 1981).

The Kamea share much in common with their surrounding Anga neighbors, including a tendency toward virilocal residence and a dispersed settlement pattern.[4] Prior to the abandonment of warfare practices during the

1950s and '60s, Anga peoples were known throughout New Guinea for their warlike tendencies and unerring skill in the use of the bow and arrow.[5] The frequency with which they conducted raids on neighboring groups earned them a reputation as being among the most hostile of all groups inhabiting mainland Papua New Guinea. Strength, bravery, and aggressiveness in one's personal style continue to be positively valued traits throughout the region.

Notwithstanding these important similarities, several notable differences exist between Anga groups. Perhaps most important for the purposes of this chapter is the fact that, unlike their neighbors to the north (most notably, the Baruya, Sambia, and Iqwaye people), Kamea initiations have never involved insemination practices.[6] Instead, maleness for the Kamea is a gradually embodied state that is brought into being through the completion of a two-stage ritual sequence. Entry into the men's cult begins when a boy is ten or eleven years old and is brought to the bush to have his nose pierced by an older initiated man. He and his agemates will remain in the cult house (*hewa anga*) for a number of weeks until their sores have healed, after which time youths are permitted to return to the house of their parents. Several years later, boys will be fed marita—the fruit of the red pandanus tree—in a secret cult ceremony that marks the final grade of the initiation sequence. Passage through both these stages is marked by the disclosure of secret narratives, including detailed knowledge of how to conduct oneself in matters pertaining to warfare and women.[7]

At the time of my fieldwork—August 1989 through February 1992—initiation was still very much an ongoing concern. Warfare has long become a thing of the past. Most children are exposed to at least some form of Western education. Rice, canned fish, wooden matches, and aluminum cooking pots are a familiar if highly prestigious accouterment of daily existence. Christian missionaries are an accepted part of the local landscape. Yet, despite these obvious, and important, components of social change, Kamea initiation practices continue unabated. Indeed, during my time in the field, I had the opportunity to witness the completion of one initiation cycle and the inauguration of a new one. What accounts for the tenacity of these rituals? Why have they managed to persist in the face of obvious impediments to their longevity? To answer this question, it is necessary to examine the basis of agency for the Kamea. This begins with a detailed look at the mother-child relation.

Embodiments of Attachment: Conceiving the Mother-Son Bond

As Bonnemère points out in her Introduction, analyzing initiation with reference to the mother-child bond is hardly new. Indeed, anthropological accounts of male initiation have long assigned women an important, if passive, role in these rituals. Forty years ago, Burton and Whiting (1961) argued that initiation serves to turn maternally attached boys into psychological beings who come to identify themselves as men. More specifically, in societies that emphasize a rigid separation between the sexes, initiation allows boys to master intense psychodynamic conflicts that have been generated as a consequence of their prolonged association with women.

Since the publication of this thesis, it has become relatively commonplace in our discipline to argue that initiation rituals detach a boy from his mother and allow him to form a counter-identification with the community of men (Chodorow 1974; Lidz and Lidz 1977; Herdt 1981). As Herdt notes in his influential account of Sambia cult life:

By the age of seven to ten years (first-stage initiation), the early months of the "critical learning" period are long since past; the formative years of childhood development are virtually complete; the core sense of identity is set; and so the late procedures of ritualized gender surgery must rattle the very gates of life and death to effect the desired modifications in even visible masculine gender behavior. (1981: 305)

In the New Guinea highlands, this has been seen to be a particularly important mandate, given the climate of endemic warfare that characterized precolonial socialities. Here, the men's cult has been seen to promote an exaggerated sense of male solidarity—a necessary condition for the creation of an effective fighting force (Langness 1967, 1974; Read 1952; Meggitt 1964; Herdt 1981).

In what follows, I intend to take this line of reasoning in a slightly different direction. I shall argue that, although Kamea initiation is geared toward separating a boy from his mother, it is necessary to understand what this underlying bond of "attachment" entails. Kamea notions of relatedness—of what connects a mother to her son—rest upon a culturally specific view of embodiment. What constitutes a body and a person in their world take on a range of associations that are not found in the West. Consequently, to understand what "detaching" a boy from his mother means, it is necessary to know how they are connected in the first place.[8]

At first glance, Kamea sociality seems to fit rather easily into the established categories of Western social science. Like most other Papua New Guineans, they believe that repeated acts of sexual intercourse are necessary to create a child. Conception is said to take place when sufficient quantities of a man's reproductive fluids (*iya coka*— "penis juice") both mix with and are encompassed by the fluids of his wife (*panga coka*— "vaginal juice"). This outer female covering will eventually form the skin and surface blood vessels of the child, while the father's semen produces the bones and internal organs. Yet, although both parents contribute bodily substance to the making of a child, this is not seized upon as a particularly compelling feature of the parent-child relationship. Unlike ourselves, the Kamea make a sharp distinction between what goes into the *making* of a person in a physical sense and what *connects* persons through time as social beings.

The Kamea term *hinya avaka* translates as "one-bloodedness" and is used to refer to a sibling set. Other than using this term, there is no way for a speaker to refer to all his or her siblings as a single undifferentiated category. All other terms in the Kapau language use sex and age to distinguish between different types of siblings. Although this chain of ideas appears to be simple enough, it is actually more complex than a cursory glance would have us believe. Any children a woman bears, regardless who the father may be, are said by the Kamea to be "one-blood" with one another. The same, it should be pointed out, does not hold true of a man. Should a man have more than one wife during the course of his life,[9] children that he has with these separate women will not be spoken about in terms of the "one-blood" relationship. Only persons born of the same womb are *hinya avaka*. To be "one-blood," then, is to have originated from the same maternal container.

This same notion of "one-blood" groupings effectively *separates* rather than connects a woman to her offspring. I initially confused the notion of "one-bloodedness" with our own ideas concerning the transmission of biogenetic substance and assumed that the expression referred to the cultural fact that blood is the female contribution to conception. The Kamea, as it turned out, did not share my views concerning the preeminence of biological connections. *Neither a woman nor a man is considered to be "one-blood" with her or his children: the term refers exclusively to having issued from the same woman's womb.* Thus, one's mother, for example, would be "one-blood" with her own "true" (<u>tru</u>) siblings, but not with any person in the ascending or descending generations (see Figure 1).

This system of ideas has a number of important implications. For while the Kamea see human life to have its origin in sexual reproduction, substance-based idioms are not used to frame human relationships through time. Despite my repeated efforts to ground lineal continuity in a process of physiological re-production, the Kamea were adamant in their claim that *children do not share substance with their parents.* Although the people with whom I worked had no difficulty specifying who their mother and father were, in the sense that these persons contributed the necessary elements toward conception, the parent-child tie is not imagined in terms of shared bodily substance. What is the defining feature of motherhood for the Kamea is not the sharing of bodily substance: it is the furnishing of a context—an enclosed environment—within which the fetus may grow.

The "containing" influence of a woman does not end at birth—it continues to define the relationship between a mother and her child for many years to come. The embodied nature of this connection is most dramatically revealed in a system of dietary restrictions. It is consequently to an examination of eating behaviors that I now turn my attention.

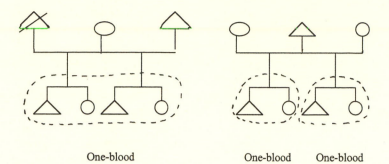

One-blood   One-blood   One-blood

Figure 1. The one-blood relationship.

Eating for Others

I first became aware of the cultural significance of Kamea food prohibitions soon after settling at Titamnga, the Kamea village where I conducted the bulk of my fieldwork. One morning not long after I had arrived in the field, I was invited to accompany a small group of women and children to hunt rat (*mataka*) along the forest edge. After several hours work, we had managed to bag a tiny handful of the rodents before beating a hasty retreat back to our homes to avoid the late afternoon rains. Later that evening Kokoban—one of the women in our party—dropped by my house, where she launched into a detailed account of how she had distributed her share of the spoils to kin. Everyone in her immediate family, it seemed, had received at least some portion of the game, although I noticed that she failed to mention her younger brother Drinda as having eaten any. When I asked Kokoban about it, she explained that rats were taboo to him. If Drinda's mother were dead, the boy could eat them without fear, but for the time being, at least, they were forbidden until he was initiated.

Rats, as it turned out, were not the only item prohibited to young boys. As I pursued the topic of food taboos in greater detail, I soon learned that boys were also barred from eating a number of other mammalian species, including several varieties of marsupials and bats. Many of these animals live on the ground, others in trees, and they are indigenously recognized as having highly variable habits and appearances. What these different species have in common is that they are all said to emit a particularly strong odor when cooked.[10] While smell is a highly salient quality of experience for the Kamea, my concern here lies less with analyzing the semantic content of these prohibitions than it does with explicating the specific form they take.[11] As I hope to demonstrate, meaningfulness for the Kamea resides less in a system of positively defined concepts than in the cracks and crevices that exist between them.

At the time it struck me as rather ironic that the more I struggled to learn about rats and boys, the more my friends at Titamnga wanted to tell me about the life cycle of women. Unlike a boy, who labors under an onerous array of dietary restrictions, Kamea girls are free to eat virtually anything they please. Indeed, some women will enjoy a taboo-free existence until the day they die: the determining factor is the sex of any offspring they may carry. Should a woman give birth to a child of the same sex as herself, her life will continue pretty much as before: both she and her daughter are free to consume all varieties of "smelly" game. If she bears a son, by contrast, her eating habits will eventually change. From the time that her son has his nose pierced onward, all the food items that were previously taboo to him now become taboo to her as well. When both stages of the initiation sequence have been completed, the boy can begin to eat these items for the first time in his life, but they will remain taboo to his mother until her dying day. Should a woman violate these taboos, it is said that her "backside would break" and she would be forced to remain in the house, lonely and sapped of her energy. A woman so afflicted eventually dies of a wasting disease.

So far, the taboo conditions I have discussed appear to fall quite neatly within the scope of the existing structuralist paradigm. A mother and son will never be eating precisely the same repertoire of foods at the same time—what is permitted to one is taboo for the other.[12] As Mary Douglas (1966) argued, food taboos are acts of separation that define discrete identities through a system of negative differentiation. The situation at Titamnga, however, is somewhat more complex. We have seen why a mother abstains from eating certain varieties of game—she follows these taboos to protect her health and physical well-being. But it remains to be seen why a son, prior to being initiated, should do the same. Although a few Kamea told me that boys avoid these items because their consumption may lead to a scabies-like condition, this was seen as a relatively minor consequence: certainly, a small price to pay for a tasty mouthful of much prized game. The principal reason given for eschewing these items is that were a boy to eat them, they would have an adverse effect *not on himself, but on his mother*. As one boy explained: "If I ate these things, my mother wouldn't be able to leave the house. She couldn't go to her garden, collect firewood, or care for livestock. She would sit in the house all day long, where she would eventually die."

For the Kamea, then, what the initial taboo conditions mark is not a *singular* but rather a *conflated* identity. In a paper that deals with the Malagasy-speakers of Mayotte, Lambek (1992: 249) discusses one of the more common features of taboo: "a taboo clearly differentiates between those who practice it and those who need not." For the Kamea, as we have seen, this is not necessarily the case. The taboo conditions that operate between a mother and son do not simply mark the two as distinct, but also establish their *essential similarity*. Taken together, they present an image of a singular body wherein the eating habits of one directly affect the health of the other. But the fact that only one half of this dual entity actually follows the taboo also has an anticipatory value—it anticipates the differentiation that will take place through the men's cult and its associated rituals.[13]

Until he is initiated, a boy is, in a sense, still "contained." During the parturition process, what the mother eats is seen to affect the health of the child. Pregnant women, for example, are enjoined not to eat either sago or watercress because both have deep root systems that will "fasten" a child to the uterus and prevent an easy birth.[14] The taboo system marks an extension of this process in that the eating habits of one directly affect the well-being of the other. It is only through initiation that a woman's son is finally "de-contained." He and his mother are no longer joined as a single entity, and the consumptive patterns of one no longer affect the other. What was once perceived in terms of its underlying similarity has now become differentiated. What was once one is now free to enter into a relationship. The son can now take a wife of his own and initiate a process of heterosexual reproduction.

The remainder of this chapter examines in greater detail the men's cult and the actual means through which this separation is achieved.

Kamea Initiation

Every four to six years, the Kamea sponsor an initiation ceremony (*apa*). When an initiation sequence is about to get underway, a men's cult house (*hewa iya anga*) will be built in a secluded clearing within the forest, far from the supposedly watchful eyes of women and children. It is here that boys will be brought to have their nasal septum pierced during the opening phase of the initiation sequence, and here that they will remain to convalesce, a process which takes from six to eight weeks to complete.

In the past, it was mandatory for all boys to be initiated, regardless whether their mothers were living or dead. Through the activities of the men's cult, boys were given the necessary strength (*yannganga*) to carry out a variety of male pursuits, including hunting game, clearing gardens, and climbing pandanus trees. The men's cult also instilled within boys an aggressive temperament—a trait that was held in particularly high esteem prior to pacification. As one man explained, "Never mind that you see everyone around you die. You cannot be afraid. You must kill people back. We strengthened boys so that they could stand up and fight."

Until recently, initiation was also a necessary precursor to marriage. It was inconceivable for an uninitiated youth to take a wife. The men's cult taught boys how to behave in the presence of women and how to avoid being contaminated by the polluting sexual substances of their brides-to-be.[15]

Within the contemporary context, it is up to the boy himself to decide whether or not to participate in the ceremonies. On the basis of my research,

I estimate that approximately 30 to 40 percent of boys will choose to undergo full initiation rites, meaning that they will sport a pierced nasal septum as an adult. It is important to note, however, that this does not give an entirely accurate picture of where things stand. A truncated form of initiation is emerging wherein boys are taught all the secrets of the men's cult and are shown the bullroarers (*mautwa*) but refrain from having their noses pierced.[16] This is done, I was told, in order to hide the men's cult from the local missionaries, who have been relentless in their campaign to put an end to initiation practices since they first began to work in the region during the early 1960s. Because these men do not embody any visible sign of their changed status, it is difficult to know how many have participated in this abbreviated system of rites.

Today, any boy who wishes to participate in an initiation sequence is free to do so. The ceremony that I witnessed in March 1990 (to be described below) exhibited marked variability with respect to both the age of the initiates themselves and the villages from which they hailed. The youngest boy in attendance was approximately ten years of age while the oldest was somewhere in his mid- to late twenties. Most participants were drawn from within a fifteen-mile radius, although I was told that persons who lived farther afield could have participated in the rites if they so desired. In the past, this system exhibited far less flexibility. Prior to the arrival of colonial agents, all boys were initiated between the ages of nine and twelve. Agemates were generally drawn from the same pool of persons who might be called upon to assist one another in times of war—a fact that sits well with one of the intended aims of the men's cult: to promote an ethos of aggressive warriorhood.

While boys are secluded in the men's house, they remain under the strict supervision of older, initiated men. In most cases, a mother's brother will take it upon himself to oversee the ritual fate of his sister's son. In addition to having their nasal septum pierced, young boys are beaten repeatedly with sticks. This is believed to promote qualities of strength and endurance and has the added benefit of teaching boys how to fight. Initiates are also shown the bullroarers for the first time and are taught how to turn them in order to produce a high-pitched whine. Notwithstanding these activities, the bulk of their time in seclusion is spent on long and arduous hunts that range over wide tracts of forest. Here, novices are schooled in the art of setting traps and tracking animals, and in the proficient use of the bow and arrow. Older men tell boys that they cannot be afraid of the dark because the night is an excellent time to hunt <u>kapul</u> (game). Boys are also instructed in the secret use of the *yangwa* tree—a type of ficus—that grows at regular intervals throughout the Kamea habitat. In addition to its publicly acknowledged use in the production of bark cloth (<u>maro</u>), the *yangwa* tree has a more compelling use which is known only to initiated men. The inner core of this tree contains a milky white sap which, if drunk, is believed to replace semen which has been lost through sexual intercourse (see Herdt 1981; Bamford 1998b).[17]

If you want to come up "new" (nupela) again, you will go to the forest. You will get the juice of this tree and you will drink it. . . . If a man wants to "make work" [engage in sexual intercourse] this juice will change him. This tree has an unlimited supply of milk. If a man drinks it, he will become "new" again.

While all these things are going on, women of all ages are strictly forbidden to approach the cult house.[18] According to one man, "If women were to see what is taking place, the noses of the initiates would break.[19] Later, the woman herself would become sick. She would lose all of her strength and die."

What I have described thus far sounds similar in all but its details to what has been written of male initiation elsewhere in the highlands of Papua New Guinea. Through the rituals of the men's cult, what is seen as an androgynous or effeminate being is transformed into a masculine form. The success of this transformation depends upon the strict separation of men from women and on the preservation of gender-specific bodies of knowledge. Yet, as I shall demonstrate below, Kamea initiation is not about reproducing a static system of gender configurations. The world is not seen to rest upon a readymade system of cultural distinctions in need of being perpetuated (see Wagner 1975; M. Strathern 1988). *Rather, it is the act of constituting those distinctions in the first place that is the aim of social action.* The symbolism of the initiation sequence reflects this difference in emphasis. Kamea women, as we shall see, figure centrally in the initiation of young boys. Indeed, it is the mother-son relationship that stands at the heart of the initiation sequence (see Bonnemère's Introduction).

While the men's house is being raised during the opening phase of the initiation sequence, a second collective dwelling is built for the mothers of the boys. During the entire time their sons are in seclusion, their mothers will be confined to this second dwelling. The women so confined are subject to a number of interdictions, particularly concerning the use of space. In the words of one man, "Mothers can't go to the bush, they can't go to their gardens, they can't collect sweet potatoes, or search for firewood in the bush. The only thing that they can do is sit in the house. If they leave the house, the noses of their sons will break."

The image we are presented with is that of a "container" tightly contained. It is only when boys are released from their seclusion several weeks later that women can quit their own confinement. Throughout this time, the fates of a mother and her son are completely intertwined.

It is during this phase of the initiation sequence that the dietary taboos discussed above undergo their first important shift. I noted earlier that, while a boy is growing up, he is prohibited from eating a wide variety of "smelly" game. Once he completes the first stage of initiation, these food items become taboo to his mother as well. Thus, for a period of approximately one to two years (until the boy is fed marita), he and his mother are united by their joint adherence to these taboos. Should either the mother or the son consume one of the varieties of interdicted game, the effect would be felt not on the consumer, but on the body of the other. After a boy has completed his final stage of initiation, he can eat these items without fear of ill effect. However, they will remain taboo to his mother for the rest of her life. A woman who eats these items risks not only illness but premature death. It is significant that it is only after a boy has completed both stages of initiation that he and his mother achieve a measure of autonomy in their eating habits. Henceforth, a mother will follow these taboos to protect her own well-being. Initiation has succeeded in separating what was previously a conjoined social identity.

In addition to the interdiction against "smelly" game, other foods also become taboo at initiation. A boy who is recovering from having his nasal septum pierced will refrain from eating pitpit, mushrooms, and marita, along with certain varieties of sugar cane. All these items are "greasy" (wel), and if they were consumed it is believed that the boy's nasal septum would never heal. After he has been released from his seclusion, the boy is free to eat these items once again. It is important to note, however (and once again indicative of the nature of mother-son bonds), that the mother of the initiate will also refrain from eating these items for precisely the same reason: were she to consume them her son's nose would "break." The mother and son operate as a single body. But, unlike the tabooed game, these vegetal items can be consumed by both of them again after the nose-piercing ceremony has been completed. Their evocation during the first stage of initiation further signifies the embodied nature of the mother-son relationship and the fact that it is this relationship that is being worked on during these rites.

I noted earlier that rituals of male initiation in Papua New Guinea have long been seen as an important vehicle of political domination. The ethnographic literature reports numerous examples in which men's control over the ritual process and sacred cult objects both validates and legitimizes an unequal balance of power between the sexes (Langness 1967; Read 1952; Herdt 1981; Godelier 1986). Within this context, it is interesting to note that one of the most important tasks assigned to Kamea women during their seclusion is to guard the bullroarers (mautwa)—the preeminent symbol of male cult life. Just before mothers of boys enter their cult house in the bush, they will be given the bullroarers by men along with instructions to watch over them carefully. The bullroarers are wrapped in leaves and pieces of bark cloth before being presented to women so that only the tip of one end is exposed. According to men, women are not fully cognizant of what they are holding on to.[20] They know they have been given an important item of the men's cult, but they are ignorant of the fact that it is this that later cries out during the final phase of first-stage initiation. One man explained:

Mautwa is something for men only. When we give it to women, it is carefully hidden. Each woman will take care of one bullroarer. When they hear the mautwa cry, they will say, "Something is calling out to our children now." Women don't know that it is the *mautwa* that cries. They think it is an insect or something like that.

Later, during the first stage of initiation, older men will retrieve the bull-roarers from women, and they will be brought back to the men's house, where they will be shown to initiates for the first time.[21] The process of recouping the *mautwa* parallels and anticipates the eventual "de-containment" of boys themselves, which is achieved during the final stage of initiation (see below). What is male must first be contained within an encompassing female environment: its engenderment as a male form is brought about by a process of extraction.[22] To be male is to have been "de-contained"; to be female is to possess the ability to act as a "container."[23]

The marked separation of mothers from everyone else in the community has a second, related rationale. It prevents the woman from becoming pregnant while her son is undergoing first-stage initiation. In the words of one man:

When a boy is being initiated, his father cannot go and look at his wife. The father must live on his own. The mother must live on her own. When the boy's sore is finished, they can live together again in the same house. But while a boy is being initiated, his parents must be separated. It would not be good if the two engaged in sex and they began to work on a new child. The nose of the boy being initiated would break. Pus would come up on the sore of the child. His nose would be infected and it would eventually rot away. A mother must go to live on her own and a father must live on his own. That way, they won't desire each other too much. When the sore is finished, they can sleep together again.

If an important aim of the men's cult is to separate ("de-contain") a boy from his mother, it makes sense that a concerted effort would be made not to evoke the woman's "containing" capacities at this time. To produce a second child would be to elicit an act of maternal encompassment at a time when every effort is being made to break this type of relation.

When the sores of the initiates have completely healed, a celebration takes place, at which time both initiates and their mothers are permitted to leave their respective cult houses. At this time a small feast is held and game is presented to the boy's maternal kin. The initiates' mothers' brothers are the chief recipients of this game, which is given to them in recognition of the assistance that they rendered in overseeing the initiation of their sisters' sons. The symbolism of this event brings to mind a related context within which the formal presentation of game is also significant. Kamea women are expected to give birth in a small house that stands adjacent to their regular domestic dwelling. As a woman's time draws near, she will retire to her birth house along with one or more female friends or relatives, who will assist her in her labor. A new mother is expected to remain in the birth house for several days, after which time a "coming out" party will be held in her honor. At this event, one of the women who assisted the new mother during childbirth will take the infant and formally place it in a string bag (bilum). The child will then be removed from the birth house and officially presented to the woman's husband for the first time. What gets emphasized at childbirth (not unlike initiation) is the removal of a child from a "container"—first, from his or her mother's womb, and then from the enclosing walls of the birth house itself. In return for her assistance in achieving these ends, the husband and his immediate kin will give the woman who placed the baby in the bilum a variety of game.

The themes of birth and fertility have long been recognized as key tropes in Melanesian male initiation (Keesing 1982; La Fontaine 1985; Whitehead 1986; Herdt 1981; Bonnemère 1998b; van Gennep 1960 [1908]). As Lutkehaus (1995: 22) points out, "Interpretations of the significance of this symbolism range from the common explanation of birth as a metaphor of the initiates' "rebirth" into a new social status, to psychoanalytic and psychological interpretations that see male initiation practices as reflecting men's envy of female reproductive capacities (Bettelheim 1962 [1954]; Mead 1949) or their desire to appropriate or control them (Langness 1967, Lattas 1989)." In this context, it is significant to note that, as Kamea boys and mothers quit their respective confinement at the end of first-stage initiation, a mixture of yellow clay and dried leaves is rubbed on the bodies of each (see Bonnemère 1996, 2001). This same mixture is spread on a mother and her newborn infant when they leave the birth house and prepare to enter the regular family domicile.

For the Kamea, then, like many other people the world over, an explicit parallel is drawn between initiation and the process of giving birth. Yet it is important to be clear about what this association entails. Kamea men (in contrast to many other Melanesians) do not use initiation rituals as a means of usurping "female powers" and channeling them toward their own political ends. Apart from providing an environment within which the developing fetus grows, Kamea women are not seen to play a particularly compelling role in conception—their contribution to the creation of a child is neither more nor less important than that of a man. Perhaps even more significant, the unification of male and female substances is not seen to result in an enduring connection between parents and offspring. Neither women nor men are seen to have substance in common with their children; it is only true siblings (the product of a similar "containment") who are united by a bond of shared bodily substance.[24] Women do not provide their offspring with anything that is uniquely "female" at conception and that is consequently capable of being appropriated by men at initiation. Initiation, instead, furnishes a context in which both sexes are equally involved in creating a gendered form. As Marilyn Strathern (1988: 332) has noted of childbirth more generally, "Women's giving birth as an act cannot be taken over by men: men can only intervene as causing the action . . . [A] mother is coerced into becoming a mother." For the

Kamea, it is perhaps appropriate to suggest that men coerce women into giving birth to a child that she has "contained" for some nine to twelve years.

Approximately one to two years after the first stage of initiation has been completed, boys undergo the final phase of the initiation sequence, which involves being fed the fruit of the red pandanus tree. It is to an account of this rite that I now turn my attention.

The Marita Ceremony

In March and April 1990, I had the opportunity to witness the second stage of Kamea male initiation. The rites were held in a small clearing approximately three hours due west of Titamnga. Fifteen initiates and several hundred of their friends and relatives took part in the ceremony.

The final stage of initiation lasts from between one and two months. Throughout this time, rites are held on a nightly basis beginning at dusk and continuing until dawn the next day. Although initiates are expected to attend each evening's festivities, the people who participate as dancers and audience members come and go as their schedule permits. The mothers and fathers of initiates generally attend the ceremonies each evening, while more distant kin drop by the danceground only intermittently.

At the time when I arrived on the scene, the second stage of initiation was already well underway. I was able to witness the last few days of ritual activity leading up to (and including) the point at which boys are fed the juice of the pandanus fruit. My consultants told me that what I saw during this period of time was representative of what takes place during second-stage initiation: it is only on the final night (to be described below) that the ritual sequence changes in both form and content.

In order to give a fuller account of what takes place during these rites, I will weave back and forth in the description that follows between a narrative account expanded from fieldnotes, and a more analytic discussion intended to situate various aspects of the ethnography. These vignettes also help to situate myself as an ethnographer and the Kamea reactions to my presence.

Engendering Male Agency: The Final Phase

We arrive at Hawabango at about six-thirty p.m., after a three-hour walk in the pouring rain. I am accompanied by Habipu, Jack, Kesiwaka, Johnson, Demi, Susan, and Philip. Hawabango is a small Catholic mission station situated five miles to the west of Titamnga. Like Kaintiba (a larger government outpost to the south), it sports a few trade-stores and is served on an ad hoc basis by flights from the coast (Kerema) and the Morobe interior. The initiation site is still an hour's walk away. Avi, a resident of Hawabango, tells me that the onset of the heavy rains will have delayed the evening's activities by several hours. We decide to rest and to dry ourselves in a small thatch house that flanks the eastern corner of the station.

Immediately after we arrive, Demi and Kesiwaka set off by themselves to ready their decorations (bilas) for the upcoming ceremony. The main item of ritual attire worn by men during the final initiation grade is an elaborate headdress made of bird of paradise and cockatoo feathers. The headdress measures approximately three feet in length and is shaped like the letter A, to which is attached an elongated center appendage made of cane and cockatoo feathers, which bobs up and down in keeping with the rhythm of the men's dance. Demi and Kesiwaka spend the next several hours straightening their headdress in an effort to ensure that it will have the desired effect when they dance.

By ten o'clock, the rain has subsided and we set off for the initiation site. The blackness of the night is filled with lit mambu torches carried by men and women who, like ourselves, have taken advantage of the break in the rains to make their way to the danceground clearing. From a distance, these lights appear to be tiny fireflies in the night sky, weaving their way up and down the sides of mountains, but progressing in the same general direction. We walk for about forty or fifty minutes and finally reach a place where a small footpath bends off to the left. From here, it spirals off in a downward direction, where it is eventually lost in the blackness of the night. I can neither see nor hear much in the way of activity down below. Demi calls out to inquire whether the singsing (ceremony) is still on. We are told that it is, and begin our descent into the awaiting darkness.

The initiation site consists of a large cleared space, roughly fifty feet in diameter, which is now packed with mud because of the extensive rain. A small fire has been lit near the center, and a group of men and women huddle around it in an attempt to cast off the chill of the mountain air. Several makeshift shelters line the perimeter of the danceground. I am told that these can be used as a place to sleep if one tires before the all-night proceedings have reached their conclusion. I am aware that my companions think I will have drifted off long before dawn arrives.

As more and more people enter the clearing, the fire at the center of the danceground is extinguished. Engiria, Pi'i, and a few other women from Titamnga with whom I am acquainted take hold of my arm and attempt to drag me to the outer reaches of the danceground. I protest that I want to see what is happening in the middle, but they are adamant that my place is with them along the outer edges of the clearing. I allow myself to be led away. Engiria grabs my hand and begins to escort me around the clearing. At first, I think that she is looking for someone she knows, but she continues to lead me in a counterclockwise direction. An old woman on my right places a <u>mambu</u> torch in my hand. I take hold of it and carry it with me as I walk. Sixty people or so are now in attendance. More enter the clearing with each passing minute.

As I become more familiar with my surroundings, I begin to notice that, whenever a newcomer enters the danceground, he or she files in with the others and begins to walk or dance around the clearing in a counterclockwise direction. When people tire of this activity, they go to watch the proceedings from the sidelines. Here, they rest, enjoy a smoke, and engage in casual conversation with friends or relatives. The atmosphere is informal and no one seems to be the least bit disturbed by my presence.

As the night progresses, I focus more on the staging of the ceremony. The initiates form a small, stationary group at the center of the danceground. Their fathers and other male kinsmen surround them, and the women move at the outer fringe of the danceground. Several of the older women carry large staffs (*cot'wa*) in their hands. Engiria explains that these women are the mothers of the boys. The staff they carry reminds me of a digging stick, but it is longer and made from an entirely different variety of wood. Men and women each have their own unique styles of dance. Men adopt a short bouncing gait as they move, which causes the third appendage of the headdress to snap up and down. Women move forward for a step or two, turn inward in a half-circle, and then move forward for a step or two again. The younger girls laugh and tease one another as they try to imitate the steps of the older women.

The bulk of the evening passes this way, with men and women moving about the danceground in the manner described above. At some point during the night—I seem to have missed the exact moment at which it occurred—a large wooden post is erected at the center of the danceground. I make several inquiries about the significance of the post and I am told that it helps to strengthen the efficacy of the <u>singsing</u>. I notice that initiates now stand with their faces turned toward the post and their hands outstretched as if supporting it. As the night progresses, a few people retire to the sidelines. The rest continue their circuit around the danceground.

As dawn approaches, a new component is introduced into the dances of men and women. The initiates and older men who have joined them at the center of the danceground join hands and begin to jump up and down. As they do so, they emit a high-pitched cry. The mothers of the boys do the same thing from their position at the periphery of the clearing. This continues off and on for the next twenty to thirty minutes. An old man, from one of the neighboring villages with which I am not familiar, explains to me that the ceremonies are about to come to a close for the night—people celebrate (hamamas) the completion of another day of initiation.

As the sun rises, people leave the danceground one by one and slowly make their way home. There, they will sleep, eat, and carry out whatever other tasks are necessary before returning to the danceground the following evening.

Despite changes in the personnel attending these rites, second-stage initiation follows the same trajectory night after night. Boys always occupy the center of the danceground, surrounded by men, who are, in turn, *encompassed* by women. The evening passes with everyone moving around in a circle. When first light breaks, everyone disbands and returns home. It is not until the final night of initiation that significant changes are introduced into the ritual sequence.

An atmosphere of excitement and tension fills the air. Tonight the boys are to be given marita. I sit on the verandah of my house at Titamnga and wait for my companions to ready themselves. In contrast to all other nights, everyone is paying far closer attention to his or her dress and decorations (bilas). Men and women sport newly made grass skirts (pulpuls)—the kind that comes to a sharp point in the front, rather than the usual style, which is cut straight across and is worn for day-to-day purposes. Honani approaches and sits down to wait with me. She is wearing several strings of shell ornaments (*nuwa*) about her neck and has put on enough armbands (*ituka*) to cover the flesh of her upper arms almost completely. Several strings of bamboo (mambu) are worn across her chest, their yellow color furnishing a dramatic contrast to the rest of her costume. She chatters happily and munches on some taro while we wait for the rest of our party.

We arrive at the danceground at about eleven o'clock. Already, it is filled with people: far more than have been in attendance on previous evenings. Those of us who just arrived from Titamnga file in with the others and begin our now-familiar circuit about the danceground. As the people move, they sing songs in the tok ples (the Kapau language). I ask David, who walks beside me, what they are singing about. He responds: "We sing of plants, trees, fruits, stones, mountains, rivers, and the forest. We comment on the beauty of the place: of the rain, of how the water flows, and of where the sun goes when it sets at the end of each day."

It is entirely appropriate that the songs sung during the second stage of initiation draw upon richly evocative images of the physical environment. Before

he is initiated, a boy is a being of undetermined gender who is strongly attached to (if not indistinguishable) from his mother. Initiation songs fore-
shadow the world that the youth will now be entering. As I discuss elsewhere
(see Bamford 1997, 1998a, b), male sociality for the Kamea is constructed less
in terms of genealogical connections, and more in terms of the relationships
men form with specific tracts of land. Through the planting of select trees (including several varieties of pandanus and ficus), intergenerational links are
formed between men who work the same ground, not on the basis of shared
bodily substance, but rather through their joint ability to share in the creation
of a humanized landscape (see Bamford 1998b). The fact that men can also
draw upon this world to supplement their own stores of semen by tapping into
certain trees further strengthens the conceptual connection in indigenous
thought between maleness, intergenerational relationships, and the land.

After a boy has been initiated, he enters a world where he can begin to act
directly upon the physical world himself. Up until this point in his life, he has
relied exclusively upon his parents to meet all his subsistence needs. Young
boys are expected to do little in the way of contributing to the family economy
and spend most of their days roaming the bush in the leisurely company of
friends. From the time that he has completed the <u>marita</u> ceremony, an initiated
youth (*hewa*) will begin to make gardens on his own. His father will assign him
a tract of land that he will begin to clear in anticipation of supporting a wife
and family. It is no accident that the songs sung during the final stage of initiation focus on naming different features in the physical environment—particularly trees, mountains, streams, and plots of ground. To sing these songs is to
give concrete reference to that domain of activity that a youth will now enter.

I ask David, who is fluent in both Neo-Melanesian and Kapau, to
speak to the mothers of boys on my behalf. I am interested in knowing
how the women perceive their own role in initiation. How does their
presence enhance the efficacy of the rites? The women smile mysteri-
ously at him and respond with what must strike them as an obvious
adage: he is a man—it is not his place to know what happens with
women at this time.

Kamea understand knowledge to have corporeal effects. It is not so much a
question of each sex carving out an exclusive sphere of influence, as that secrecy is seen to represent a health-related issue. In the wrong hands, knowledge
becomes a toxin—a poison. Should either sex learn what is appropriate only
for the other to know, sickness or death would be the inevitable outcome. To
keep a secret, then, is to demonstrate concern for the welfare of another.

At the top of a hill, roughly seventy-five feet from the danceground,
stands a medium-sized cult house where the boys will be fed <u>marita</u>. I do

not remember seeing this structure on any of the previous nights, and, when I ask my companions about it, they explain that it was built only recently in anticipation of the very final phase. The cult house will be razed in the morning when the second stage is complete.

At about two o'clock in the morning, the ceremony undergoes an abrupt change. The men at the center of the danceground begin to jump up and down. They take hold of the initiates and race toward the cult house on the hill, but before reaching their destination, they turn on their heels and reenter the danceground. This is repeated several more times. On the fifth charge, the older men disappear with the initiates into the cult house. Those of us who remain down below continue with our circular pilgrimage. I ask where the initiates have gone and receive two different answers: (1) they have gone to cook different varieties of game; and (2) they are being given marita by older, initiated men.

One of the most carefully guarded secrets of men at initiation concerns what actually takes place in this cult house on the hill. The official and public account (what is known to women and children) holds that youths are fed the bright red fruit of the pandanus tree. Through this act of consumption, they are finally released from all of their dietary taboos, and the second stage of initiation all but draws to a close.[25] What actually does take place in the men's cult house is notably different from the official canon. Instead of the initiates being given pandanus fruit to eat, the juice of this fruit is rubbed on their faces and bodies. Boys will be fed marita only later—after they have first been thoroughly coated with this substance from head to toe.

To grasp the significance of this rite, it is necessary to understand something of the importance of pandanus fruit (marita) in Kamea thought. On several occasions, I was told by my friends at Titamnga that marita had "come up" (originated) "from the blood of all men." The Kamea myth of origin holds that long ago, in the distant past, a man named Akeanga was killed in a house fire. His bones were collected by his two wives and deposited in a pool of water. There, they underwent a series of transformations, eventually metamorphosing as tiny humans who took shelter in the trunk of a tree. When the wives of Akeanga heard voices calling out from inside the tree, they made a series of incisions in the trunk, each time releasing a group of human beings. As the men tumbled forth from the tree, afterbirth spilled in all directions. Wherever it fell on the ground, a pandanus fruit tree subsequently sprouted.

Marita then, is explicitly associated with afterbirth in indigenous thought. It is significant that this substance must first be rubbed on the skin of boys before their own bodies can come to contain it through an act of ingestion. An encompassing female form must first contain that which is "male"—it is only later that the capacity to act with a measure of autonomy is achieved.

The light from a fire illuminates the cult house on the hill. From down below, the house appears to be an incandescent beacon, glowing brightly against the velvet blackness of the night. I long to be with the boys and men myself, as much to warm myself as to catch a glimpse of what is going on. Instead, I walk in a circle. Engiria bites down hard on the tough outer skin of some betel nut and wraps her bark cape more securely about her shoulders. A few children doze in the makeshift shelters along the sidelines. I fidget distractedly and wonder when the monotony of going around in circles will end.

At about four o'clock, a number of <u>mambu</u> torches appear on the hillside. One of the men who has chosen to remain down below instructs me to keep well out of the way—otherwise, I am likely to get hurt in the upcoming commotion. I retire to the outer reaches of the danceground along with other women.

The cry of bamboo flutes fills the air. The initiates, along with several older men, storm noisily into the danceground. Their arms are linked at the elbows, and they are crouched low to the ground in a squatting position. As they begin to fill the clearing, they fan out to form an ever-widening circle. As the circle expands, they begin to bash into the spectators on the sidelines. I am glad that I was warned to stand a respectable distance from the goings-on. Almost as abruptly as it began, this phase of activity ends. Everyone resumes their accustomed positions of the previous nights: boys in the middle, women along the outer edges. Our journey around the circle begins anew.

At dawn, several things take place. Two large posts are carried into the clearing and placed horizontally on the ground. The initiates are instructed to sit on these posts, which form two parallel lines facing the cult house. Mothers and sisters stand behind their sons and brothers. The rest of us watch from the outer perimeter of the danceground. The atmosphere has suddenly become tense. A number of the older men have returned to the cult house on the hill, where they begin to sound the bamboo flutes again. Suddenly, two men rush into the danceground. They run a circle around the seated boys and then tear back to the cult house again. The youngest initiate begins to cry. Ten minutes later, this sequence of activities is repeated. It occurs for a third, fourth, and fifth time over the next half hour. Each time the men charge into the danceground, the mothers of novices emit a piercing cry and begin to jump up and down. The overall effect is quite dramatic. Those of us who watch from the sidelines are mesmerized.

Suddenly, everything comes to a halt. Nearly an hour goes by with no further sign of activity. The initiates begin to look bored, and one boy dozes from his perched seat. Malo, seated beside me, complains about the heat. Now that the sun has risen, it is beginning to get quite warm. One of the mothers of the initiates leaves the danceground and disappears along a footpath that leads off into the surrounding forest. She returns a short time later with a wet cloth and proceeds to mop the face and upper body of her son. Several other women follow suit. We seem to be waiting for something, but I do not know what.

<u>Mambu</u> flutes are once again heard from the hillside. As before, two men race into the danceground. This time, however, they do not return immediately to the men's house: they bend close to the initiates and seem to be giving them some kind of instruction. More men pour onto the danceground. The initiates rise and begin to run with the men to the cult house on the hill. Almost as abruptly, however, they stop and reenter the danceground. This pattern of activity is repeated several times. The howls of the youngest initiate have reached a frantic peak.

Several men bearing steel knives race into the clearing. They begin to run in circles around the boys moving in a clockwise direction. The mothers of boys circle in the opposite direction, forming a barrier that contains the ritual action. This continues for several minutes. Then the men, accompanied by the initiates, make a dash toward the cult house on the hill. A number of the women attempt to follow their sons, but they are chased back by knife-wielding men. For the first time, I notice that a post has once again been erected at the center of the danceground. Five women, coated from head to toe in mud, are supporting it.

I noted earlier that shortly after a woman gives birth, both her body and that of her child are rubbed with mud. The Kamea assert that this offers them a measure of protection against would-be sorcerers, who are known to prey upon persons in a weakened condition.

The symbolism of the final phases of the initiation sequence emphasizes a process of extraction whereby boys are detached from the containing influence of their mothers. Throughout the bulk of these rites, women—in particular, the mothers of boys—form an outer wall by virtue of their positioning along the periphery of the danceground. Women collectively envelop the bodies of others, just as a mother envelops the body of her child throughout gestation. At the penultimate moment of the initiation sequence, the containment of women is finally, and irrevocably, broken. Initiates in the company of older men break through the line of women who continue to dance in a circle. The staging of the rite mirrors its intended consequences.

Conclusions

I have argued that Kamea rites of initiation effectively separate what is otherwise a conjoined entity: the inherent singularity of a mother and son. Up until the time that he is initiated, a boy's identity is fully enmeshed with that of his mother. The nature of this attachment is strikingly revealed in the consequences of their respective eating behaviors—that is, by the capacity of each to affect the corporeal well being of the other. Bodies are not perceived by the Kamea in exclusively individual or relational terms, but can exist as both singular and composite states (M. Strathern 1988). One of the key ways in which bodies are brought together (as in sexual relations) and taken apart (as through initiation) is by being gendered, a process that eventuates, in part, through the performance of the initiation/taboo complex.[26]

To be "male" in the world of the Kamea is to be "de-contained"; to be "female" is to possess the capacity to act as a "container" oneself. This distinction helps cast light on a significant contrast between the Kamea and what has been written of their Anga neighbors to the north. Many Anga groups initiate women as well as men (see Godelier 1986), but the Kamea perceive such a practice as erroneous. Whenever I questioned men and women about their views concerning the feasibility of initiating women, they found the entire idea to be quite unimaginable. In terms of the argument being advanced here, it can be seen that such a practice would make little sense. A female child will one day be a "container" herself—one hopes to elicit (rather than deter) the development of this quality in girls. Cultural understandings of gender and kinship are inseparable from the ritual system.

The last thirty years have witnessed many important changes in the initiation/taboo complex. Yet, significantly, instead of challenging the ideas that underlie the ceremonial sequence, they have buttressed what is seen as being its primary aim—"de-containment." Within the contemporary setting, if the mother of a boy is no longer living, he need not adopt the dietary restrictions that prohibit the consumption of "smelly" game. Safeguarding the health of his mother has ceased to be an issue, and he can eat the tabooed items without fear of ill effect. The son has, by his mother's death, already been "de-contained," and this state has important consequences for male cult life.

While living at Titamnga, I had the opportunity to befriend a young boy whose mother had died several years earlier. Habipu was approximately ten years old and had yet to be initiated. However, unlike most other boys his age, he was well versed in the goings-on of the men's cult and was given to turning the bullroarers whenever the opportunity presented itself. When I expressed surprise that a child such as Habipu had any knowledge of the bullroarers given that they were normally hidden from women and children, I was told that motherless boys are not barred from secret male proceedings, but are free to take on many of the rights of older men without having to undergo initiation themselves.[27]

Kamea initiations are intimately bound up with the ways they see bodies and the connections between them. We have seen that the parent-child relationship is not imagined in terms of a tie of shared bodily substance. This car-

ries with it a number of important implications. Much of the published literature on Highland initiations takes the existence of a substance-based universe
as its analytic baseline. Rituals such as bloodletting and insemination are understood, on the one hand, to "remove" the maternal (female) part of the individual (see M. Strathern 1993; Herdt 1981; Read 1952), and to replace it
with an exclusively masculine counterpart. Initiation, in other words, achieves
its efficacy by acting directly upon the alchemy of bodily substances.

While this analytic model has proven to be highly useful in understanding
the initiation systems of many Melanesians, the Kamea fit rather awkwardly
with the prevailing paradigm. Here, the tie between a woman and her child is
not substance-based. Indeed, as we have seen, substance *disconnects* rather than
conjoins persons in proximate generations. This is not to say that the connection between a woman and her children is not embodied—rather, it is based
on the very act which brought the relationship into being in the first place: the
act of containment itself. It is this containing influence that comes to be acted
upon within the context of Kamea initiations. What initiation does is to separate one from the other and, in the process, to engender male agency. Both
men and women are central to this process, and the end result is not the reproduction of an enduring political hierarchy, but rather the ongoing creation
of culturally meaningful social distinctions (see Wagner 1974, 1975, 1977).
Understanding women's participation in these rituals is more than mere "ad-
ditive analysis"—a simple insertion of otherwise missing ethnographic facts. It
leads to a fundamental change in perspective concerning the meaning of these
rites and ultimately of their consequences. What gets produced in this system
are a shifting assemblage of identities and relationships rather than the abstract configuration of "society."

Chapter 3
When Women Enter the Picture: Looking at Anga Initiations from the Mothers' Angle

Pascale Bonnemère

In November 1994, in one of the three valleys they occupy, the southern Anga people known as the Ankave performed initiation rituals for all boys between ages eight and twelve or so. During my first stay in 1987, I learned from talking with them that the women living in the area played a role of some sort on such an occasion, but our discussions on the matter never went very far because in the end "initiations are men's business," a women's utterance perfectly symmetrical to what is said by men when asked about anything having to do with babies and procreation.

Although I tried to get my female friends to talk about what they used to do when the boys were initiated, it was really only when all adults in every hamlet were preparing this big communal event (some fetching forest products, a few repairing old shell necklaces, and many making new bark capes and loin-cloths) that the women began to feel more at ease discussing the question with me. In fact, comments about and explanations of their part in the male rituals were forthcoming when the preparations for the events were actually in progress, as well as during and after the events, as if sharing the experience with them was a condition for my being able to hear about it.

Having read the ethnographic work on northern Anga peoples, I was somewhat surprised to learn that during Ankave initiation rituals all the novices' mothers were secluded together in a large shelter made of leafy branches and had to respect taboos of various kinds (on several types of food, on drinking water, on going outside the collective house except at a particular moment at dawn, hence on their usual activities). In the analyses of Baruya, Sambia, and Iqwaye male initiations published by Maurice Godelier, Gilbert Herdt, and Jadran Mimica respectively, the prevailing view is that these events are a strictly male affair and that women have nothing to do with them. The exclusion of women, girls, and uninitiated boys is a key element of almost every article or book published on New Guinea male rituals, be they initiations or any other kind of ritual concerning and involving men (like so-called bachelors' cults, spirit cults or even fertility cults).[1] Local people say that, if the women were present, the objectives of the rituals would not be attained, whether maturation and strengthening of boys, preparation for sexuality and marriage, or human and general fertility.

Given the exclusion of women from the ritual scene in the forest—and the discourse of the men on female pollution in general and the bad effects women have on their boys, who need to grow and become strong, brave adult men—sexual antagonism and warfare have been considered the two contexts underpinned by Anga initiation rituals. These rituals have been shown to occupy a central place in the reproduction of male domination: "male and female initiations are two complementary aspects of a social practice that establishes and legitimizes the domination of men over women" (Godelier 1986: 62), which the Baruya view "as a gathering into the men's hands of both male powers and female ones, and the female are thus made masculine" (76).

In a not-so-remote past, being an adult man implied being a warrior fierce enough to protect the community from enemy raids.[2] Intertribal warfare was a normal state of affairs, and, as Herdt writes, "truces were infrequent and usually short-lived" (1987b: 53). For boys to become strong warriors, they have to be separated from the female world for several years, since it is thought that women's bodies produce dangerous and highly polluting substances that would prevent the boys from reaching full manhood and the strength associated with it.

Although warfare ceased several decades ago, the Anga still view initiations by men as the only way for the boys to mature and acquire strength, and ultimately to be able to dominate women. Women are absent from this picture, then, or, more accurately, they are present as figures men have to oppose in order to make the novices grow and become strong. Moreover, during the rituals the men teach the novices that the subordination of women is something legitimate that they must perpetuate for the welfare of the community, given that female bodies are potentially dangerous to all.

Among the Ankave, a southern Anga group of about one thousand persons, the picture is slightly different. There, even though the male rituals are organized in secret places in the forest beyond the view of the women, it cannot be said that women are excluded from the ritual process. Women are excluded only from the site of performance of the male ritual, not from the ritual itself: the boys cannot be initiated without their mothers (and, to a much lesser degree, their sisters) being present. This involvement takes the form of seclusion, taboos, and required behaviors, which last the time of the boys' seclusion. But women's participation clearly differs from that of the men.

Since women's activities and behaviors have not been taken into account in the existing analyses of Anga initiations, either because women do not intervene at all or because their participation is much less visible than that of men, it seems quite reasonable to wonder whether, when women enter the picture, the view of the male rituals as the place where male domination is legitimated and reproduced can be sustained (see Roscoe 1995: 222 for similar remarks about female initiations). In other words, when we focus our attention on what women do during these male ritual events, does this imply that we need to challenge the results of the previous analyses, which emphasized sexual antagonism and the reproduction of male domination in these rituals? In short, do we have to suggest an alternative interpretive model when introducing this new (ignored, underestimated, or whatever) parameter, or should we, on the contrary, regard the existing one as still valid, but in need of some adjustment?

In the perspective adopted here, the male ritual is seen primarily as a cultural practice dealing with the ontogeny of the male person (see Herdt 1982b: 211 15, 1989: 361; Juillerat 1995: 253). Focusing on the collective phases of several Anga male rituals, those which concern boys only, since a different logic is at work in the rites performed when a young man is about to marry or have his first child, this chapter uses ethnographic material collected about what the novices' kin in general and their mothers in particular do in the course of the rituals, and puts this material side by side with what is asked of the novices themselves at the same moments.

I look at the participation of women in male rituals from three different perspectives: procreation theories, the mother-son link, and fantasies concerning the production of human beings.

Such a comparative exercise shows that, in the course of the rituals they perform to make boys grow, Anga men unconsciously enact female physiological events, but also that, in each group, this process takes a specific form that varies according to local conceptions about human reproduction and intra-uterine growth.

The chapter also suggests, on the basis of the Anga ethnography but also with the support of general psychoanalytical findings, that the mother-son bond is conceived as a symbiosis that continues well beyond the separating events of birth and weaning and can be transformed only through initiation into a dyadic mode of relating.

The analysis then moves on to an interpretation of male parthenogenesis myths in light of the recourse to a female physiological model to make boys grow and of this representation of the mother-child bond as symbiotic. Finally, some comparative hypotheses are advanced concerning links between women's involvement in male rituals, the aspects of motherhood that are stressed in the imaginary metamorphosis of the boys, and gender relations.

Some Ritual Patterns Shared by All Angans: Variations on the Female Physiological Model

The Nourishing Ankave Mother

Although it would certainly be true that mothers are seen as the nourishing figures par excellence in most New Guinea societies, in their views about procreation and growth, the Ankave assign them a very important role with implications in several areas of social life. Not only is the production of human beings seen to owe much to women, given that intra-uterine growth as well as the blood of the fetus are owed to the pregnant woman's blood alone, but maternal milk is also seen as a substance produced independently of the father's semen (a rather peculiar position in Anga groups). In fact, semen is seen as harmful for the child (fetus or baby) in general.

In the case of behavioral characteristics and naming practices as well as marriage prohibitions, this substantial link between mothers and children stands out in the explanations given by Ankave men and women. A special term, *amenge'*, may be used as an address term between people, male or female, whose maternal grandmothers were sisters. Given that maternal milk plays the same roles for the baby as menstrual blood for the fetus (making it grow and giving it blood), and since this term also means breast and maternal milk, it can be said that persons who are *amenge'*-related share some bodily substances. Between people who call themselves *amenge'*, as with all maternal kin, conflicts are carefully avoided and gifts frequently exchanged (Bonnemère 1996: 145).

Moreover, not only is marrying someone related to you through female links (*amenge'* or other) prohibited, it is the most respected of all negative rules, lineage exogamy included (Bonnemère 1996: 86). In other words, being linked to someone through women appears to carry a stronger sense of sameness than being of the same clan or lineage. Finally, there are special appellation terms that are totally dependent on the clan affiliation of the mother as well as on the sex of the person. Two men whose mothers belong to the same clan will be addressed by the same term, which refers to a plant. These terms are always employed in cheerful contexts, when welcoming people, inviting them to share a meal, and on the whole expressing benevolent feelings toward them.

All these ethnographical facts indicate that the Ankave place a particularly positive emphasis on the relationship with the mother.

What, then, of male initiations and the role played in them by women? As in many New Guinea societies, Ankave boys have to be initiated in order to become adult. I have already given a description of these rituals elsewhere (Bonnemère 1996, 1998a), so I will simply recall here the most relevant events (according to the people themselves) and the role of women on this occasion; then I will present the major themes of my analysis.[3]

Among the Ankave, the sets of rites we commonly call initiations can be divided into three main stages. When boys are between eight and twelve, a radical resocialization (see Herdt 1987: 81) occurs for which there is no equivalent for girls: the boys have their nasal septum pierced (first stage). From several weeks to a year afterward, the second stage is held, consisting mainly of the (violent) smearing of the boys' bodies with red pandanus seeds. The third and final stage is organized when a man's first child is born; the pregnancy itself is surrounded by specific behaviors that can be considered part of these rituals.[4]

Throughout the period when the initiates' septums are healing, in other words during the first stage of the rituals, the boys' mothers are secluded in a large collective shelter and obliged to respect numerous daily behavioral constraints and food taboos, which, for the most part, are similar to those imposed on the initiates in the bush. Mothers and initiates alike must also soak their new bark capes in stream water every day at dawn before putting them on their shoulders. Whenever the mothers hear the cry of a certain bird, they immediately spit out whatever food they may have in their mouth, exactly as their sons do when hearing the same bird. In the forest, next to the initiation hut, men often comment on these restrictions and particular behaviors of the novices' mothers, which they consider to be an absolute condition for the success of the male ritual. Men even add that this is so "because they gave birth to the boys in the first place."

Many of the taboos the novices' mothers must respect are the same as those they had to obey when pregnant. Red pandanus juice is the principal food eaten by a pregnant woman, since it adds to the amount of blood she has in her body, on which the fetus feeds. In effect, as already said, for the Ankave the mother is solely responsible for the intra-uterine growth of her child. However, at initiation, it is the boys, and not their mothers this time, who consume the red pandanus juice between the first and the second stages of the ceremonies. Moreover, when the boys eat this plant substitute for blood, they do it in utmost secrecy (Bonnemère 1994: 25–27).[5]

The main rite of the second stage of initiation, the one that gives it its name, is the violent rubbing of the boys with red pandanus seeds. The initiates are put next to an intense fire in a tiny shelter. This shelter is built next to the entrance of a corridor of branches, both ends of which are decorated with red leaves and beaten bark dyed with red pandanus juice. Pushed by their sponsors, who are preferably real or classificatory mother's brothers, the young boys advance into the corridor, while being beaten by men posted on the outside. As they emerge, a man flings cooked red pandanus seeds onto their face and shoulders, which he rubs in together with a reddish ochre.

I suggest elsewhere (1996: 349) that these two adjoining frameworks of foliage are metaphors for the uterus and the vagina respectively. The difficult progression of the initiates through the narrow passage—which, because they are pushed, can literally be called an expulsion—can be interpreted as their rebirth to a new state. The red elements at the entrance and exit of the corridor are metaphors for the blood which they believe fills the uterus and of which a small amount spills out at delivery. And like a newborn, whose head is the first body part to emerge at delivery, only the head and shoulders of the initiates are rubbed with red pandanus seeds.

When this rubbing is completed, the boys go back to the village and are treated like newborn babies. Two women coat their bodies in the yellow mud with which every infant is rubbed soon after birth. The charm employed is exactly the same on both occasions. Then the initiates distribute the rats, birds, and small marsupials they have caught in the forest to their sisters and mothers, which parallels the gift of game by the husband and male kin of a woman soon after she gives birth. In both cases, the same name is used ("marsupials for a birth").

Thus initiation can be seen as a rebirth, preceded by the enactment of a gestation process (the secret consumption of red pandanus juice). Since growth is the main concern and goal of these rituals, and since, for the Ankave, the main agent of growth is blood, which is provided by the mother, I suggest that gestation has been "chosen" as the most appropriate metaphor for making boys grow.

The Defiling Sambia Mother (and Fertile Women)

The Sambia system of representations of procreation and growth is different from the Ankave view. Here the father's semen alone is responsible for making the fetus grow, and so sexual intercourse is maintained throughout most of the gestation period, while it is absolutely proscribed among the Ankave. Moreover, "the most female act—giving birth—arises from semen injections into the blood pool" (Herdt 1981: 193). These two Anga groups have opposite views about semen: Ankave think that it has bad effects both on the fetus and on the mother's milk, which it causes to dry up; while for the Sambia it has nourishing capacities and contributes to the production of women's milk. Impairing the nourishing role of the mother for the newborn in one case, semen is the source of it in the other.

As Herdt himself writes, "the masculine viewpoint tends to deride femaleness while also denying its procreative function" (Herdt 1981: 193). And generally, in discourse at least, women are considered to have a negative impact in many ways: the substances placed in their sons' bodies through breastfeeding block the boys' maturation, vaginal fluids can impair male health, and female pollution weakens men so much that physical contact between spouses was totally prohibited in times of war. Menstruating women are the most feared of all and are relegated for several days to a lower part of the village, where no man or boy ever goes and where they are fed by their female relatives.

This consistently negative view of femininity engenders problems with regard to mothering, which in part is negatively connoted (at least for male children) but at the same time essential for the baby's life. "For months, the baby owns the breast, has no rivals for its milk, is constantly, blissfully cuddled, remains enveloped and nameless, a piece of his mother's body and existence" (Herdt 1981: 304). This prolonged exclusive relationship generates in men a "nagging fear that one is less than masculine, that one could change into a female. This anxiety I have labelled the transsexual fantasy in masculine behavior" (278). Herdt adds that "the nature of the child's tie to his mother is so powerful and seductive that it has life-long effects on a man's capacity to sense himself unequivocally as the kind of person Sambia warfare, ritual, and women demand" (290). According to these ideas, Sambia boys have to be abruptly separated from the female world. This separation takes place at the time of the initiations, and it is not an easy process, since "boys must not only separate from their mothers but must also disidentify from them and early symbiotic union" (313).

All these ethnographic details indicate that the Sambia attribute a rather negative image to femininity and that the mother-son relationship is pervaded with ambivalence. How are these views about masculinity and motherhood framed in the course of the male initiations?[6] The Sambia male ritual cycle comprises six different phases in two distinct segments: "the first segment consists of collective initiations done by the hamlets acting together. This involves first-, second-, and third-stage initiations, [and] bachelor ceremonies" (Herdt 1987b: 107). The second segment is organized locally and "depends on a youth's maturity and the elders having obtained a woman for him, which is often several years after his third-stage initiation" (108). Between the two segments of initiations is a period when all the initiates live in forest houses.

Sambia boys do not have their nasal septum pierced during initiation rituals; instead, the operation is performed in early childhood on boys and girls alike (Herdt 1987b: 131). What happens during the first-stage ceremonies is the giving and inserting of a new noseplug. The main rite of this stage is the nosebleeding, done in great secrecy, after the initiates have been "thrust into a green barricade and through a muddy, narrow, inner chamber that leads only one way into an even narrower cagelike . . . passageway" (141). As with the similar corridor of Ankave rituals, pieces of red bark are tied into the branches of the green mass. Herdt adds that "approaching from the distance, it appears as if blood were dripping from the branches" (141). Actually, the only difference in the two leafy structures is the moment of their use. In Sambia rituals the initiates are pushed into the structure by their ritual guardians in the first stage, before any ritualized homosexual practices have begun, while, in Ankave rituals the ordeal occurs in the second stage, just before the violent rubbing with red pandanus seeds.

The nosebleeding itself takes place a moment after the corridor ordeal, near a stream in order to let the blood flow into the water, so that "women cannot discover any signs of blood, and it also allows the boys to wash themselves off" (Herdt 1987b: 143). Two hours later comes the "stinging-nettles ritual," intended to "make way for the growth of a new masculine skin" and consisting of rubbing fresh nettles onto the boys' bodies (144). The flute ceremony follows, which is an instruction about fellatio and about semen as a nourishing substance. It is also the occasion to teach the boys about the fatal consequences of breaking the secrecy of these practices.

Apart from the nosebleeding and the boy-inseminating practices, there are several other Sambia ritual events that do not occur among the Ankave. The most striking features in this respect are the extreme dramatization of the separation of the boys from their mothers and the violence of the ritualized interactions between men and women, ending with the proclamation of the "mothers' harmful effects" on their sons, which make the male rituals necessary in the first place. In short, women are held responsible for the painful events the boys have to endure and are therefore addressed and treated with considerable aggression (Herdt 1987b: 151–52).

The second-stage Sambia rituals are "the simplest of all collective ceremonies." Food taboos are less numerous than in the preceding stage and, in particular, red foods are now permitted. Boys are told about the importance of continuing to take in male seminal substance: "the elders implore them to ingest as much semen as possible, to grow strong," writes Herdt (1987b: 126). The focus is then on the ingestion of semen and, although the rites "stretch over several days and are colorful" (125), not many different events take place during second-stage ceremonies.

The gateway of branches hung with red objects used during the first-stage rituals can be interpreted, I think, in the same way as for Ankave rituals: a difficult passage through a vagina and then a delivery. The flow of blood in the collective nosebleeding that immediately follows this painful progression would consequently be similar to delivery blood, and the two events are actually considered equally dangerous (Herdt 1987b: 140). Afterward the Sambia initiates are rubbed with nettles, possibly in the same way their mothers were when they gave birth several years earlier.[7] We would therefore have here a ritual act similar in meaning to the smearing with yellow mud among the Ankave since it is performed on both newborns and initiates.

About the following lessons on semen and the necessity of fellatio taught by men during the flute ceremony, Herdt writes that the "tree sap [that the adult men must ingest to replace the semen lost in heterosexual intercourse] is symbolized as 'milky mother's sap'" (1987b: 164). And it is not the only time semen is equated with the maternal nourishing substance since, in the teachings concerning fellatio, men say: "If you try it [semen], it is just like the milk of your mothers' breast. You can swallow it all the time and grow quickly" (150).

I propose that boy-inseminating among the Sambia are modeled on breast-feeding,[8] in the same way that ingestion of red pandanus juice among the Ankave is modeled on pregnancy. This would explain why the symbolic rebirth occurs respectively before and after this growth process in these societies. In short, for some reason probably related to differences in ideas concerning pro-creation and babies' growth, the Ankave have recourse to the metaphor of intra-uterine growth, while the Sambia use a metaphor based on postpartum growth to make boys mature.

To summarize, we can say that, for the Sambia, the boys' maturation is con-structed on breastfeeding as the focal point of reference (see also Elliston 1995: 858). This metaphorical maternal nourishment enacted in fellatio starts during the first stage of the initiations, just after the rebirth scene and the collective nosebleeding, and goes on in the second-stage set of rituals. In a sense it lasts as long as real breastfeeding does, several years. In the next stage, the initiates will become the bachelors from whom boys will in turn take their vital sub-stance.

The second collective nosebleeding is performed during the third stage of the male rituals, when the boys are between ages of fifteen and eighteen (Herdt 1987b: 107). These rituals are the last to be held collectively, and Herdt qual-ifies them as "puberty rites . . . which transform the pubescent initiates into bachelor youths" (Herdt 1981: 242).

Now, although this paper does not deal with individually oriented phases of Anga male rituals, a brief description of some of the Sambia phases is needed to sustain my argument that the men unconsciously enact female physiological events in their life cycle rituals.

Subsequent nosebleedings are done on an individual basis at specific mo-ments: when the man's young wife menstruates for the first time (fifth-stage ini-tiation); at the birth of his first child (sixth-stage initiation); and finally at each of his wife's periods. Thus, "the final three (ego-centered) initiations carry the youth into full-blown manhood based on marriage, cohabitation with his wife, and fatherhood" (Herdt 1981: 242).

Given Herdt's assertion that the Sambia consider women as "innately healthier and longer-lived than men" (1981: 191) and menstrual blood as the substance which keeps them healthy (192), I would propose that all these nose-bleedings reveal that female bodily functions are used by men as an uncon-scious model for the maintenance of their own good health.[9] This is not unusual in New Guinea. Donald Tuzin wrote, concerning the Arapesh living in the Sepik region (1995: 299–300), that, although a girl experiencing her first menses is secluded for a month, none of the rites performed on this occasion are "thought to be essential to the maiden's procreative powers. Rather, they are meant to celebrate the manifestation, or unfolding, of powers that have been a part of her since birth."

Plainly stated, then, after having been reborn and having grown through the ingestion of semen, the initiate would then "menstruate" for the first time at puberty, during the third-stage rituals. The subsequent ritual events depend on the maturation of the young woman who has been designated as his spouse and is "of similar or younger age" (Herdt 1981: 39). When she has her first period, the fifth-stage rituals, which end with a nosebleeding, are held for the young man. And from then on, he will have to nosebleed himself each time his wife "disappears to the menstrual hut" (Herdt 1982b: 209). "Sambia men thus engage in private bleeding for many years, till they halt coitus or their wives undergo menopause and stop having periods" (210).

The birth of a man's first child is the occasion to organize the sixth and final stage of the initiation rituals, which comprise a nosebleeding performed voluntarily by the young father. Then, "following this initiation, most men do not nosebleed themselves again until . . . they resume coitus with their wives following the child's breast-weaning" (Herdt 1982b: 208–9).

What seems clear from all these statements is that, in adult life, men stop bleeding themselves when their wives do not bleed (during breastfeeding and at menopause). This confirms the idea that it is through the imitation of female bodily functions that men seek maturation and good health. The Sambia say that they perform nosebleedings in order for boys "to rid them of female pollutants that block 'male growth'" (Herdt 1982b: 192) and for adult men to "remove female contaminants from the body" (Herdt 1987b: 140). But if this were the case, we could legitimately wonder why in adult life men make themselves bleed only at the time of their wives' menses. In effect, getting rid of female pollution does not itself impose matching the women's cycle; it can be done any time.

So, for all these reasons, rather than accepting Sambia men's discourse at face value, I would suggest the following alternative reading of their nosebleedings: men ritually accomplish what occurs naturally in women (see also Herdt 1981: 190). Women being "biologically gifted" (192) and the female body being "a body capable of reproducing itself" (193), their functioning constitutes an adequate model for thinking and operating the maturation of men's bodies, which lack this capacity. So, as Per Hage wrote, "the relation between these [initiation] rites and female physiology is based not on envy but on analogy" (272). To which I would add "not necessarily on envy" since the discussion is by no means closed.[10]

Previous analyses of Anga male initiations by Herdt or Godelier have not emphasized rebirth, but clearly these authors were both aware of the strength of this symbolism (Herdt 1987b: 141; Godelier 1986: 53). Although it may be regarded as patently obvious by some since the publication of *Les rites de passage* (1909), this symbolism is evidenced in so much detail among the Ankave that it cannot be simply said to conform to Arnold van Gennep's model without further qualification. What the comparative study of several Anga collective male rituals shows is that a female physiological model[11] is fairly widespread among these groups, and that it means much more than simply the enactment of birth. The female physiological events referred to are highly varied (breastfeeding, menstruation, or gestation, or a combination of them) and are linked to local conceptions of human procreation, growth, and fertility.

Representations of the Mother-Son Link

For the Sambia, relationships with mothers are highly problematic in the male child's developmental cycle because the strong dependency created by maternal bonding has the effect of feminizing the child's body. "What is constant in New Guinea societies," Herdt writes, "is close proximity to mother in childhood. The mother is invariably the primary caretaker until weaning, and often up until the child reaches age five or so" (1989: 339).

New Guinea peoples are not unique in regarding this physical and nourishing dependency of children on their mothers as a relationship whose rupture when the children grow older poses a problem. Male children are especially concerned here, given their sexual difference. Being symbiotically close to their mothers is less problematic for girls because their sexual identity and physiological roles are continuous with their mother's. For boys, things are more difficult because they have to disidentify from early symbiotic union as well as separate from their mothers.

Many psychoanalysts together with a few social anthropologists trained in psychoanalysis have raised the issue of maternal bonding as a difficult relationship from which to free oneself sufficiently, in adult life, to establish good relations with sexual partners and children. The pediatrician Aldo Naouri writes that, far from being changed, the relationship with the mother remains identical throughout one's life, and this often generates trouble in relationships with others (1994: 79). In spite of themselves and unconsciously, mothers play a key role in making of this largely symbiotic bond limited in time an enduring one (107–9). This is the reason for the necessity of interposing the father or any substitute figure to which the mother is related affectively, thus producing the configuration that psychoanalysts call the "Oedipus complex."

If one accepts, as I have chosen to do in this particular chapter, that male initiations are a cultural practice that deals with the ontogeny of the male person and when one hears the general statements about mother-child relationships, then the ethnographic fact of Ankave mothers being involved when their sons are initiated seems much less odd than it does in analyses of New Guinea male rituals as an exclusively male institution.

In Baruya male initiations, the novices' mothers are involved.[12] They are not usually secluded in a shelter built for the occasion, as is the case among the Ankave; rather, each stays quietly in her own house, or in another house that bears the same name as the novices' communal shelter. As they cannot go out, they receive cooked tubers from other women. They have to respect taboos on water and leafy greens just as their sons do. In addition, they may not scratch their skin with their own nails but must use a special stick, the same restriction applying to the boys. Before the rituals, the mothers make a bark cape for their sons, and more generally, it is the women who make the body decorations and loincloths for the return from the bush. The mothers wear an additional bark cape on top of their own. Taboos are the same during the first, second, and third stages of the rituals, except for the scratching stick, which is an object of concern at the end of the first stage only.

After these ceremonies, the novices' mothers take the burned skins of the tubers they have eaten during the seclusion period, as well as a big stick that has just been given to them in exchange for their small scratching sticks, and go into the forest, under cover of their bark capes. It is just before dawn. There, a man climbs a tree (ideally a wild pandanus-nut tree) and ties the women's scratching sticks to the trunk.[13] Soon afterward, another man fells another tree. When he begins to cut its trunk, each woman shouts and throws away the big stick she was given. Two comments are made concerning this ritual act: that it is done, first, "in order to kill the boy's name" and, second, to lift the taboo imposed during the rituals on talking openly, letting their face be seen, and scratching themselves with their fingernails. When the mothers go back to the village, they wash in the river before putting on a new bark cape and skirt. Their final gesture is to rub themselves with yellowish-gray clay. A big meal is then held to close the first-stage ceremonies, and every person concerned can now drink water and eat the usual foods.

Before attempting any interpretation of these particular ritual acts and restrictions, let us listen to the Baruya people themselves. The women make an explicit link between the male rituals and several major events of their own physiological cycle: they mention the pain they endured when giving birth to explain why they do not do anything when their sons are in the forest and why they wear an additional bark cape on top of their heads. They say that they also put on new pieces of clothing after they wash in the river at the end of the menstrual seclusion period or after they have given birth. Like the Ankave women, Baruya mothers spontaneously draw a parallel between these different events. Similarly, in explaining why the novices' sisters do not have to respect the restrictions imposed on their mothers, they say that they are not the ones who gave birth to the boys. In short, Baruya women consider themselves to be involved in the initiation of their sons, and they link their participation to the fact that they gave birth to them.

As stated above, the idea of initiation as rebirth, widely recognized as a "key type in Melanesian male initiation" (Lutkehaus 1995: 22), is also present in the analyses of northern Angan male rituals, although it is not fully developed. Some Baruya men even say something that leads me to propose an alternate interpretation of the rituals. They say that the novices are as though they were in an egg and that the initiation rituals, and especially the blows the men give the boys with the *kwaimatnie*, break the egg in which they were enclosed and give them a greater capacity for understanding. It is the men, collectively, who make this egg hatch. By contrast, women give birth individually.

In saying this, they may be emphasizing the idea that physical birth does not succeed in getting the baby fully born, and that only initiation can do this. Pursuing the same line of reasoning, I would propose that, contrary to all expectations, birth is not for the Baruya the time a new being is brought to the world; instead, it should be viewed as not impeding the perpetuation of the symbiotic relation which begins at conception and lasts during pregnancy. In short, birth does not entirely succeed in breaking the link the male child has with his mother and in establishing him in the outside world. Men also speak of their role with regard to the boys in terms of acquisition of a greater understanding that their mother has not given them. Clearly, this is another occasion on which Baruya men "complete and perfect what woman had begun" (Godelier 1986: 72).

So, until weaning and probably beyond, children may perhaps not be considered to be separate from their mothers, a statement that is consistent with general hypotheses formulated by psychoanalysts or pediatricians (see above). Among the constants of "oedipal symbolism," defined "in its capacity of founding a universal principle" as "the establishment of a structure whose invariables may be organized in a variety of ways" and made distinct from "on the one hand, its neurotic expressions, and on the other, its various cultural elaborations," is the "fusional bond with the mother received as the pre-oedipal legacy of the child whatever its sex" (Juillerat 1993: 726). This view matches Baruya and Sambia ideas, since they say that boys have to be abruptly segregated from the female world. The separation takes place at the time of the initiations and is not an easy process.

Among the things Anga male rituals do, clearly is deal with this link. But the cultural manifestations of this concern with the mother and male child bond vary from group to group. Local discourses on mothers and their impact on their children differ as well. For northern Angans (Baruya and Sambia), maternal influence is at least potentially harmful, and residual pollution in the boys' bodies has to be eliminated in a strictly masculine environment. Although necessary, the mothers' presence is minimal, noncollective, and therefore hardly visible for an outsider. For the Ankave, maternal influence is primarily nourishing, and it is to its imitation that men collectively turn during the initiations. Moreover, the mother's presence is made highly visible by being collective, and is recognized as essential to the very success of the male ritual process, as we have seen above.

While Baruya and Sambia people say they perform initiation rituals in order to rid the boys of the harmful influence their mothers had upon their bodies, the Ankave do not express things this way. The influence the women have on their children is instead thought of as positive since it is above all a relationship of nurturance. Similarly, beliefs about female pollution are expressed differently: among northern Angans, they lead to the relegation of menstruating women and of those having recently given birth, to the outskirts of the village for weeks, while Ankave newborns are brought back into the family house only a few days after birth. On the whole Ankave do not regard menstrual blood as a lethal substance.

Now, in an attempt to go beyond northern Angans' discourse with its emphasis on the need to remove maternal substances from the boys' bodies, I suggest that it might be relevant to take into account another of their discourses. The Baruya say that the ritual breaks the egg, a statement that might allow us to interpret male initiations in these groups as the time when boys are truly and fully born, since their first, physical birth did not sever the link with their mother.

It is through male initiation that this breaking off is effected.[14] As Godelier wrote, "all that this world of women has already deposited in them, incorporated into their personality . . . must be driven out of them" (1986: 74). That the Baruya initiate receives a new name is consistent with such an interpretation. Then, when he has been born in the hands of men, he is nourished by the semen of elders, which contributes to his masculinization. A boy cannot become an adult man without the intervention of the male community. This is made very clear both in discourse and in ritual practice.

In such a view, if women have to be part of these rituals, it is simply because they are one of the components of the symbiotic relationship that links them to their sons. They need to be detached from them as well. But this process of detachment takes various forms. Among the Ankave, the mothers of the boys being initiated are placed in the conditions that obtained when their sons were inside their womb. In order to detach the boys from their mothers, the process of gestation needs to be repeated, and a gift of game from the novices to their mothers marks the transformation of their symbiotic relationship into a dyadic one. For northern Angans, the imitation of female physiological processes does not involve reiteration of the imitated event with the presence of the real characters.[15] Women are there only to participate in the breaking off of relations with their sons. What is emphasized is the feeding and growth of the reborn initiate with male substance, rather than their rebirth.

Consideration of the mother-novice link must extend to the extremely different outcomes of the ritual: whereas an Ankave boy can sleep in his parents' house or frequent his mother and other women, a Northern Angan initiate avoids all women and systematically hides himself from his mother for years.

In sum, the Ankave, where a novice becomes a man through a ritual enactment of a gestation process with female substance, merely *transform* the mother-son link and allow the initiates to continue relations with their mothers. On the contrary, northern Angans (Baruya, Sambia), who emphasize all-male nurturance of the novices in order to complete them, abruptly *sever* the mother-son relationship for several years. Not only does the mother "kill the name" of her son, but the two persons previously linked by a symbiotic relation are forbidden to meet again for an extremely long period of time, during which the boy lives in an entirely male world. These highly contrasted ways of considering the future of the mother-novice bond find an echo in the way various Anga societies fantasize about the respective procreative abilities of each sex.

Fantasy and Imaginary Constructions About Reproduction

The analysis of male initiations has revealed that the transformation of boys into men was unconsciously enacted through a female physiological model. For Angans in general, boys are at risk of being feminized by the time they spent in the womb, of being like girls since they were like them in the intra-uterine environment and were born the same way. And "femaleness is a self-propelling, competent principle in natural species and humans" (Herdt 1981: 277).

This model and these two discourses are built on a representation of female physiological functioning, which may hark back to a fantasy found in many cultures about female parthenogenesis, or "reproduction without concourse of opposite sexes or union of sexual elements" (*Shorter Oxford English Dictionary*; see also Spiro 1968: 249). That females are seen not merely as self-reproducing but also as capable of reproducing the other sex is a widely shared system of representations, because, as Georges Devereux wrote in *Femme et mythe*, "it is easier to believe that a woman can engender a child by herself than to believe that semen can produce a child on its own without the help of a woman or some equivalent" (1982: 175).[16]

This representation of the ability of women to engender beings of both sexes could easily be associated with myths, so common in many cultures, which depict a time where only women existed (Moisseeff 1987: 127).[17] Such myths are found among the Ankave; it is therefore most remarkable that northern Angans have, rather, elaborated extremely rich male parthenogenesis myths, as a whole chapter of Herdt's *Guardians of the Flutes* (1981) shows. Sambia men used to tell the adult men a secret myth recounting that Numboolyu, the first ancestor, "an unfinished pseudohermaphrodite with a small penis and female breasts" (Herdt 1981: 272), created both masculinity and femininity. As he copulated with his partner (an agemate with no definite sex at the beginning of the story, but progressively becoming identified as a woman) using her mouth, his own breasts fell flat while those of the "woman" grew larger. She became pregnant afterward and, as she was in pain, he made a vertical slit in her pubic area with a bamboo knife, letting out a female child. The other consequence of his act was that he could now copulate with the woman using her vagina. They soon begot another child, a son this time, who, when he was grown, asked his father what he should do with his erect penis. His father told him to go and copulate with his younger brother. And here is the origin of ritualized homosexuality ("boy-inseminating practices"). What the myth says is that fellatio created both masculinity and femininity since "being a homosexual fellated masculinized the hero; being a fellator feminized his mate" (292).

Among the Iqwaye, a northern Anga group inhabiting a territory between the Sambia and Ankave countries, the theme of parthenogenesis is carried even further. The primordial being "is closed in upon himself, with his fingers and toes completely interdigitated, and his penis firmly lodged in his mouth. . . . His vital conjunction holds together the sky and earth. Throughout this originary bodiliness of the cosmic man circulates his semen, which makes him grow" (Mimica 1991a: 40). A few paragraphs later, the author writes: "Omalyce, the cosmic man, is androgynous . . . his bodily gender is the source of human bodily gender in the realm of the differentiated world" (41). Omalyce then created other human beings from clay: five men, the fifth being without genitals. He brought them to life and invested them with procreative substance by creating a chain of inseminators (by fellatio) from himself to the youngest brother, who was without a penis. This last son became pregnant as a result and, having had his womb slit open, became the first woman. But this myth clearly says that the primordial beings appeared without the mediation of a woman.

Iqwaye people regard the Omalyce story as "the basis of the subsequent practice of institutionalized male homosexuality, the organization of bachelorhood, and the initiation ceremonies" (Mimica 1991a: 42–43). But during the rituals, the movement is reversed: the initiate into the fifth grade "has therefore finally become the true equivalent of Omalyce, the self-creator, precisely because he has himself procreated his own child, whereas as a young novice in the first initiation ceremony he was the equivalent of the first mud-men created and inseminated by Omalyce" (1991b: 99).

As far as we know, the Baruya have no such male-parthenogenesis oriented myth, but, for them, "Sun, the supernatural father, is the father of all, without distinction of sex or social origin" (Godelier 1986: 68). These all-male reproductive fantasies shared by the three northern Angan groups referred to here clearly parallel the exclusive use of semen as a maturation-inducing substance in male ritual. They are also exemplary of men's "minimizing the importance of, or even denying, the fertilizing powers that apparently belong only to women," as Godelier wrote (69). In short, northern Angan ideas about intrauterine growth with semen as *the* nourishing substance, boy-inseminating practices, and the male parthenogenesis myth all relate to this exclusively male reproductive fantasy world (see also Tuzin 1995: 295). They are the only modes of thought that offer an escape from the frightening implications of the male nightmare of female parthenogenesis, which, as we have seen, does not disappear from the male rituals in these groups, since breastfeeding and menstruation models are unconsciously used as models for the transformation of boys into men.

Comparative Hypotheses

To sum up, the present comparative analysis shows that Anga initiation rituals express diversely, or are variations on, a single theme of making boys into men via a physiological female reproductive model that is culturally denied or acknowledged. Looking at the details of what women do during Anga male initiations (the nature of their involvement, its significance in the gender relations, and the acknowledgment of this role) leads us to distinguish two highly contrasted configurations.

Among the Ankave, maternal blood is considered to be the only nourishing substance for the fetus; in male initiations, the physiological model for growing boys is gestation through the ingestion of red pandanus juice, a vegetal substitute for blood. Ankave mothers are essential to the achievement of the ritual process: they are collectively secluded while their sons are in the forest; they must respect the same taboos and make the same gestures as the boys. Their lengthy collective seclusion and the daily repetition of ritual acts similar to those imposed on their sons are conditions sine qua non of the success of their sons' metamorphosis into adult men. As for the crucial mother-son bond, the Ankave merely transform it whereas other Angans endeavor to sever it dramatically.

Northern Angans, by contrast, consider semen to be the substance that must be given to the boys for them to reach adulthood, a clear parallel to their ideas about procreation, which assign semen the primary role in the development of the fetus. By equating fellatio with breastfeeding, they emphasize a process that takes place after the "rebirth" of the novices and that they can handle themselves. For northern Angans, even the comments about their mothers' seclusion minimize their role. Baruya men say that a mother should stay in the village for fear of disturbing the capture of spirit familiars by the master of the initiations (Nunguye Kandavatche 1997). And male rituals aim to sever rather than transform the symbiotic mother-son bond. The Baruya, for example, literally "kill the boys' names." After the rituals, mothers and sons are not allowed to meet again for many years. The denial of women's procreative powers is also expressed in myths of male parthenogenesis, which they regard as the basis for their boy-inseminating practices.

These representations and practices represent two opposing patterns that clearly parallel the differences already noted in gender relations. It would probably be irrelevant to ask if women's participation in the rituals was the basis or the result of gender relations among the Anga. All one can do is to note that, in those societies where it is considered and acknowledged to be necessary, women fare better (Bonnemère 1996: 369–83). Women's participation in male rituals is a fundamental aspect of the highly complex sets of representations and practices on which gender relations are built and by which they are structured in Anga societies.

Among these societies at least, the rituals are obviously closely related with everyday life; I say obviously because we see these correlations, even though we cannot explain them entirely. In some way or other, the general climate of violence against women that characterizes northern Angan life (Godelier 1986: 148–49; Bonnemère 1992) corresponds with the overwhelming demonstration of male superiority during the rituals. Conversely, among the Ankave, there is no systematic depreciation of women's activities and specificities, in ritual life or beyond (Bonnemère 1996: 369–83). Nevertheless, male domination remains crucial in explaining Anga initiations, and there is not much to justify a total rejection of the existing analyses of this aspect.

Looking at what women do during male initiations certainly adds a crucial dimension to the analysis of these rituals. It leads us to focus on the relationship that links the boys to their mothers already taken into account by Herdt (1982b: 211–15). In this respect, the present chapter reveals that the very way this bond is thought and acted upon during the rituals reflects the way representations of women's procreative abilities inform the sequencing and symbolic content of ritual events. It also has crucial implications for the future of the daily relations between the boys and their mothers, which in turn have major consequences for gender relations among the Anga.

Chapter 4
Ujawe: **The Ritual Transformation of Sons and Mothers**

Marta A. Rohatynskyj

It is to some extent a matter of perspective whether one sees male initiation as an instrument of male domination and oppression, as Bonnemère notes in the Introduction. The analysis of male ritual within the context of the sexual antagonism literature of the 1950s and 1960s along with what Strathern and Stewart (this volume) see as the male exclusivity model is associated with a set of problems largely defined by issues of gender inequality and male domination. In what was termed a "new Melanesian ethnography" at the time, many of these issues were made to disappear, as Josephides (1991) puts it, largely as a result of the deconstruction of the social person into the locus of gendered relations (M. Strathern 1988). However, Ellen (1998: 147), commenting on collected papers dealing with sociality and environment in Melanesia, links the reluctance to engage in systematic and regional comparison in Melanesian ethnography to an overenthusiastic commitment to the uniqueness of the local. What seems important to say about the local "up close" is often quite different from what needs to be said about it from the distance necessary for comparison (M. Strathern 1991).

Also, the nature of the data itself has an influence on the interpretation given it. For example, speakers of the Ömie language, comprising 1,500 people residing in the Kokoda district of the Northern (Oro) Province, practiced a form of male initiation which required that novices be secluded in an underground structure called the *ujawe,* egg or bird house, until sometime in the mid- to late 1940s. When I conducted my initial research in the mid-1970s, groups of *a duvahe* (mature men of recognized social standing), who had experienced the initiation some thirty or so years earlier, were eager to reconstruct from memory the various phases of the ritual, the details of the underground seclusion structure, and so on. They also offered bits of exegesis that still shape my understanding of the meaning of the whole ritual complex. However, there is a distance here, both for them in looking back at an important experience of their adolescence and for me in trying to understand a ritual complex from the memories of informants. I have no direct experience of these ritual enactments, and the memories presented in the course of our intensive sessions are tempered by time and the setting in which they were asked to codify them into a coherent, symbolic structure. This type of data tends to evoke a formalism, even a functionalism in analysis. Had I a more direct experience of the drama, noise, and emotion of the ritual on the part of the novices, their mothers and sisters, and the adult males who conducted the ritual, my interpretation would be compelled by a much richer sensory experience.

In attempting the reconstruction, I worked with small groups of men drawn from those who claimed to have experienced the *ujawe* at least once. There was a gravity with which they undertook the task of recounting to me the structure of the ritual from the perspective of the all-knowing narrator. There was a sense in which men competed with each other to demonstrate traditional authority and degree of esoteric knowledge. I did gather some accounts of personal experience and there were moments when the group of four or five of us would be struck by nostalgia for these long ago events. These men were recognized as the personification of traditional values of leadership and maleness by the community at large and, at that time, having experienced the *ujawe* contributed to the respect awarded them as elders and leaders. They saw the lack of this experience as contributing to the "softness" of younger men and would deride their ability to speak with authority on matters of common concern: "How would you know? Have you been in the *ujawe*?" In spite of my efforts to gain as accurate a description as possible of the rituals, it is clear that their depiction must be seen as no more nor less than "statements by [relatively] acculturated natives to a European woman," as Herdt (1984b: 43) said of the ambiguity with which Manus islanders greeted Mead's questions concerning homosexual practices. I am not suggesting that there was any dissembling in the accounts of my informants; rather, I wish to underline that I have no personal experience of these events even as an indirect observer and that the recountings of the experiences themselves were structured by informant's perceptions of me, the task at hand, and the implications of the material they presented beyond the confines of the moment. Interestingly, when I returned to the Ömie in 1990, only one man survived who had undergone the initiation. When asked to talk about it, he was overcome by sadness and nostalgia for the dancing partner with whom he had entered the village danceground after emerging from seclusion, and I recorded much more emotionally charged accounts and reactions from him and the younger men who were present. I am belaboring the point of the specificity of the conditions under which such accounts of long ago experiences are recorded, not just because they fundamentally affect the nature of the accounts themselves, the perspective taken, and so on, but also because they influence the type of analysis possible of past practices as representative of a particular group's culture. A related problem of representativeness and comparability is also present when trying to deal with extant rituals, which have been modified as a result of mission, administration, and other influences of the metropolitan culture.

Finally, my presentation of the *ujawe* is informed by a larger concern with the rare rule of group affiliation that I documented among the Ömie in the initial fieldwork period. This rule was termed sex affiliation by the government anthropologist F. E. Williams in the one intact case he encountered among the Sogeri Koiari (1932). Unfortunately, he was unable to learn much about it from the Keveri, who reputedly had given it up in the face of the Rev. Charles Abel's Kwato Mission (Williams 1944). This practice of group affiliation simply means that a girl belongs to the group of her mother and a boy to the group of his father. I have interpreted the prevalence of such a practice in terms of beliefs of parthenogenesis on the part of gender-neutral persons, both male and female being seen as able to reproduce themselves. The practice of the *ujawe* I have interpreted as males reproducing themselves in imitation of the hornbill (Rohatynskyj 1990). The theme of male parthenogenesis is evinced in the detailed ethnography of the Sambia as well as other peoples, and Gilbert Herdt sees the Sambia as a limiting case (Herdt 1981). But in these cases, women are not credited with parthenogenetic capability and this is linked to their passive growth, the "naturalness" of their physical development and reproductive functions. Gillison's work (1980, 1993) posits an endless argument or competition between men and women over "the *indivisible* power to reproduce the world" (1980: 171) and thus provides an instance where both male and female parthenogenesis do have bearing. Gimi equation of male identity with features of the high mountain forest is similar in many ways to Ömie understandings, and significantly Gillison reports that men model their rites of male initiation "upon the emergence from its nesting hole of the fledgling Hornbill" (1980: 146). Bonnemère's (this volume) carefully argued discussion of parthenogenetic myths and the value placed by some groups on same-sex reproductive competence touches on many important issues, and her hypothesis is not incompatible with the Ömie material. However, the approach that I would like to develop to address the question of parthenogenesis proceeds from the current reconsideration of the relationship between human beings and the nonhuman environment yielding notions of co-evolution and interagentivity (Descola 1992; Ellen 1996; Ingold 1996). An understanding of Ömie totemism moving beyond Lévi-Strauss's (1963, 1966) metaphoric rendering decenters human physiology as the currency of gender differentiation and identifies gender distinctions as "emanating out of the relationships that people form with the non-human environment." (Bamford 1998: 46). This is a task for a larger project. For now, I would like to make two observations about male initiation and what I see as a social manifestation of beliefs about parthenogenetic reproduction among the Ömie, the rule of sex affiliation.

First of all, the form male initiation took among the Ömie historically was linked to the practice of sex affiliation. When I returned to the Ömie after an absence of fifteen years, sex affiliation was no longer practiced (Rohatynskyj 1997, 1998). Second, like Williams (1944), I find that colleagues find the notion of sex affiliation "difficult to swallow," as also they find the notion of female parthenogenesis. However, gender distinctions are becoming more recently understood as not predetermined by our idea of physiological reproductive processes, and it is in appreciating the different embeddedness of Ömie males and females within the natural environment that both sex affiliation and the entertainment of male and female parthenogenesis as a model of Ömie sociality and of the indigenous conceptualization of gender incommensurability can have currency.

The *Ma'i Ma'i*, the *Anie*, and the Human Life Cycle

There are two basic concepts that Ömie traditionally use to define their social identity, their claim to specific tracks of garden and hunting land and their tie to the ancestors. These concepts are the *ma' i ma'i*, land-based totems and the *anie*, "plant emblems," much as described for the Orokaiva by Williams (1925). The *anie* are used to express the Ömie notion of sex affiliation, which underlies a parthenogenetic view of gender reproduction. The *anie* are exhibited as the leaves of various trees and shrubs that stand for the individual in her/his absence, for example, on a forest path indicating direction of travel or as a "signature" left behind in a garden upon the removal of some garden foods by a relative. It is also the *anie* that are conceptualized as a land-based group, and adherents of a given *anie* are referred to as "people of" the particular type of tree. It is said that the *anie* groups came into being when the people first emerged from the ground. The weather was fine and then suddenly it started to rain. People scattered to find shelter under trees and from then on came to be identified with the tree that protected them. For males, the *anie* identity tends to reflect the set of *ma'i ma'i* that a man takes on in his exploitation of hunting and garden lands. This process commences after his initial experience of the *ujawe* and the range of his *ma' i ma'i* set grows as does the intimacy of his identification with them as he moves through the life cycle.

Bonnemère (1996, 1998b) emphasizes the importance of trees in Ankave-Anga ritual life. Rival (1998: 24) notes that tree symbolism materializes the living process at three levels: that of the individual, that of social groups, and that of life itself. Ömie make use of these levels of symbolization, seeing individual men as trees, the social group of the *anie* itself as embodied in the various parts of trees, and the human life cycle as the movement through the various stages of tree growth and maturity. For both male and female the growth of the tree is the predominant metaphor used to discuss movement through the life cycle. Ömie identify eight parallel stages in the life cycle. Tables 1 and 2 present the

TABLE 1. Female Life Cycle Stages

Term	Chronological age	Physical characteristics	Social characteristics	Point in ritual cycle
I. *magana harihe*	newborn–3	immobile, needs constant tending	cannot speak coherently	(naming)
II. *asoso'e*	4–10	mobile, can look after self	speaks coherently, useful in minor tasks	
III. *aboride*	11–15	puberal	making own garden	
IV. *aboride duvahe*	16–18	post-puberal, secondary sexual characteristics	aspiring to adult female role	hair-tying, nose-piercing, menstrual seclusion
V. *aboride juvije*	18–?	"breasts have dropped," physically mature	marriageable	
VI. *magana bune*	18–?	bears child	married	
VII. *magana duvahe*	30–?	mother of several children, prime of strength	known for generosity, competence, and knowledge	
VIII. *magana mavoje*	55–?	post-menopausal decline in strength	withdrawal from social life	possible relation with supernatural powers

age, social, and physical characteristics and ritual marking each stage (Rohatynskyj 1978). The terms used to describe each stage for each gender evoke key metaphors that make reference to the parallels between personal maturity and the life stages of plant life.

Stages three and four for males are termed *ase simano buno'e* (boy head short or stump) and *ase duvahe* (boy mature) and physiologically represent the periods from pre-puberty to the onset of secondary sexual characteristics. For women the stages are termed *aboride* (girl) and *aboride duvahe* (girl mature) and mark the same physiological stages in life.

Ritually, both males and females were said to undergo the hair-tying and nose-piercing rites in order to move from one stage to the other. Females also will have undergone menstrual seclusion. Interestingly, in light of Bonnemère's discussion (this volume), Baruya and Sambia pierced the nasal septums of both males and females. Stages six and seven are termed *ama'e/ae bune* and *ama'e/ae duvahe* for the male, and movement into stage six is defined by marriage and fathering a child. Movement into stage seven is defined by fathering several children and the development of proficiency in *dame*, hunting and garden magic. For the female, stages six and seven are termed *magana bune* (woman short or stump) and *magana duvahe* (woman mature). Movement into stage six is defined by marriage and the bearing of a child, and stage seven by the bearing of several children.

Bune refers to the stump of a tree or the point in the trunk before it bifurcates into the major branches. *Duvahe* refers to the point in the trunk where the major branches diverge. This term signifies maturity as opposed to immaturity of the social person whether of boys (*ase*) or girls (*aboride*), men (*a* or *am'e*) or women (*magana*). It was said that social maturity for men and women depended on the network of ritual exchanges they entered into, and that the spread of the branches of a tree symbolized this multiple network of ties. In this sense, the use of the adjective *duvahe* in these terms indicates progression along the life course as well as the social placement of people. An *a duvahe* was said to be at the crux of the tree where the major branches started to diverge. The ancestors were said to be the roots, and the children and grandchildren were seen as the smaller branches, twigs, and leaves. Although when speaking thus, informants were referring to the physiological reproduction of an *anie*, they often collapsed this into a parallel depiction in terms of exchange relations.

Competitive exchange and the "making" of kinship through reciprocal obligations are well-developed themes in Ömie feasting and exchange obligations. The felling of a large tree is seen as an occasion for the singing of *ture ture*, laments or mourning songs naming various totemic sites and the experiences of ancestors and relatives at these places. The death of big men is seen as comparable. It was said that a man will grow old and suffer and become weak, and suddenly like a large tree will crash to the ground and be no more.

The term *juvije* means "ripe" in the sense of a ripe fruit. The term is used for both male and female in stage five of the life cycle, marked by marriageability, both sexes having had their nasal septums pierced, the boys having undergone the *ujawe* ritual and the girls having experienced menarche. Their bodies are seen as ripe for reproduction, the skin tight, shiny, and smooth. The beauty of males at this stage of life was not likened to a fruit, however; rather, young men were said to be as shiny and smooth as an eel or were likened to trees with smooth, light colored bark. I have classed the eel with the minor fauna *ma'i ma'i* even though it is charged with intense male mystical power. It was the young women who were likened to a fruit, specifically the *siha'e* (hog

TABLE 2. Male Life Cycle Stages

Term	Chronological age	Physical characteristics	Social characteristics	Point in ritual cycle
I. *ase harihe*	newborn–3	immobile, needs constant tending	cannot speak coherently	birth ritual and naming
II. *asoso'e*	4–8	mobile, minimally self-sufficient	speaks coherently, useful in minor tasks	
III. *ase simano buno'e*	9–15	puberal	making own garden	
IV. *ase duvahe*	16–20	post-puberal, secondary sexual characteristics	aspiring to male adult responsibilities	hair-tying, nose-piercing
V. *ase juvije*	20–27	fully mature physically	marriageable	*ujawe* experience
VI. *ama'e/ ae bune*	25–?	fathers child	married	
VII. *a/ama'e duvahe*	36–?	at prime of strength	several children and exchange ties	proficient in *dame* and other magic
VIII. *a mavoje*	55–?	declining strength	withdrawal from social life and labor	perfection of *ha'erive* and secret knowledge

plum, *Spondias dulcis*), a yellowish orange fruit growing wild and eaten by both humans and cassowaries. The initiation rituals were seen as making male adolescents grow big and capable of reproduction, but the production of children cannot be seen as the culmination of Ömie notions of maleness.

Although the movement to the final stage of the life cycle is one of declining physical strength into the infirmity of old age, the supernatural power of the individual male augments until stage eight, where men have control over *ha'erive*. This form of supernatural power was explained as emanating from the male body itself, expressed in the spoken word, the breath and very presence of the *ha'erive ae* (man with *ha'erive*). Men became the embodiment of the power of the ancestors, pure agency. It is at this point in the life cycle that men have accumulated in their bodies the power drawn from the various totemic sites that act in hunting and gardening ritual as sources of ancestral agency. It is at this stage that men develop a complete identity with the whole range of *ma'i ma'i* that reflect the history of their movement over the land and with the land itself. A similar notion could be seen as expressed in the Siane practice (Salisbury 1965) of spreading the spirit of important men over the whole clan territory by the separate burial of each limb at different sites. The Siane, like the Ömie, equate the body of important men with ancestral spirit and the land.

The *ma'i ma'i* can be grouped into four categories: (1) the major fauna, including a named New Guinea eagle, wild pig, snake, bird of paradise, and at times the Vulturine parrot; (2) trees, including the large banyan-like *marove*, the home of ancestral spirits, other aged and imposing trees of the hunting grounds, as well as various fruit- and nut-bearing trees; (3) geographical features, such as rivers, creeks, pools of water, waterfalls, caves, hills, large boulders and rock walls; (4) minor fauna, including small snakes, cuscus, frogs, eels, flying foxes, and so on. Each adult male of recognized social standing, *a duvahe*, ideally bears a full complement of the major fauna *ma'i ma'i*. This is the most inclusive category of totems and reflects the three territorial units resident in the Mawoma valley. The sets of totems are associated with myths of migration from the origin place in the Wawonga valley and particular territorial unit sets, comprised of the New Guinea eagle, pig, snake, and bird of paradise or Vulturine parrot, are believed to reside on high mountains marked by a major totemic tree and sacred pool. Within the pool lives the totemic eel, but this minor fauna totem is also said to reside in various pools and creeks of land claimed by less inclusive groupings and individual men.

A duvahe also claim totems from the other categories, indicating their own personal land claims. Speaking the name of a *ma'i ma'i* in public marks the situation as a confrontation of male political authority and interests. The use of the name of any particular totem makes claim to the land with which the totem is associated, to the magico-religious knowledge contained in the myths and *kine'e joe* (bush spirit stories) in which the *ma'i ma'i* figures, and to the collective power of the spirits of the dead who are believed to reside at the various *ma'i ma'i* sites. The speaking of these names is thus a supernaturally and politically charged event and men in 1990, after most of the *ma'i ma'i* names had fallen into disuse, said, "It was our way of praying."

Males would take on the complement of major fauna *ma'i ma'i* of the man on whose land they grew up. This could be a father or other paternal relative, or it could be a maternal relative if the boy grew up on maternal land. This process of male children taking on the totemic names of the father, as the male who fed them from his land, was in keeping with the tenet that boys follow their fathers on the land. Men would take both male and female children with them and show them the totemic sites that belonged to them, teaching them the names as well as associated myths and histories of naming. It was also generally held that "women did not have *ma'i ma'i*" because, given patrilocal marriage, women left the lands of their fathers. However, this statement was contradicted by adult female informants who did claim to have *ma'i ma'i*, at times pointing to distant trees of the places where they had grown up. Although I could find no instance where women had direct claim to land in their own right, male informants, when pressed on the point, conceded that women did have claim to the *ma'i ma'i* of their husbands. Each gender focused on a different aspect of women's life in relation to the use and exploitation of land, but there is an ambiguity in these contradictory perspectives. There were two instances that women did invoke *ma'i ma'i* names in their own right, as far as I was able to establish. One instance I witnessed. On the death of a three-year-old female child, the mother directed the spirit of the child to her own (her father's) totemic *marove* tree. When I asked whether it would be the case that a mother would invoke her father's totem at the death of both male and female children, neither male nor female informants were able to answer definitively. The second instance about which I have information was provided me by senior male informants in the context of the *ujawe* ritual. The ambiguity of whether the named *ma'i ma'i* is in fact the mother's father's or the father's will serve as a focus of my discussion of women in the male initiation.

A Description of the *Ujawe* Ritual

The reasons given for the discontinuance of the *ujawe* ritual were several. First, pressure was apparently exerted by the administration, seeing the long seclusion of boys as harmful to their health, although several officers included detailed reports of the tattoos and the underground structure in their patrol reports. Early mission patrols during the immediate postwar period also expressed disapproval, saying the ceremonial complex was a "heathen" practice. Also, several disruptive events made it impossible to organize such largescale celebrations. Continuing warfare with the neighboring Orokaiva led to loss of large tracts of land. The Japanese/Australian battle for the Kokoda Trail drew many ablebodied men into supporting roles, and some had started to work on coastal plantations. Finally, the eruption of Mount Lamington in 1951 forced many groups of Ömie into relief camps. The men who underwent the *ujawe* recalled an attempt to organize the initiation some years after the eruption, but they found that "all the old people had died" and there was no one to "help" them with the matter. They lamented, "Before we had the *ujawe*, we had great feasts and we worked very hard for them. Now the government has given us coffee and chillies and we work hard at that. It is easier work, but before it was a better life."

Up until then, the *ujawe* took place on a seven- to twelve-year cycle. None of my informants had undergone it more than once. All boys who had reached the status of *ase duvahe*, who had passed puberty and showed secondary sexual characteristics such as hair on the face and chest, were considered ready for initiation. Those of the previous stage of life, *ase simana buno'e*, were also included, and most of my informants had been at this stage when they were initiated. Usually, it was said, boys entered the *ujawe* twice, in the belief that if the boy was strong enough at the *ase simana buno'e* stage the ordeal would do him good and help him grow. These younger boys were generally not tattooed, as it was believed they could not bear the pain. Sometimes the first tattoo on the chest over the sternum was attempted, just to see if they could stand the pain, but further tattoos were left until the *ase duvahe* stage.

An *ase duvahe*, once he entered the *ujawe*, left with the full complement of tattoos on the chest, back, arms, and thighs. Then he became an *ase juvije*, a mature, marriageable man. Men recalled the fear they experienced at the long seclusion and the pain of being tattooed. They said that if a young man entered the *ujawe* for a third time, he would leave with tattoos covering his forearms and calves as well. It was said that this third round of tattooing was "like washing," the initiate no longer feeling the pain. This would allow him to be called an *a duvahe*, a mature man of social standing, a stage usually signaled by marriage and the development of exchange networks.

Large gardens were planted one growing season in advance of the planned feast. Pigs were marked to be paid for the tattooing, and large amounts of game were accumulated and smoked. Extensive gardens were necessary not only for the emergence feast that hosted guests from other villages but also to maintain the boys in seclusion. The novices were responsible for aiding in the clearing of land for the "feasting villages," which were built close to the site of the proposed *ujawe*. The last observance of the feast recalled by several informants involved the consolidation of three groups of boys, who had been secluded separately, into one *ujawe* for the ritual emergence. About thirty boys were involved in that common emergence. The informant with the most extensive tattooing recalled that feasting platforms were built between the hamlet and the *ujawe*, which was off in the bush. He had experienced the *ujawe* only once, at about age eighteen, after the Japanese war. He recalled similar large-scale preparations as a very small boy.

The actual construction of the *ujawe* took place at the end of the rainy season about April or May. The structure had to be built and the boys secluded within one day. A ditch was dug into the ground about four feet deep, the exact size dependent on the number being initiated. In one instance it was said that a ditch approximately ten feet by five could accommodate about a dozen novices. A frame of saplings was built over the ditch and covered with sago palm leaves. This in turn was covered with two more layers of specifically named leaves and then with a layer of bark. The whole structure was packed with earth, so that no light could get in. The only opening was a low door facing west, low and narrow enough that a fully grown boy had to twist his torso and crouch to get in. No fire was built in the structure, and there were no platforms. The floor was strewn with sweet-smelling leaves.

The *ujawe* was built to the east of the feasting village. A small structure was built in front of the doorway to provide a place for tattooing and for eating. Then a tall wall of leaves was constructed around the whole to hide everything from view. The bush behind this palisade was used by the boys as a toilet area and for washing with the juices of various vines.

As the structure reached completion, the initiates bid farewell to their female relatives especially, and to male relatives they would not see for the duration of their seclusion. Informants stated there was a fear that some people would die during the seclusion period, and that they would not be seen again. Female relatives were said to undertake the full mourning ritual, wailing and throwing themselves on the ground. Mothers and fathers' sisters were said to retreat to their houses and conduct themselves as if a death had taken place. Aside from this, I have no information about the activities of the mother, and at the time I did not ask whether these women were seen as in seclusion as well. It was stressed, however, that the responsibilities of the father and the mother's brother were to keep the novice supplied with large quantities of game, *mie*. This food was seen as essential to making him grow, and it was said that the game would be fed to the mother as well as to the novice. Frequently, I was told in other contexts that it is the husband's and the mother's brother's responsibility to provide a woman with game while she is pregnant.

The novices were led by a few senior men to the bush behind the *ujawe* area, where they were directed to circle around very tall trees with fine smooth bark. They would strike these trees with their hands and then strike their chests, saying "I will grow as great as this tree." Then they would call out their ancestors' name. The guardians would take lengths of a particular vine, *bore*, split down the middle with the ends left attached, and place them in the path of the initiates. Each boy would pass through the vines and leave them on the ground for the next one to pass through. The initiates washed in a pool of a river or stream and rubbed their bodies with rough leaves. They donned a specially made perineal band given by their fathers, leaving the abandoned clothes tied to the roots of a tree at the edge of the water. This band was called the *kine'e uhe* (bush spirits' band). They donned armlets and stuck leaves of the red croton in them. They painted around their eyes and down the sides of their mouths with red clay. They rubbed the juice from the vine on their bodies to make them fragrant. This process was meant to change their appearance. They were said to be *sibimirove*, a word translated as "mocking themselves" or "pretending to be other than what they were."

The ritual washing signaled the start of the prohibitions that must be observed. Each initiate at this stage would prepare for himself a small reed flute that he would use to communicate with others, to signal need to the guardians but also to warn people, should he find himself outside the *ujawe* for any reason, to avoid him. The high whistling sound made by this instrument was identified as the noise that *kine'e* (bush spirits) made in their encounters with men.

A ritual meal was eaten before entry, composed of red banana, various flavorful herbs, and ginger baked in a ground oven, served with game and various early yams.

There was some disagreement on the period of time the novices were actually secluded in the *ujawe*. Periods as long as ten months to a year are named in my notes. One informant claimed that the ritual meal eaten prior to entry was actually the one eaten at the first yam harvest ceremony. This is significant because several informants agreed that the meal eaten upon emergence was made up of the last yams to be harvested. Boys entered the *ujawe*, then, in about May and emerged by October. This period when yams are plentiful is seen as the feasting season, while the rest of the year is referred to as *vadune*, famine time.

As far as could be ascertained, the initiates spent their time in seclusion crowded into a small, sweaty space. They were not allowed to touch each other and were supposed to stay very quiet, communicating with the guardians only with the flutes. Informants emphasized that the goal of the seclusion was to make the boys grow big, that is, fat. Inactivity was seen as contributing to this. The major prohibition during seclusion was eating pig and cassowary and any contact with females. Even hearing the voices of females was seen as detrimental to the novices' development, and the use of the words for female entities was forbidden. Ritual words were used instead for females of the various life cycle stages and for pig and cassowary. Several varieties of greens, "cabbages," were also prohibited because it was generally believed they would stunt the growth of ritually vulnerable individuals. Emphasis was placed on the ingestion of male foods such as "white" bananas, yams, and sugar cane, as opposed to the "red" varieties. Smoked game was also emphasized. Initiates could have no water to drink, drinking the juice of the *bore* vine instead. Nor could they bathe in running water; rather they were encouraged to find pools of still water or use the juice of vines to wash. All their foods were roasted or smoked.

A kinsman, *o'muene'e*, was responsible for making the tattoos. This individual was compensated with a pig for contact with the initiates' blood in the process of tattooing. When the boys were judged fat enough and their skin light enough, as a result of extended seclusion from the sun, several were led out to be tattooed. The tattooist was assisted by another close kinsman of the boy, and as the skin was quickly punctured with a large thorn and the blood wiped away, a mournful lament was sung. This lament was classed in the genre *ture ture*, which included all mourning songs.

There was an order in which the tattoos were applied. First, a diamond shape was outlined over the sternum, which was seen as the seat of the *aru'ahe*, the spirit. This diamond shape was said to represent the fruit *siha'e*, to which the beauty of sexually mature girls was likened. This initial tattoo was extended along the sternum, at later stages or with more stoic novices, to link the initial diamond to a circle, which in turn was linked to another diamond. It was said that the circle was a tree with the fruit on either side. Tattooing would stop there with younger boys, of the *ase simana buno'e* stage. For older boys and if the boy was agreeable, the tattoos would extend to just above the navel and along the pectoral muscles to the upper arm. The next day, the lower abdomen would be outlined, then the front of the thighs, the upper arms down to the elbow, and finally the back. Thus, tattooing of one individual could take several days depending on ability to bear the pain. Some novices had to be held down in order for the men to work, and others quickly gave up. If a large part of the body had been tattooed, the boy was allowed to sleep outside the *ujawe* for a few nights. But it was emphasized that the structure could never be left empty. A few boys had to stay in it, in order to "keep it warm." Boys remained in the *ujawe* until their skin had healed. If a man had just the diamond shape over the sternum, he could say he was *soru'e*, tattooed, in opposition to those with no tattoos, who had skin "like that of the pig." It was emphasized by informants that a boy could not be considered a *juvije duvahe*, mature but unmarried male, until tattoos covered the back of the thighs and the inside of the forearms. This ideal was seldom attained, mostly because few mature men remained unmarried. However, such cases were seen as a matter of the number of times a boy entered the *ujawe* and a function of individual stoicism.

Emergence occurred in three steps: breaking out of the *ujawe*, presentation of the boys to their mothers and fathers' sisters, and presentation of the boys to the public in the feasting village. The final meal that the boys ate while in seclusion was a ritual meal composed of the last yam to reach maturity. This yam was roasted and cut into small pieces and presented to the initiates on a black palm leaf. The leaves of this particular palm were traditionally used to wrap the bodies of the dead. Each boy took only a token piece of this yam. They all returned to the *ujawe* and the youngest boy was selected from among them. Informants recalled that this boy could be as young as nine years old. A hornbill beak was tied onto his head, and he was directed to a spot where some of the earth and bark had been pulled away from the top of the roof of the *ujawe*. The youngest poked his head through the intervening leaves and worked his way out of the top of the *ujawe*. He was then called the oldest, the first to emerge or to be born. The other boys followed suit, climbing out the top of the structure, with the oldest boy among them emerging last. This oldest would then be considered the youngest. All males would have gathered around the structure to watch their young relatives emerge. They sang the fighting songs of the ancestors of these boys as they emerged. These songs fall into the genre of *marove doe*, feasting songs, and dances. All men were dressed in full fighting regalia and there was a great drumming, singing, and shouting as the boys emerged.

The initiates were then led back to the stream where they had washed before entry, each accompanied by his father and his namegiver, who was often his mother's brother. There they underwent a further ordeal. The guardians had prepared many rough waist bands made out of cane and purposely made too small to fit over the hips. The *ase simana buno'e* were given only one of these to put on, whereas the *ase duvahe* were given up to six or seven. What occurred next was a type of tug of war, with some men pulling the band up the boy's body and others pulling it down. This was very painful, and they cried out for their mothers and their fathers to help them. To ease the pain they were carried to the mud of the stream and rolled around in it until they and their guardians were entirely plastered with it. Significantly, women experiencing difficulty in labor were similarly treated. All the waist bands were cut off except one, which was wrapped in bark cloth and worn for an indeterminate period of time. The boys then washed in clear running water and donned feather and shell decorations provided by their fathers and mothers' brothers.

Once they were properly adorned, the novices were led to a garden house not far from the feasting village. There they were directed to recline against the walls, careful not to disarrange their feathers, and wait for nightfall. As the sun set, the mothers and the fathers' sisters assembled and with cane pith torches entered the garden house to see their children after the long separation. I will use a direct translation of one of the senior men's description.

The boys are all sitting in two lines against the wall of the house, pretending to be asleep. There is no fire in the house, it is dark. The mothers and the fathers' sisters come to the door, and the guardians silently indicate where each child is reclining. The two women grope over the bodies to reach their child, and the mother takes her son in her arms as if to give him the breast. The boy, with eyes closed, reaches out and touches the offered breast, saying "*Mamo, nasi ame*" (Mother, my breast). The mother answers "*Nasi jiebe, nasi Asapa jiebe*" (My eel, my eel from Asapa creek). [This is an example. The mother would name the relevant totemic creek.] She then hugs him silently to her and withdraws.

At daybreak, the emergence into the village started. At the eastern end of the feasting village, a special structure to house the boys was constructed. People lined either side of the public space to allow for the entry of the initiates from the west. The initiates' fathers and namegivers/mothers' brothers fetched the boys two at a time. As the boys emerged, their grandfathers' fighting song was sung. It was said that there was much shouting, women crying with joy at seeing their transformed sons and drumming and singing. Mothers, at this time, indulged in a bit of *sibimirove*, mocking themselves or pretending to be other than what they are. They would run at their son with their bark skirt flying loose as if to expose their genitals, only to have another skirt tightly wrapped underneath. As they did so, they again called out the name of the totemic creek inhabited by "my eel." The boys' younger sisters would trail behind him, hanging on to the tags of his bark cloth band. Informants spoke frequently of the initiates as newborn children, some requiring help in walking because of their added weight and long period of inactivity. The younger sisters looked after the initiates and guarded them throughout the feasting against the touch of mature girls, which was dangerous to the boys in their ritually vulnerable state. The emergence feast was seen as the occasion of major ritual exchange by informants in their mid-seventies, and they lamented this loss of grandeur.

Ujawe and Male Parthenogenesis

The group of men I worked with to arrive at this reconstruction were eager commentators on the significance of this ritual complex. They readily offered interpretations of the meaning of the ritual acts, often delighting at my tentative attempts to suggest linkages and parallels. Although, the word they used to describe the ritual enactments was *sibimirove*, which I have translated as "mocking themselves" or "pretending to be other than what they are," they categorically identified the novices while in the *ujawe* as (1) *kine'e*, spirits of the dead; (2) fetuses in their mother's womb; and (3) baby hornbills in the nest. Each of these identities implies a different set of understandings of the necessity of literally growing boys in the ground.

Yams in the ground, like boys in the *ujawe*, are *kine'e*. It is men who grow yams. They perform the necessary garden magic that calls upon the *kine'e* to grow the yams, and in their ritual formulas the yams are implored to go straight down and search the water of boundary creeks. *Kine'e* manifest themselves in the very growth of the yams. Women and children are forbidden entry into the yam gardens for days after these ritual enactments, and the major contribution of the women in the growth of yams is in the two weedings seen as necessary. It is forbidden at any time to say the word *kine'e* in the gardens by the same logic that forbids the saying of the word in the *ujawe*: it would spoil the growth of the yam or the boy. And of course, sexual intercourse is forbidden in the garden. However, yams grow well and the *kine'e* are pleased when the rich repertoire of *kine'e joe* (bush spirit stories) are told in garden houses in the months that the yams are in the ground. These are myths that recount fantastic events: the transformation of real men into *kine'e* or trees and animals of the forest, horrific deaths, dismemberments, and reconstitution in totally different guises drawing on the full pantheon of totemic sites and beings. Ömie grow dozens of varieties of yams in an array of shapes and sizes, some reaching more than two meters in length. They challenge each other as to which man will grow the biggest yam of the season. Once the yam is judged to be fully grown it is carefully excavated, carried from the garden by the group of agnates, intricately painted and decorated, and displayed on the feasting rack. In the years that the *ujawe* was held, as the yams were starting to be taken from the ground, boys were being placed in it.

Tuzin (1972) documents a similar equivalence between yams, spirits, and children for the Ilahita Arapesh. Yams are seen by these people as the only plants with spirits, and they are accorded an active life underground, moving about and visiting friends in other gardens. Yams are equated to the human body and treated as children. In pantomimic episodes among the Siane (Salisbury 1965: 65–66), the players who "are *korova*," a term Salisbury translates as undifferentiated ancestral spirits, enact an equivalence between the production of children and large piles of vegetable food. The Ömie practice of growing boys like yams and in the growth process equating both with spirits of the ancestors is paralleled by similar beliefs and practices among the Ilahita Arapesh and the Siane.

Boys are *kine'e* in another sense as well. I translate the term itself as spirit of the dead or as bush spirit. It is believed that the spirit of a living person, *aru'ahe*, leaves the body upon death and lingers in the vicinity of her/his home for a few days or weeks. Eventually, it finds its way to a *ma'i ma'i* site that seems appropriate; once in the bush it is referred to as *kine'e*. They thus form a pool of ancestral spirits. Entry into the *ujawe* is treated as a death by the novice's relatives, and emergence is treated as a rebirth in the form of the boy's *hije*, ancestor of the grandparental generation. Queries as to whether the grandparent replaced by the boy is maternal or paternal would always be met with the same response, "It is one and the same." Frequently, Ömie explained to me that the *anie* distinctions hold for one's own generation, that of one's parents, and that of one's children. After that it is all *hije*, a term used for all consanguines of the +/−2 generation. A number of issues impinge on such statements, not least of which is the form of marriage prescription; however I cannot explore them here. My point for the purpose of this chapter is simply that the *ujawe* recycles spirits and cancels fragments of lineality and history of bi-sexual reproduction in the person of the novice.

"Because they are in mother's womb, they can't say female words," one informant explained. These words include those for woman, girl, mother, pig, and cassowary. Novices could not be seen or see any of these female beings while in seclusion. The logic of these word avoidances was similar to that of the word *kine'e*; because this force is at work, it cannot be named. Men readily volunteered interpretations of the ritual as rebirth. "*Ujawe* is like mother's womb and they struggle to be born again," one man said. The struggle to pass the coarse waistbands over the hips after emergence was likened to the passage through the birth canal. Rebirth was further emphasized by another informant: "It is a newborn child. They go in where the sun sets and come out where sun rises. Go in, they die; come out, they're born."

Seeing the hole in the ground as mother's womb equates the earth itself with the mother of men. This is so in the Ömie cosmology in two senses. Humans originated by emerging out of a hole in the ground in the Wawonga (Upper Kumusi) valley. This myth is shared by a number of neighboring peoples. The light shining through a small hole from the outside into the underground world shone first on the sternum of the first man. By following this ray of light, humans discovered and entered the aboveground world. In a very real sense, then, the earth mothered men and allowed them to be born into the larger world. The placing of the first tattoo, the diamond shape on the sternum, the seat of the *aru'ahe*, was explained by some men as an evocation of this primal awakening.

Also, there is a way in which the landscape itself is seen as female. Gillison's (1980, 1993) powerful evocations of Gimi rivers of menstrual blood and dark, boggy places as wombs come to mind. Ömie made an equivalence between still bodies of water called *a'a* and blood. These lakes, several of which are permanently red in color due to a particular alga, were in all instances sacred, *mairi'e, ma'i ma'i* sites. Some informants explained that the clothes discarded by the novices and tied to the roots of the tree by the pool in which washing took place acted as an umbilical chord. The drinking of water was itself prohibited and novices were instructed to drink the juice of the vine, *bore*. And while the Sambia were eager to preserve the level of semen in a man's body and, unlike the Ömie, saw semen alone as producing the fetus, the image of Sambia males drinking tree sap (Herdt 1981: 251) and Ömie novices sucking juice from a forest vine both point to the nurturance of trees and other forest plants. I am less concerned here with the gender of the substance taken from the plants than with the nature of the act.

Although not included in the repertoire of *ma'i ma'i*, the hornbill is seen as everyone's *ma'i ma'i*. It was the hornbill that led people out of the ground in the primal emergence, and Ömie say that its name, *bubuore*, is a *ma'i ma'i*. Hornbills lay their eggs in holes of trees some sixty to one hundred feet above the ground. There the female with anywhere from one to three eggs is sealed in the compartment and fed through a slit by the male. It is the male who breaks away the seal and allows the fledglings to emerge. Ömie recapitulate human emergence from the ground in the *ujawe*, returning to their mythic origin to reincarnate novices as the embodiment of their grandfathers.

The Mother's Eel

Discussing the eel trapping ceremony held to mark the end of the mourning period among the Ankave-Anga, Lemonnier (1993a: 80) concludes that "the eel functions here as the equivalent, or marker, of a piece of territory held through the male line." He notes its mythic male origin as the severed remains of a giant penis. The phallic nature of the eel is noted by the Ömie as well, and it is associated with the most powerful forms of yam magic. The slime from the skin of the eel, or even the water plants from the pool the eel inhabits, is collected and inserted in the hole in the earth made for the placing of seed yams. This is done sometimes using the ancient stone pestles Ömie treasure as "magical stones," and men explained the ritual as like human copulation. The equivalence between semen and the mucous-like covering of the eel's body was noted. Lemonnier speaks of the fatty-flesh of the eel as forming the human body's fat.

The eel is the most highly localized of *ma'i ma'i*, believed to reside in a particular pool of a creek or a river and is associated with garden land claimed by a number of agnatically related men. Creeks form the most clear boundaries of garden land and the male substance of the eel is directly fed to the yams growing in the ground. Given this, the mother's *sibimirove* at the emergence of the initiates brings to mind the equivalences that Gillison (1993), in her psychoanalytic analysis of myth and ritual, notes for the Gimi between menstrual blood, the primal penis and the child. In her analysis women have penises within them, as they have a child within them before they actually reach maturity, marry, and conceive. It is in these terms that the Ömie mother, running at her newly emerged son, playing at exposing her genitals, and evoking her eel *ma'i ma'i*, can be understood.

Whitehead (1986) distinguishes male fertility cults in Papua New Guinea that emphasize a common ritual manhood as opposed to the reinforcing of solidarity within kin-defined units. She identifies regional social structural features that underlie the two differing emphases but admits that some societies seem to demonstrate a combination of both clanhood and manhood themes. She sees the more westerly Eastern Highlanders such as the Kuma, Chimbu, and Siane as manifesting ritual foregrounding the clan, but writes of the Siane that their male initiation "strikingly reveals the intrusion of clan-oriented meaning into the procedures for making men" (1986a: 93). Salisbury (1965: 60) is himself clear about the clanhood aspect of the initiation, stating that "A boy is initiated into his father's group." But clanhood for the Siane, probably more so than for any other of the highlands groups described at that time, involved the transmission of ancestral spirit through the food grown on specific tracts of land and enlivened by the clan pool of ancestral *korova* (spirits of the dead). As a result most rituals centered around the eating of pork or vegetable food that was termed "spirit food" in that it was sacrificed to the *korova* but also contained the spirit of the ancestors adding to the spiritual substance of the man and the woman who consumed it. These clanhood fertility rituals were very much about specific tracts of land, the spirits associated with them and their produce.

The Ilahita Arapesh, on the other hand, are classified as partaking of the northern bloodletting, manhood-emphasizing type of fertility ritual by Whitehead (1986a: 87–88). Although I do not want to deal with the ritual itself, it is interesting to note that the Ilahita saw parallel pedigrees to people in the yams brought to the marriage by the husband and the wife. In the initial part of the marriage the yams had to be kept separate although, Tuzin writes, "The sharing of vital fluids involved in sexual intercourse establishes a spiritual harmony between an individual and his spouse's yams which permits each of the parties to relate to the other's ancestral yams" (1972: 236). It was in the latter stages of the marriage that such distinctions became less important to the point that at the marriage of the couple's first child only token efforts were made to keep the yams separate in that "for all practical purposes the spirits of the old couple and the spirits of their yams have fused" (236). Ömie women were given seed yams by their mothers to take to their husbands' land and to plant in their own garden plots. Informants envisaged a pedigree of yams paralleling the line of women who transmitted from mother to daughter seed yams to be grown on the lands of their husbands.

Without resorting to too mechanistic an explanation or reducing the complexity of relations, at issue here is a conceptualization of local identity as based on spiritual substance contained in the produce of the land. The clanhood/manhood themes played out in the *ujawe* complex underline that, in the instance of sex affiliation, male identity and kin group identity are in fact the same. Returning to the notion that yams parallel human group distinctions, understanding women's participation in the *ujawe* forces a consideration of the ambiguity of women in relation to the land and the pool of ancestors that sustains them. The recycling of men, by growing them as *kine'e* within ancestral soil to emerge as embodiments of their grandfathers, contrasts with the growing of women, who emerge from their mothers' wombs and who are nurtured on the surface of the lands of fathers and husbands. The ambiguity of women's relation to the tract of land on which she is living as an adult emerges in my notes concerning whose *ma'i ma'i* the mother actually calls out at the sight of her son in his reincarnated form. Initial answers were always "Her *ma'i ma'i* eel," which I understood to be the one of her father's land. When asked for clarification, informants always answered "The *ma'i ma'i* eel of her husband's land." One way of resolving this ambiguity is to allow that for the Ömie, as for the Ilahita Arapesh, there is a moment when the spiritual and material stock of the husband and wife become fused. The woman speaks the name of her husband's totemic eel as a product of her own body, as having emerged from her own genitals, as having been fed by her own breast milk. This transformation is signaled just as the product of their relationship, their first-born son, is transformed into the embodiment of an ancestral spirit of the land on and in which he was grown.

Male Initiation as a Transformation of the Mother's Status

I had always been puzzled by the ritual sequence enacting the reintroduction of the boys to the mother and the father's sister. When I asked informants about the significance of this sequence, they answered that it was to show the mother how the boys had grown and to give them an opportunity to reacquaint themselves with their sons. When I asked why the father's sister was also included in this ritual, the general answer given was that she was "like the mother and like the father." The way the father's sister is like the mother is a problem that preoccupied the classical descent theorists, as is the problem of how the mother's brother is like the mother. Marilyn Strathern's dividual person is compatible with and indeed grows out of descent theory's attempts to come to terms with the conflictual claims of lineage identity and gender identity. Strathern has simplified the problem by disregarding the significance of lineality, clan, and specificity of land-based groups and by focusing on gender identity, which she defines, in its complete form, as inherently androgynous. Using a fantasized, mythic incestuous tie between the girl and her father, the male child placed within the girl by the father and expelled as menstrual blood at menarche, Gillison expresses a notion of claim by the father's group on the product of female fertility similar to that recognized by descent theory (1993: 244–45). In Ömie terms, patrilineal identity would be expressed as identity with a set of *ma'i ma'i*. The same sex pair of the mother and the father's sister would share an experience of being nurtured by the same land. Normatively, the father's sister would have eaten off that land until her marriage, and the mother would have commenced to do so upon her own marriage. Their similarity would thus be in the shared mystical substance of the land. Similarly, the mother's brother would be living on the mystical substance of the land that nurtured the mother until her marriage. These partial juxtapositions of mystical substance, interrupted by the requirements of patrilocal residence and the probability of hamlet exogamy, serve in Ömie terms to encode in the bodies of the mother and the father's sister, and of the mother and the mother's brother, what descent theory saw as the problem of gender identity in unilineal systems, the male component of women's fertility in Gillison's psychoanalytic rendering and the inherent androgyny of persons according to Marilyn Strathern.

In the sequence of struggling to pass through the series of bands prior to the emergence into the village, the mother's brother was said by some informants to be pulling the band up, while the father was pulling the band down, working to allow the boy to be born. The mother's brother, at some level a representative of the mother, is working against this male rebirth. Under conditions of sex affiliation where the gender of the individual becomes determinative of the *anie* identity, the mother's brother is attempting to claim the product of his sister's body for their pool of ancestral spirits, for his patrilineage.

The participation of the father's sister in the garden house reintroduction of the boy to his female relatives was not elaborated by informants. It was said that the same act was performed by the boy with the father's sister—the grasping of the breast, the pretense at suckling, the evocation of the father's eel *ma'i ma'i*. The general expectation of the *mu'e*, the father's sister, was that she acts like the mother and feeds the child. It was said in other contexts that the arrival of the *mu'e* was heralded by cries of joy by children because they knew she would be bringing food for them. As much as the *ma'i ma'i* allow for a sharing of identity between brother and sister and between wife and sister-in-law, the *anie*, plant emblem, separates brothers and sisters. It is possible under some conditions that the wife and sister-in-law could share an *anie*. Informants recognized that men had claim to both their mother's and their father's *anie*, but that eventually the *anie* of the father or another male relative, depending whose *ma'i ma'i* set was passed on to the boy, became more important. It became more important because it is associated with the land-based totems that provide the individual male right to land and identity with the line of ancestors who claimed and in many cases named the set of totems.

Even though I have included the eel in the category of the minor fauna, it is the one totem most associated with male mystical agency. The "slime" from the body of the eel, or even the weeds growing in the creek where the eel resides, is seen as powerful garden magic. Eating eel is a ritual act. The invocation of the totemic eel is a way of invoking the most intense *woroe*, male mystical agency. The fact that the mother in two sequences of the post-seclusion ritual calls the boy the totemic eel from the creek belonging to the boy's father's totemic repertoire signals a number of transformations of the boy's status. He is clearly now identified with a "male" entity; the phallic symbolism is evident. He is identified with an entity charged with *woroe*, male mystical agency. He is identified with an entity that places him, locates him on the land, within that totemic set of his father. It can be argued that this ritual for the boy of the *ase simana bune*, or later, stage of life provides him with the core symbolic association with a particular area of land delimited by a complex hierarchy of totems defining an agnatic group. The *ujawe* creates the capacity within the boy to act effectively in the world, to practice the hunting and gardening magic, *dame*, which is seen as necessary for the production of food. The progress for the male through the life cycle can be seen as the cumulative and progressive development of the capacity to deploy *woroe*, male mystical power, through various forms of magic and ritual manipulation. Hunting and garden magic are a basic component of this capacity, with various forms of sorcery, divination, and curing being further elaborations. It is in the eighth stage of the male life cycle, old age, that men are said to develop the power of *ha'erive*. This is power that comes from within the man himself. It is the power of the spoken word, which can stop all gardens from growing, cause feasts to be finished quickly, and arrest the development of children. It is considered both ultimately powerful and ultimately dangerous and is seen as an identification of the living man himself with the ancestors and the land that grew them.

What is the significance of this for the mother? How does her invocation of the eel totem of the land on which she now lives in reference to her own son affect her status? Women's life histories involve a transition in dependency from their natal lands to those of their husband. It is possible to argue that the ritual sequence in the garden house where the woman recognizes the product of her own body as a manifestation of male mystical power rooted in the land of her husband is a transformative moment for her as well. Her work on her husband's land, in giving birth and having the blood of parturition enter that land is now recognized in its male manifestation, her son. Her female substance at last becomes male and belongs to the place. The importance of this work is recognized in her own status. Given the age of marriage at about eighteen and the fact that most young boys entered the *ujawe* for the first time in their early teens, I believe it is possible to ritually mark the transition of the woman from the status of *magana bune*, which informants classified as a women eighteen or older who was married and who had borne a child, to that of *magana duvahe*, which informants described as a women aged thirty or more, who had borne many children and was in the prime of her strength. It is upon the completion of the *ujawe* ceremony for the first-born son that the mother develops an incipient claim to the land and *ma'i ma'i* of her husband's place, and this is the transformation that takes place in the ritual realm for women as they become *magana duvahe* living on the land of their husbands.

Significantly, it is the father's sister, who would have grown up on the same land as the boy and had been fed by the same magic, who shadows the mother's action with her son. Throughout the *ujawe* ritual, same-sex bodies grown on the two *ma'i ma'i* sets that produced the mother and the father jointly minister to facilitate the movement of male neophytes from one level of human agency to the next.

The *Ujawe* and Male Domination

I have developed an argument about the role of the mother in the *ujawe* male initiation by drawing on ethnography from other parts of Papua New Guinea, not so much in comparison but to add plausibility. The ethnographic examples from the Anga groups, other Eastern Highlands peoples, and the Sepik resonate in the manner spirits of the dead, vegetal growth of trees and tubers, and the transference of ancestral spirit is conceived. I have focused on the different relationships of identity between men and the land, and women and the land in the form of claim to totemic plants and animals. These relationships are not metaphoric, but animic and metonymic as Descola (1992) would have it. Men and women orient themselves to their appointed tasks and life courses through relationships formed with spirits of particular places and nonhuman entities and this determines the range of their political power and influence. It also determines the material resources at one's disposal. Ömie women's ties are truncated in comparison with those of men as they are not taken into the earth itself to be grown as spirits of the generalized ancestral pool. In the mother's evocation of the eel from her husband's pool of water she identifies not with the eel but with the land that contains it. Although initiation can be seen as making novices incomplete by giving them a single sex identity and enabling them to physically reproduce (M. Strathern 1988, 1993), the *ujawe* also commences a process of intimate identity between males and the spirits of the land from which they are fed and in which they are incubated. Given the degree to which human agency itself stems from the power of the ancestors in Ömie thought, women never recover from the disadvantage of not being mothered by the land in the same way that men are. By allowing nonhuman differential agency in the formation of the human male and female person, a view of gender differences based solely on the details of human reproduction gives way to one that encompasses processes of production of both human and nonhuman material aspects of the world.

Bonnemère notes in her Introduction that the inquiry concerning the role of women in male initiation rituals took place as anthropologists moved from the focus on individuals as independent of the social relations in which they participated to a focus on the social person as a microcosm of social relations (citing M. Strathern 1988). In my interpretation of the significance of the *ujawe* ritual for both initiates and their mothers, I am suggesting that the relations that are manipulated in this ritual are not just those between people, but also between human bodies and the nonhuman entities that surround them. The manipulation of these relationships suggests that for the Ömie, and possibly other peoples, the dividual person is a composite not just of social relationships as we conceive them to be, but also of relationships of identity and interaction with the very earth and its vegetation. The acceptance of these relations as equally social to those with human beings is integral to grasping something of the particular import of what the Ömie struggled to communicate to me in their recounting of this former practice.

It is possible to see the two approaches to the analysis of male initiation rituals as incompatible. However, the understanding of the sexual antagonism model as growing out of the particular conditions of the fieldwork period that produced it, is an inevitable luxury of hind sight; while the overlay of the dividual person model has caused a melting away of concerns with cross-culturally comparable conditions of gendered lives. Because the rule of sex affiliation is unable to deliver the promise of gender equality in relation to the control of land and other resources, my interpretation of this ritual highlights its prefiguring of male domination. The opening of the dividual person to the agency of nonhuman entities and relations with them allows for a consideration of the real material conditions that differentially constrain the lives of Ömie men and women throughout the life cycle.

Chapter 5
The Bachelors and Their Spirit Wife: Interpreting the *Omatisia* Ritual of Porgera and Paiela

Aletta Biersack

In memory of Kenneth D. Biersack

Gender first became important in New Guinea research when anthropologists discovered elaborate male initiations that seemingly reflected a sexual politics of gynophobia and "antagonism" (Herdt and Poole 1982). Among the early texts, Mervyn Meggitt's "Male-Female Relationships in the Highlands of Australian New Guinea" (1964), which reported on a central Enga clan ritual called the *sanggai*, was perhaps the most influential. In the *sanggai*, the bachelors of a particular clan retreated from the residential area and assembled in the forest, where they purified their eyes, learned magic, and grew bog iris plants. The purpose of the ritual was largely prophylactic, a matter of shoring up defenses against female powers of destruction at a critical moment in the male life cycle. Fearful of women, the bachelors believed that they were vulnerable to their "pollution" and sought to protect themselves until such time as they married, when they would require still stronger defenses against those same female powers (1964: 217). Meggitt would conclude that the *sanggai* ritual reflected "the anxiety of prudes to protect themselves from contamination by women" (221).

Just west of Enga speakers live the Ipili-speakers of the Porgera and Paiela valleys. The *omatisia* ritual traditionally performed in these valleys paralleled in key respects the *sanggai* ritual Meggitt described almost forty years ago. In the *omatisia* ritual, adolescent boys stole away under cover of night to the forest, where they learned spells, performed magic, and cultivated plants representing their bodies. One of the plants was *omatisia*, a plant that I shall refer to here as bog iris; the other was bamboo (*uiyapa*).[1] Like the Enga *sanggai* ritual, the Ipili *omatisia* ritual was designed to purify and grow the bodies of the male participants.[2] Yet, despite a clear emphasis upon sexual purity, the *omatisia* ritual paradoxically centered on the relationship that the boys entered into with a female spirit—varyingly referred to as the *omatisia* woman (*omatisia wanda,* "the bog iris woman"), the *uiyapa* woman (*uiyapa wanda,* "the bamboo woman"), and, since she was the boys' wife, the "*omatisia* wife" and the "*uiyapa* wife."[3] In fact, this spirit wife was thought to be the indispensable helpmate in the boys' project of growing and beautifying themselves. The ritual's ideal yield—the growth and beautification of the bachelors and, by implication, their success in attracting a real wife and becoming fathers—depended in large measure upon this fantasy conjugal relationship. How do we explain the paradoxical presence and efficacy of this phantom marriage (see Biersack 1982 for early reporting and analysis)?[4]

We may begin answering this question by recognizing the extraordinary efficacy attributed traditionally to Ipili marriage per se. Conjugal couples controlled the plants and animals they domesticated; they also controlled or domesticated each other, performing magic and observing taboos on behalf of each other in the interest of safeguarding each other's health and well-being and promoting each other's fertility (Biersack 1987). It would not be an exaggeration to say that human life in its reproduction and maintenance—along with the life of the plants and animals that, by virtue of domestication, sustained that life—fell largely under the sway of married couples (Biersack 1987, 1995; see Wiessner and Tumu 1998: 227). Attributing the growth and beautification of young males to the powers of a spirit wife, as the body of belief underlying the *omatisia* ritual does, extends this putative conjugal power into the ritual sphere.

But is there an informing logic that underlies this attribution of extraordinary power to conjugal couples? I believe that there is—to wit, an indigenous philosophy concerning the nature of the human condition that places conjugal couples at the hub of a universe of causation centered on fertility and its related outcomes: death and regeneration (see Bloch and Parry 1982; Buchbinder and Rappaport 1976; Gregor 1985: 78–79). This philosophy is implicit in traditional pollution-related beliefs and practices, which conjured menstrual blood as both lethal and fertile, which made intercourse so risky that new husbands used to learn an extensive battery of spells to protect both themselves and their wives from the consequences of it (Biersack 1987), and which in sum attributed aging and death no less than fertility and growth—indeed, all corporeal processes—to reproductive activities, substances, and agents. Underlying these beliefs and practices is a handful of propositions: that human life is mortal, that regeneration is therefore necessary, that death is not only the cause but the effect of reproduction, and that death and regeneration are inextricably linked in the human sphere (Biersack 1995, 1996, 1998a, b, 1999, 2001).

Much of the literature on New Guinea male rituals is preoccupied with the sociology and gender politics of these rituals (see Bonnemère's Introduction) rather than with meaning. My account begins with the sociology and gender politics of the *omatisia* ritual, yet it closes with a "thick description" (Geertz 1973) reading of its meaning. The chapter opens as so many accounts of so-called rites of passage (see Biersack 2001) open: with a description of the separation of ritual participants from ordinary space and ordinary people (see Turner 1967b; van Gennep 1960), a separation that immediately poses questions about the sociology and gender politics of the ritual. Yet the female spirit is a mythic figure, someone who, according to local narrative, has a determinate cosmic locus, fate, and work, and it is only in interpreting her as a mythic figure that it will be possible to understand the undergirding philosophy and meaning of the ritual.

It is upon this philosophy and meaning that the chapter closes. Key to the chapter's shift in perspective from issues of sociology and gender politics to meaning is the middle section, which interprets traditional pollution beliefs in terms other than the purity-and-danger themes of so many analyses, themes that direct our attention inexorably toward "male-female relationships" and sociological analysis. My argument in this section is that pollution beliefs and practices are part of a wider system of beliefs and practices that envision human life as inherently risky—filled with danger but also opportunity. Cowards refuse these terms; they shun risk and never marry. The only people who stand to merit the esteem of their peers are those who marry and shoulder their responsibility as mortal beings to "replace" themselves, accepting life's risks in pursuit of respectability and prestige. The proposition that human life is inherently risky follows from the perception that death and regeneration are inextricably linked and the philosophical anthropology that underlies it, directing our attention away from sociology—and, incidentally, away from gynophobia and "antagonism"—and toward meaning.

While the *omatisia* ritual may be distinguished from some other New Guinea rituals in terms of its heterosexual focus (Lindenbaum 1984, 1987), the phantom rather than flesh-and-blood nature of the female presence in it, the focus on conjugality rather than motherhood (but see Biersack 2001), and so on, much of the symbolism and intent of the ritual is not exceptional and does resonate with other cases—most notably with the Sambia case (see Biersack 1998a: 89–90, 2001: 78–81). Accordingly, the journey from sociology and gender politics to meaning that attending to "unseen characters" has inspired me to take may be more generally applicable (Biersack 2001).

Although *omatisia* participation was not restricted to the membership of a particular line (Biersack 1998a: 85), the ritual was staged by particular lines of descendants, and the details of ritual performances vary somewhat from line to line. I have discussed the ritual with both Paiela and Porgera people. Koipanda and Kualata described the *omatisia* rituals of Anga and Maipangi lines respectively, lines that are based in the Porgera valley. Luke's knowledge is of the Yokone *omatisia* ritual in the Paiela valley. Despite the variations, there is an unmistakable conceptual and thematic commonalty in all versions of the Ipili *omatisia* ritual that allows me to offer a general interpretation for both valleys.

Growing Up the Ipili Way: The *Omatisia* Ritual and Related Procedures

The *omatisia* ritual had a distinct sociology. In ways that I will describe, boys gave bridewealth for a spirit bride whom they all shared. They also gathered under the leadership of an older but still unmarried boy, who was the spellman of the ritual. This boy was classified as a *kinambuli*, a term that refers to someone who is old enough to have married and to have borne children but who remains childless.[5] Participants were divided between "old timers" (*ba yo atene*), those who had participated before, and "newcomers" or "novices" (*wene yo atene*). Between these two classes of participants, and between these and the leader, plants, bamboo tubes, and ritual knowledge flowed.

The *omatisia* ritual began when the participants harvested sweet potato at dusk in the gardens of the residential area and withdrew to the upper forest, a pure and virginal realm "where adult females and males do not go" (*wanda akali na pene nga*). The categories *wanda* and *akali*, adult woman and adult man, oppose the category *kinambuli*, a term that signifies an infertile but physically mature person of either sex. *Kinambuli* also contrasts with all terms for younger males and females (for example, *iwana* and *wana*, young male and female or *iwanana* and *wanana*, boy and girl). The boys departed under cover of night to avoid detection, and they took all precautions to prevent any sentient being from the residential area below (even domesticated dogs!) from discovering their hideaway. Those living in the residential area had "seen bad things" (a woman's vagina and its blood, for example) and were defiled as a result. Should they look upon the boys' magical plants or upon the boys themselves, the ritual would lose its efficacy.

The first night in the upper forest was spent at a halfway or threshold house on the edge of the forest. This house was not as pure as the *omatisia* house in the forest proper, but it was purer than the ordinary houses of the residential area below. At the threshold house, the boys shed their ordinary clothing (which had been "seen" and thus contaminated by the adults in the residential area below) and dressed in makeshift bush clothing. Then they traveled on to the main ritual structure, the "*omatisia* house" (*omatisia anda*), where they purified their eyes. Kualata, the man who described for me a Porgera version of the ritual, told me that when he was born his mother's wombal and vaginal "juices" ruined him, and that he had also been defiled when he glimpsed inadvertently exposed genitalia (male as well as female). The purpose of washing the eyes was to rinse off this filth (see Meggitt 1964: 213), so that the boys might look upon their magical plants and bamboo tubes without damaging them.

The person through whom the ritual participants actually grew was a female spirit. While she was associated with all ritual paraphernalia and their power and with the ritual per se, she was housed in the bamboo tubes (*uiyapa pene*), which a boy did not receive until his second season of ritual participation. The most elaborate description of the preparation of the bamboo tubes that I have collected comes from Luke, who led the Yokone *omatisia* ritual in the Paiela valley for many ritual seasons. According to Luke, the tubes were divided into two lots. The "long" tubes were "our skin tubes" (*nanimana umbuaini pene*), in the sense that they were associated with the health and scale of the boy's skin. The spirit woman "sat" in the single "short" tube. The tubes were grouped as a "bamboo house" (*uiyapa anda*) and roofed using the bark of the *makua* tree (*Cunoniaceae, Schizomeria* sp.; Ingemann 1997: 44). The roofing procedure was elaborate. To prepare the bark for cutting, the spellman used a pearl shell to etch the point of incision as he addressed the boys as "wealthy men (*akali amango*) one and all," the pearl shell symbolizing the wealth the boys would eventually accumulate (see Wiessner and Tumu 1998: 229–32). Every season a boy attended the ritual, he would group and roof a new batch of bamboo tubes, and before leaving the upper forest he would make sure that the bamboo batches from prior years were all properly roofed, such "houses" accumulating over the seasons of ritual participation.

The tubes, gathered and roofed, were placed in swampy ground, and water tended to accumulate in them.[6] Upon returning to the upper forest for another ritual season, those who had already prepared bamboo houses would check to see whether the water in the single short tube was discolored and whether it contained a spider web, signs that the spirit woman was menstruating and that the tube and its water were contaminated. Only fresh water helped the boy grow. Any soiled water was discarded; fresh water was poured into the new tubes that the spellman supplied.

The boys also planted and weeded the *omatisia* itself. Newcomers (*wene yo atene*) received their *omatisia* plants from the spellman himself or from the old-timers (*ba yo atene*). In the Yokone version of the ritual from Paiela, as each boy received his plants, a spell was said to encourage growth in various body parts: hair, eyes, shoulders. Those who had attended the ritual at least once before already had a bed of bog iris under cultivation and needed to weed it. The two men with whom I have discussed Porgera versions of the ritual, Kualata and Koipanda, told me that in the spells they said as they weeded their gardens, they beseeched the spirit woman to help them grow. "O bind my hair / Come sleep in it and make my hair as round and full as a sweet potato mound," Koipanda said, while Kualata implored, "Sit in my calf / In my side and middle back / In my shoulder / In my eyeball / In my belt / In my hair / You who lie concealed in the tree ropes, don't run away, come to me."

Women of courting age also cultivated plants, called *sialangai* (sometimes also referred to as *kandolopa*, perhaps a synonym for *omatisia*). My information here is restricted to the Paiela valley, where first Mata and more recently Kongolome taught me about the female traditions that paralleled male magical procedures. Like a boy's *omatisia* plants, a girl's *sialangai* plants had to remain invisible if they were to work. They were planted in out-of-the-way garden corners, where they were penned with a fence of cordyline plants to better conceal them. The plants were weeded regularly as spells were said. The purpose of the girls' plants was the same as that of the boys' plants: to make the skin and head hair big. When the plants had matured, some of the leaves were stripped off, doused with dew, and rubbed on hair, face, and body to mature the girl. Pig fat might be combined with charcoal and smeared directly on the hair or enfolded within *sialangai* leaves. With or without the pig fat, the *sialangai* leaves were rubbed over the skin in the morning as a spell was said. The spell Kongolome gave me for the occasion alluded to various trees that have smooth bark (*sia umbuaini*, "tree or wood skin")—as smooth as the skin that the girl hoped to have—and to the various body parts she aimed to enlarge. After Kongolome rubbed the leaves over her face and hair, she placed them in the rafters of her house. Whenever she went courting, she carried *sialangai* leaves with her in her netbag to assure that she would attract sweethearts and eventually receive a handsome bridewealth offer from the man she desired.

Marriage as Theme and Goal

The account so far has suggested that heterosociality and in particular heterosexuality threatened the efficacy of the *omatisia* ritual. The boys withdrew from the residential area, where adult females and males copulated and reproduced; they hid themselves from the view of those living in the residential area; they cleansed their body of its filth, acquired through birth itself and years of cohabitation with (hetero)sexually active adults. Moreover, intercourse was strictly forbidden during the years of ritual participation.

However, from start to finish, the Ipili *omatisia* ritual promoted the physical maturation of the boys by enlisting the aid of a female spirit. This spirit woman, moreover, was the boys' "wife." A boy gave a modest payment for his *omatisia* plants and bamboo—a cowrie shell at the time these paraphernalia were received and a pig upon return to the residential area—to the ritual leader, and this was deemed a kind of bridewealth. (Real bridewealth is collected among the groom and his relatives and given to the bride and her relatives.) The spirit woman was thought to move with these paraphernalia, "going" to her various boy husbands. The efficacy of the ritual, moreover, depended upon the spirit woman's performing certain uxoral duties, a matter I discuss in the next section.

From the very beginning of the ritual, the spirit woman was addressed as if she were the boys' wife. In a spell that was said as the boys approached the main ritual structure or their bed of *omatisia* plants, the *anda wai* spell, the spirit woman was reminded of the importance of conjugal propriety. Luke, a veteran *omatisia* spellman from the Paiela valley, uttered his *anda wai* spell as he led the boys from the threshold house to the *omatisia* house: "If a man comes cutting wood to see you / If a man comes from home to see you / Sit to the side in the clouds / Sit to the side in the rain / If he comes to see the woman whose face is covered by a netbag / You sit decorated behind a closed door." Kualata's Porgeran *anda wai* spell, said as he approached his plants, clearly indicates his sense of conjugal proprietorship with respect to his spirit wife. "Who is that in the water? / Who is that in the mud? / If you hear wood breaking / It's a thief who has come / A thief will come [the implication being that the woman should prepare herself and hide]. . . . / Hide . . . / Hoist your netbag up / Get your netbag [and run away] /I myself, a man, want to come / I, your owner, want to come."

Not only was the *omatisia* woman the *omatisia* wife, but the ritual's purpose was to grow and beautify the boy so that he would compete successfully for a bride. A boy typically began attending the *omatisia* ritual before he had begun to court, initiated courtship sometime after his first ritual season, continued courting throughout the period of ritual participation, and suspended participation once the purpose of the ritual had been achieved and he had decided upon a bride-to-be. This goal was reached through the assistance of the spirit wife, who effectively transferred him from herself to a real wife and who facilitated that shift by promoting the boy's growth and beautification. Thus, marriage was both the medium and the goal of the *omatisia* ritual (Biersack 1998a, 2001; see Langness 1999: 135ff.).

Throughout the period of seclusion, the possibility of marriage with a real woman was very much on each participant's mind. A favorite pastime at night was to say "woman *kale*" (*wanda kale*), spells, a kind of love magic that was designed to make a preferred girlfriend smitten. Traditionally young men and women courted by decorating themselves and attending dance parties (*mali*). During the day, they danced and displayed themselves, but at night they sat in pairs, the boys proposing and the girls accepting. Anyone who was courting, male or female, typically had multiple fiancés or fiancées, leaving the question of the eventual spouse undecided. *Wanda kale* spells were said to make girlfriends, particularly the one the boy favored, lovesick and eager. A love-magic procedure that Luke described to me employed *omatisia* leaves. A vine was attached to a tree and run into the *omatisia* house, where the boys sat chanting their spells at night. *Omatisia* plants were draped over the vine. As the vine was tugged and the plants danced (simulating the boys at a courtship dance?), love magic was said in the hope that the fancied fiancée would swoon with desire. Luke, who had supervised multiple cohorts of *omatisia* participants in the Paiela valley, emphasized the importance of the evenings spent saying love magic. "The boys were thrilled to say their love magic. . . . We say love magic when we are attending the *omatisia*. We say the name of our sweetheart, and we poke a leaf with the bone of a bat [one of the rites associated with the love magic]. . . . Our fiancées should be obsessed with us. That's why we say the magic."

The saying of love magic was not merely incidental to the ritual—a nocturnal pastime that filled out days focused elsewhere, on bog iris plants, bamboo tubes, and other magic; it was *integral* to the ritual's purpose. A "big" and "beautiful" boy was a competitive suitor. Among Ipili speakers, skin and hair are considered sexual bait, and the purpose of all the procedures was to make the boy sufficiently handsome and wealthy to catch the eye of a girl. As Luke explained to me, "When the boy went to a courting party, there should be two girls there who think, 'My, he's handsome,' and they should fight over him, hitting each other over the head. The two girls should fight over him, each one saying that she wanted to marry him." Luke himself had great success courting, and he attributed that success to his many seasons of attendance at the *omatisia* ritual and also to the fact that when he courted he rubbed the leaves of the plant over his skin and hair as he said the following spell: "When I go to a pig kill, say that I am handsome / When I dance, say that I am handsome / When I travel far, say that I am handsome / When I talk to you, say that I am handsome / The hair should be beautiful / The eye should be beautiful / The shoulder should be beautiful." Luke told me that whenever a boy who was participating in the *omatisia* ritual attended a dance party, his audience should admire his appearance, "saying that the *uiyapa* woman, alive, sits." In this context, puberty ceased to be a biological process and became instead a theatrical effect—the beauty in the eye of the beholder. Any one ritual season culminated in a display of the ritual's efficacy. The boys decorated themselves in the leaves and nuts of the forest and returned home, where they were greeted by young girls of courting age, including their various fiancées.

Because the goal of the ritual was marriage, ritual participation continued until such time as the boy had a sign that he would soon marry. If a *yange* bird ("a long-tailed bird of paradise, variously identified as Taeniaparadiseae mayeri, Epimachus meyeri, Paradisornis rudolphi, and Trichoparadisea guilielmi"; Ingemann 1997: 82–83) flew overhead as the boy weeded his plants or a frog was found on or near his plants or tubes, the boy surmised that the girl of his choice was ready to accept an offer of bridewealth. The Porgeran sage Kualata told me that the *yange* bird symbolized woman. Much to the same effect, Koipanda explained that the *yange* bird symbolized the woman's grass skirt, which itself signifies women's fertility. The direction from which the *yange* bird approached could indicate the location of the sweetheart who had decided to accept a marriage offer, thus disclosing the identity of the future wife.

The break with the ritual was definitively made when the boy passed his *omatisia* plants on to a successor, a "newcomer" (*wene yo pene*), telling the spirit wife to get various shell wealth and "go" to whoever had paid for her. Much as in leviratic remarriage, then, the spirit wife circulated from one male to another. Having left the heterosexual residential area, zone of sexual reproduction, to engage in homosocial (although not homosexual) bonding, the boy returned for good to the residential area to take up a new life: no longer merely a boy, a virtual husband, he would become a man (*akali*) and a "real" (*enekeya, angini*) husband.

Boys grew and beautified themselves to marry; and, just as boys participating in the *omatisia* ritual said magic to make their sweethearts want to marry them, adolescent girls magically seduced their chosen ones. In the spell that the Paiela woman, Kongolome, gave me, she said: "I am a good girl / My skin should be good like the pearl shell / I am a good girl / My fiancé, the one from Yokopia should propose to me / That boy from Yokopia should summon me / . . . My skin should be beautiful like a pearl shell." The place name Yokopia indirectly alluded to the man whom Kongolome married. The magic was said while Kongolome was courting to assure that the man she had chosen would make an offer of bridewealth.

The *Omatisia* Ritual in Life Cycle Perspective

As the boys themselves knew, the spirit woman was not a "real" (*enekeya, angini*) wife; she was a *bamboo* wife. In what ways was she like a "real" wife, and in what ways did she differ from a "real" wife, and what might the differences tell us about the *omatisia* ritual as a moment in the male life cycle?

Prelude to Reproduction

Ipili marriage is contractual, a matter of the principals agreeing to exchange objects and services, the various gendered "work" (*peape*) of Ipili conjugality (Biersack 1995). The contract is initiated through bridewealth, which obligates a real wife to perform conjugal duties as a "return" on the husband's bridewealth. The male produces the bridewealth; the female engages in the domestic work of production and reproduction, closing the circuit of the transaction. To determine how the spirit wife differed from a real wife, it is necessary to compare the contract initiated with ritual bridewealth with the contract initiated with actual bridewealth.

A wife co-owns pigs with her husband, and her kinspeople ideally share wealth with him. Through a wife's labor and kin, a man accumulates the wealth that will allow him to garner prestige in the wider community. The spirit woman was a "rich woman," and like a real wife, the spirit wife brought wealth to her boy husband. When the bamboo tubes and the bark used to roof them were cut, the incision was first etched on the bamboo and bark with a pearl shell as the leader said the spell beginning "wealthy men one and all." Similarly, when a boy received his first batch of bamboo tubes, he paid for the tubes and the spirit woman, who was thought to travel with them, as the cult leader said a spell that told the spirit woman to "get pearl shell and go to the boy," to make the boy rich.

Also like a real wife, the spirit wife grew her boy husband. Although married men had good reason to fear their wife's menstrual blood, menstrual blood properly deployed promoted a husband's health and appearance, along with his acquisition of wealth and safety in war. Traditionally, married women collected their menstrual blood and carried it to the base of a special tree, where they performed magic over it (Biersack 1987). The day after a wife performed this magic, her husband gave her magically prepared mud, which she used to purify her eyesight and speech. Once purified, a wife was sexually available to her husband, and she used the rest of her monthly cycle to conceive. In this non-menstrual phase of the cycle, menstrual blood was also crucial. According to local notions, a woman conceives when sperm wraps around menstrual blood, binding it and keeping it from "coming outside" (Biersack 1983). Ipili speakers attribute procreation to the heterosexual mix of sperm and menstrual blood. That which is reproduced, the body, is itself a combination of paternal bone and maternal body blood (*tunduka*, *tundupa*, which is different from *tatama* or menstrual blood).

The bridewealth the boy gave for his spirit wife was relatively sparse—nothing like the twenty-eight or more pigs of traditional bridewealth—and the spirit woman's contractual obligations were concomitantly narrower than those of a real wife. The spirit wife neither gardened nor tended pigs for her boy husband, for example. Moreover, whereas a real wife was required, by virtue of the bridewealth, to "bear and give" children to her husband, the spirit wife was under no such obligation. Her infertility was subtly stipulated in the *omatisia* ritual itself. A real wife becomes fertile once she stops menstruating and becomes sexually available to her husband again. Real women traditionally exploited periods of menstrual flow to grow their husbands, but periods of menstrual intermission to *conceive*. In sharp contrast, the *omatisia* woman was useless as a menstruator, and she used the periods of menstrual intermission to grow her boy-husband, *not* to reproduce. Upon returning to the upper forest, a boy would examine his bamboo tubes. Was there a spider web in them? Was the water brackish? If the answer was yes, the spirit woman was menstruating, and the boy would not grow. But if the answer was no, the spirit woman was not menstruating and she could come "sit" in the boy's hair and body and make them grow. The spirit wife thus performed the same service that a real wife performed, growing her husband, but she did so during the segment of her cycle that a real wife used to conceive and remained sterile as a result.

Throughout the ritual, the boy husband performed certain spouse-like services. Should the boy discover that his spirit wife was menstruating, for example, like a real husband he would give her some mud with which to purify herself, putting it near the bamboo tube in which she was thought to "sit."[7] He also roofed and reroofed his spirit wife's house and gave bridewealth for her. But this house, a bamboo house, was not a real house, and the bridewealth was paltry by traditional standards. He also never had intercourse with his spirit wife, nor did he say the special spells (the "woman *tingini* spells") that a real husband said to protect his wife and himself from the dangers of intercourse (Biersack 1982, 1987).

The spirit woman's failure to "return" a child to her boy-husband at the same time she fostered his maturation and success in courtship established her position within the male life cycle. The goal of the various adolescent procedures I have described was to assure that those who performed them married and bore children. The key axis in the boys' ritual was the quasi-conjugal relationship established between the female spirit and her boy husband. As the seasons of a boy's ritual participation wore on, he would begin courting in the hope that the female spirit would "sit alive" in his skin and make him attractive to members of the opposite sex, particularly in moments of courtship. The boy performed love magic to induce the sweetheart of his choice to desire him. But it was the female spirit as wife, as someone who would grow the boy husband out of a sense of conjugal duty, who was crucial to the ritual's ideal outcome, which was marriage. The ritual thus created a practical bridge between childhood, with its bachelorhood and immaturity, and adulthood, with its marriage. Real bridewealth obligated a woman to bear not only offspring but kinspeople for her husband and her husband's kin. Children are a woman's principal "return gift" or *paini* on the bridewealth. Reproduction is thus staged *sociologically* as an exchange between bride and groom, making fertility a contractual conjugal function.[8] To marry is to give bridewealth and obligate the recipient to reproduce. The *omatisia* ritual is best understood, then, as a precursor to and enabler of reproduction.

Adolescent girls also appear to have prepared themselves magically for marriage and parenthood. In Kongolome's love magic, she targeted the beau of her choice, the one she wished to marry. As an adolescent girl Kongolome also magically grew her breasts, especially the nipples, rubbing dew on them as she said a spell that alluded to the back, wing, breath, eggs, and offspring of various birds that she thought pure and strong. Maturing ("ripening") breasts are considered sexually alluring, but they are also indispensable to the reproduction project, and girls grew their breasts to prepare themselves for both courtship and motherhood. Kongolome also said other spells to assure that she would grow and marry (*akali peakale*, "for the purpose of going to a man"; *akali poyale*, "readying to go to a man"). Kongolome also said magic to forestall the onset of menstruation. This spell had two purposes: to prevent menstrual embarrassment in the delicate process of courtship in particular and also to assure that the girl's finite, fertile fund of menstrual blood would not be drained off before she was ready to use it for procreative purposes. As a mature woman and mother, Kongolome used this same spell to postpone the resumption of menstruation after she had given birth so that she could continue to nurse her child until the child was "big" and ready to be weaned. Kongolome's various spells—to retard the onset of menstruation, to promote breast growth and a more general bodily growth, and to snag the boy of her choice—ultimately had a single aim: reproduction.

Beyond Paradox and Gynophobia

If the *omatisia* ritual promoted heterosexual activity and its fertility, it cannot be understood primarily with respect to male fears of heterosexual contact and its dangers. How, then, must it be understood? My answer to this question will involve reconceptualizing pollution in terms of an indigenous understanding of the nature of the human condition, a reconceptualization that will allow me to understand maturation as a cultural process. I lay the groundwork for that argument by recasting pollution and the life cycle itself in terms of risk, risk-taking, and risk-based careers. I then discuss the human condition as I believe Ipili-speaking people understand it, and I interpret the entire enterprise of the *omatisia* ritual in that context.

The outcomes of Ipili pollution-related practices were always dual. If taboos were breached, if the magic that could have been performed was not performed, if the magic was performed incorrectly or with malice, as black rather than as white magic, then the consequence was negative. However, if taboos were observed and if magic was performed correctly, the consequences were positive. Thus, however dangerous women were to their husbands as menstruators, as menstruators they were also their helpmates (Biersack 1987).

The two-sidedness of the domain of practices that bear upon pollution is apparent in the *omatisia* ritual itself. If the boy looked upon his plants with impure eyes, if he had intercourse with any of his fiancées, if someone from the residential area chanced by and saw him, his plants, or his bamboo tubes, the boy's plants would wither and die and he would remain puny. However, if he preserved his purity, if he learned and performed the magic, and if he manipulated the paraphernalia correctly, the boy would become sexually alluring and catch the girl of his dreams.

If the outcomes of pollution-related practices were dual, the term *pollution*, which reflects the negative outcome only, is inadequate as a global term, and the system is more aptly described as a system of risk-taking. Every risk poses a real danger, but it also creates an opportunity, and there is no opportunity without danger and no danger without opportunity. The risks and opportunities pertained specifically to fertility in all its aspects—from intercourse to child-bearing to the infertile interlude when menstrual blood "comes outside" and women menstruate. In sum, risk and opportunity inhered in heterosexual activity.

There is ample evidence of the connection between pollution and fertility in the *omatisia* ritual itself. The boys participating in the *omatisia* ritual were considered contaminated through their contact with the fertile adults of the residential area, in particular with their genitalia. If any of these same reproductive adults discovered the ritual site, the ritual would abort. Every precaution was taken to extricate and insulate the boys from the contaminated zone of reproduction lying below. The boys secluded themselves, changed their clothes, and cleansed their eyes. They hid away until they were ready to decorate and return, displaying themselves before an audience of such adults and, more important, their admiring, lovesick girlfriends.

It is possible, in fact, to view the very growth that the ritual promoted as a continuation of the act of reproduction that each boy's mother initiated in giving birth. While a boy was secluded in the forest, his mother lent him support back home. She observed certain taboos designed to promote her son's transformation. For example, she collected and hid her potato peelings lest they be eaten by ants—which, being small, might sympathetically impede the boy's growth. She buried this refuse in mud on the sympathetic principle that the boy would become juicy like the mud and grow. She also observed food taboos lest she consume anything that was too dry and might sympathetically undermine her son's fat- and water-based growth. In effect, these practices perpetuated the mother's role as nurturer. No longer at her breast, the boy nevertheless benefited from her as if he were still suckling at her breast and being fed at her hearth (Biersack 2001).

This system of risk-taking in which reproduction and pollution were two sides of the same coin supported risk-based careers. Those who risked the most were called "mature males" and "mature females" or "fathers" and "mothers"; and it was these who, despite their impurity, were—indeed, who still are!—the bulwark of Ipili society. Only through risk-taking did a person gain renown. Males began cutting a figure, even before they married, as courageous warriors. The *omatisia* ritual prepared young men for marriage and reproduction. Participation signaled a readiness to run risks, for the ritual culminated in the giving of bridewealth to a woman who was thereby obligated to bear children as a return on the bridewealth, and the process could only be consummated with marriage and parenthood. The older bachelor boy who organized the *omatisia* ritual did indeed garner prestige as *primus inter pares*. But a bachelor who never married, who became a lifelong *kinambuli* instead of a risk-taker, was (and still is) an object of ridicule, a man of no account (*ko takawa*, "bad, rubbish").

Since women bear and nurse children, and since their menstrual blood and milk are material to the process of reproduction, women rather than men are the greater risk-takers in this system of pollution-related practices and risk-taking (Biersack 1987, 1995). A woman risks her life in giving birth, a fact of which all Ipili speakers, I dare say, are aware; and there is some sense among women that breastfeeding drains away vital fluids, desiccating and elongating the breasts. As women frequently remark, the breasts of a woman who has nursed a child are "dropped." Women attribute their aging—the elongation of their breasts, the wizening of their skin—to reproduction and breastfeeding as well as to the progressive exhaustion of their supply of menstrual blood. More-over, wives as well as husbands are at risk in intercourse. The *wanda tingini* ("woman *tingini*") spells that a man learns in preparing to marry are designed to protect the wife, and not just the husband, from the dangers of intercourse. Indeed, a husband's fertility-related risks are relatively episodic and trivial—re-stricted to coitus and menstruation, which are themselves episodic. Once a woman conceives, she ceases to menstruate and to have intercourse, and she does not resume intercourse until, ideally, she has weaned her child some two or three years later. Having risked death in bearing the child, the woman nurses the child, using up her vital "juices" to do so. Becoming a mother is an act of heroism.

Since pollution is a possibility that arises whenever the opportunity for pro-creation presents itself, and the effects of pollution are physical decline and even death, there is never regeneration without the risk of physical deteriora-tion and death. The implication of all Ipili pollution-related beliefs and prac-tices is that human beings are vulnerable *as propagators*. In the course of bearing life, propagators expend life. Semen is siphoned off, menstrual blood is spent, adults age as parents—and then they die. That propagation requires an ex-penditure of life, that regeneration has as its tariff mortality—these proposi-tions undergird the Ipili understanding of the human condition. In the Ipili worldview, growth and decline, birth and death, reproduction and mortality are two sides of a single coin: human life. Women waste away from procre-ation; they die so that they can give life to others. The same link between fer-tility and death informs the attribution of male aging and even death to heterosexual encounters, including contact with the menstrual blood of the heterosexual partner and wife.

Underlying these beliefs is what I call a "sacrificial principle," that life must be lost to gain life, that every act of procreation requires a concomitant death, that death is the condition of life's renewal (Biersack 1995: 257–61, 1998b, 1999; see Buchbinder and Rappaport 1976).[9] The principle not only trans-forms the "facts of life" into *significant* data, into a stipulation of human life as intrinsically finite and heroic, but it creates a powerful intersection between two temporal trajectories: the time of the particular life, which begins in birth and ends in death, and the time of the particular line, which begins in an ancestral figure and continues indefinitely through a series of regenerations. By the sacrificial principle, particular deaths are paradigmatically linked to the transgenerational continuity of particular blood-and-bone lines (Biersack 1999). (The exception that proves the rule is the marked case of the infertile but physically mature *kinambuli*.) Among Ipili-speaking people, a person belongs to the lines of *both* parents and is thus anchored in *multiple* ancestors, the various "roots" or "sources" (*tene*) of the various descent lines of which he or she is a member. All filiation involves an exchange of the particular life for offspring and also for descendants. By the same token, offspring are born in debt to their parents, who expended their own life bearing them. Thus, children, even today, give their mothers a special payment to compensate them for the toll that procreation has taken on their body (Biersack 1987, 1998a, 1999). Parents, for their part, must "replace" themselves, assuming what is ultimately a cosmic burden—the burden of perpetuating the line in the face of the fragility and finitude of human life.

The purpose of the *omatisia* ritual was to prepare a boy for marriage and reproduction, and attending the *omatisia* ritual was a crucial step toward assuming this cosmic burden and the responsibilities of adulthood. The ritual must therefore be understood as a veritable benchmark in a maturation process that culminated in procreation, with its risks and opportunities. The ritual unfolded in a pure zone away from the contaminations of sexuality. Every precaution was taken to preserve the purity of the forest retreat and to purge the boys' bodies of the contaminations of the zone of fertile adults lying below. Yet the purpose of the ritual was to mature participants physically so that they could marry and risk just those contaminations they had fled; the ritual phase of purity, with its insularity and prohibition on intercourse, would ideally culminate in marriage. Shifting from the upper forest to the residential area, the boy also shifted from the bamboo wife to a real wife and learned a new battery of spells: the *wanda tingini* spells, which would equip him as a husband to protect both himself and his wife from the dangers of reproduction.

Looked at this way, the centrality of the female spirit to the *omatisia* ritual ceases to be paradoxical, for the spirit woman functioned as a transitional figure in a career of risk-taking related to heterosexual activity and reproduction. She represented the duality of the adult phase, its dangers but also its opportunities, albeit in a scaled-back way. Neither mother nor wife, she was interstitial: the virginal, opposite-sexed partner in projects of domestication and self-growth (Biersack 2001). In this regard, the spirit woman signaled an *escalation* of risk in the male life cycle. Participating in the ritual created the opportunity for personal bodily growth, but it did not guarantee that outcome. If a participant violated the taboo on intercourse during his various ritual seasons, or mishandled the ritual paraphernalia, or misspoke the magic, his growth would be stunted. Through a panoply of magical procedures, Ipili-speaking people convert natural into human processes, awarding individual agents a range of responsibilities that derive from cultural contrivance. More-over, since the ritual paved the way to marriage and reproduction, participat-ing in it embarked the boy on the specific risks associated with marriage. For a variety of reasons, then, ritual participation evidenced bravery and an unmis-takable zest for heterosexuality (Biersack 1998a, 2001), not gynophobia and prudishness (see Meggitt 1964). Those who did not muster the courage but who remained bachelors for life, the shunned *kinambulis* of ordinary Ipili dis-course, were cowards rather than "prudes"; they had no balls.

From Ritual to Myth and Cosmology: The Meaning of the *Omatisia* Ritual

Ipili myths frequently focus on beings that lived a long time ago, "when the ground originated," or on a category of being called the "sky people" (*tawe wanda akali*), those mythic beings who ultimately leave the earth and ascend to the sky. The bog iris or bamboo tube woman is a "sky woman," and her iden-tity as "sky woman" is crucial to placing the *omatisia* ritual in cosmic perspec-tive, the ultimate purpose of this section.[10] I set the stage for this interpretive work by recounting the myths (*tindi*) I have heard about the *omatisia* woman. I then return to the beginning of the account and cosmologize the matter of rit-ual location and the spatial oscillation involved in all *omatisia* participation. Fi-nally, I interpret the spirit wife as a ritual, mythic, and cosmic figure.

The Spirit Woman in Myth

What stories, then, do Ipili-speakers tell about this female spirit and the origin of the *omatisia* ritual? The stories that I review here were told to me by Simion (né Toyo), a man who lives in the Paiela valley, and Koipanda, who lives today in the Porgera valley. A term that occurs in these stories is *tawe toko*, "sky bridge." *Tawe toko* is associated with mountain tops and access to the sky. At the end of some Ipili myths, "sky people" ascend to the sky along *tawe toko*.

Simion's first story concerns two men, Kima and Ponala, and three women, Ponala's sisters. One of these, Ume, is the *omatisia* woman. Ume wanted to marry Kima, but he marries her two sisters instead. Ponala is a "sky man" (*tawe akali*). "He had a hole in his rib and wind came out of it. In fact, Ponala is the hidden word for wind [*popo*], and he is the sky man who is responsible for thun-der and lightning." Ponala and Kima agreed to exchange sisters, and in that context Ponala and two of his sisters—but, importantly, *not* Ume, the *omatisia* woman—as well as Kima decorated and went to a dance. Based on the ap-pearance of Kima, Ponala, and Ponala's two sisters, the audience predicted that they would all go to *tawe toko*. The four returned home and prepared a pig feast. Peoples from all around—the Huli, the Waka, and the Enga, in addition to the Ipili—came to eat pork. The story ends with Kima and his two wives ascending to *tawe toko* while the *omatisia* woman stays behind.

At dawn, Kima and his two wives, Pepaka and Pake, got pigs and bog iris and they went off. They went to *tawe toko*. . . . The *omatisia* woman stayed behind. . . . She told the three to go to *tawe toko*. She said that she was staying behind where adult people who bear adolescent boys stay. The *omatisia* woman cut her knee and from the blood that flowed out, a lake where the bamboo tubes are placed formed. Wherever she lay down her head, bog iris sprang up.

In thematic content, Simion's second version of the story is substantially the same:

There was once a good boy named Kima who was still unmarried, and there was also a girl who wanted to marry him. Kima went to hunt marsupials, and another boy joined them. Then a sister of the girl who liked Kima came and joined them. Kima and Pange, the sister, went to a courtship dance. The little sister, the one who first liked the boy, made decorations for Kima, decorations that Pange liked. The boy and Pange performed at the dance, and they liked each other. Kima decided that he wanted to marry Pange, and he did marry her. The couple went to *tawe toko*. But the younger sister said that she didn't want to go to *tawe toko*, that she wanted to stay in the upper forest. She wanted to become the *omatisia* woman. She said that men who would carry children would come through her. She broke her ankle and the blood became the lake in which the bamboo tubes are placed. She told Pange, her older sister, and Pange's husband, Kima, to go to the sky. She wanted to stay behind to be the source [*tene*] of all men. She said that she would stay in a particular flower: *kulealepaka*. "I am the bamboo woman" she said. Wherever the younger sister's hair or legs touched, bog iris sprang up.

In both stories, the *omatisia* woman wants to marry a bachelor boy who hunts marsupials in the upper forest. But she yields to her sister or sisters, who marry him instead. There is a sense in both stories, and particularly in the second version, which has the *omatisia* woman decorating the successful bachelor, that the *omatisia* woman promotes her beloved's efforts to court. It is her sister or sisters—her older sister—who becomes the bachelor's actual wife. Both stories suggest that the *omatisia* woman remains unmarried and chaste, and that she does so in order to promote adolescent male growth as a preliminary to courtship and marriage. She sacrifices herself several times over: first, in giving Kima up; second, insofar as the paraphernalia of the *omatisia* ritual stems from her own fractured body; and, third, in choosing to stay in the upper forest rather than in realizing her manifest destiny as a sky woman and ascending to the sky. In Paiela myth, culture heroes escape death and ascend to the sky, achieving immortality, but the *omatisia* woman refuses this fate and uses her own body to promote the bodily growth of bachelors.

Simion lives in the Paiela valley. Koipanda was born in the Paiela valley but has lived most of his life in the Porgera valley, where he attended the *omatisia* ritual of the Anga line. His version is different from Simion's two versions, but there are unmistakable similarities. As Koipanda tells the story, an immature male goes to the upper forest to hunt possum. There he comes upon a beautiful woman, who takes him to see an *omatisia* house. The two wash their eyes. In the context of hunting possum, a bamboo plant penetrates the girl's toe, and the girl tells the boy to cut it out. When he cuts the bamboo out of the girl's toe, she bleeds, and her blood is collected in the bamboo cylinder. The two travel on and find a swamp where two kinds of bog iris are growing. The bamboo tube containing the girl's blood is placed in the swamp, and the bamboo tubes are ringed with *makua* bark. "The woman tells the man that if he sees a spider web in the bamboo tubes, that means that she is menstruating; if he does not, then she is not menstruating. Then she gives him spells. . . . The two go inside the house and say spells there." Fearing that the boy's mother and sister would worry about him, the girl decorates him with the materials of the forest and sends him home. As a final decoration, the girl gives him a bird to sit on his head and hair (presumably beautifying these). The girl then tells the boy: "You will go to the sky [*tawe toko*, "bridge to the sky"]. I will bear [*mandi*] men; I will carry them here." She also tells him: "I won't go to the sky myself. I am the seed [*waini*] of all young men, and I will sit on earth as a result." She tells the boy that he will go to the sky with the girls, but that she will stay behind as the source of manhood (*iwana waini*). The storyteller pointed out to me that the girl's blood was in the bamboo tube.

This version of the myth dwells on the spirit woman's revelation/invention of the ritual and is even more emphatic than the previous versions about her refusal to ascend to the sky. Had she ascended, she would have become immortal. She chooses instead to continue living in the upper forest of the earth, where she becomes the "seed" (*waini*) of boys of courting age (*iwana*) and the reproducer of reproducers (Biersack 2001). She does so like real women, out of her own body, for the liquid in the bamboo tube is her own blood. The blood is her body blood, her *tunduka* or *tundupa*, not her menstrual blood, and body blood symbolizes life. Her blood/body/life is exchanged for the blood/body/life of the pubescent male. The sacrifice of the spirit woman parallels the sacrifice of real women. These now menstruate, now have intercourse and conceive, and in both cases they deploy their blood to (re)produce flesh of various sorts—that of their husband or children. As a female whose work is quasi-maternal, quasi-uxorial, the *omatisia* woman symbolizes the risks that all women take as propagators, deploying their bodies in self-consuming procreative projects. As a mythic figure, the *omatisia* woman symbolizes the heroism of all women. Her specific project is to spawn a male adult, father to the next generation, a project that her various boy-husbands have contractually conscripted her for, through a bridewealth of cowrie shells and pig.[11]

Spatiotemporality and Life Courses

In keeping with much of the reporting on so-called rites of passage (Turner 1967b; van Gennep 1960), this account opened with a description of the moment of the boys' withdrawal from the residential area and their seclusion in the forest. What appears on the surface as merely spatial, a matter of relocation, is actually also temporal. The mid-altitude residential area (referred to in this context as "inside," *andaka*) is "where adult females and males [that is, parents] live." The upper forest is associated with hunting rather than with the (paradigmatically conjugal) domestication of plants and animals, and with the *omatisia* ritual, through which boys magically cultivate their youthful bodies and enter into a quasi-domestic fantasy arrangement with a sterile female spirit. The lower forest and its waterways are associated with the spirits of the dead. The vertical gradient of the earth is thus ordered from youth at its apex to middle age in the mid-altitude region to death at its nadir point, an axis that spatializes the life cycle itself.

Viewed on the scale of the individual life, this spatiotemporal scheme appears linear—a matter of shifting from youth to middle age to old age and death. Yet it is actually circular. Life begins in the middle tier, the home of adult "women and men," the married reproducers who are the bulwark of Ipili society. It is here, in the middle tier, that reproduction occurs, here where there are vaginas and birth canals to see, here where risk-takers rather than play-safe *kinambuli* prevail. Participation in the *omatisia* ritual occurred some time between infancy and marriage and functioned as a bridge between the two periods. The series of ritual participations and any one ritual opened with an attempt to cleanse the boy's body of the contaminations of birth and ready him for his ascent into a pure zone. However, the series and any one ritual ended with the boy returning to the zone of sex-caused pollution, with the implication that he would incur the risks of the middle tier. In the upper forest, males matured, and they deployed their new allure in courtship as they competed for brides. After a boy's final participation, he returned as a young adult ready to face both the dangers and the opportunities of conjugal life. He did so as a resident of the mid-altitude "inside."

The *omatisia* ritual was thus poised between two moments of contamination—birth, which jeopardized the infant, and the various aspects of reproduction, which jeopardized the couples who were party to it. The boy who entered the upper forest to cultivate magical plants did so in flight from the middle tier but also in anticipation of returning to the middle tier to marry and father children. Reentry, but as a real bridegroom, soon to be a fertile adult, was the entire purpose of the ritual. During the *omatisia* ritual, the contaminations of infancy are shed, new risks are taken, and a boy prepares to enter a phase of maximum dangers but also maximum opportunities—the middle reproductive years.

But for that reason the temporal horizon of the ritual process was not the intragenerational horizon of the individual life cycle but the transgenerational process of filiation. Moving from the upper forest to the residential area, the boy, now man, would father sons who would follow in his footsteps, ascending to the upper forest in search of ritual purity and a fantasy heterosexual relationship—but only to return to the residential area and father their own sons. The up-down perpetual motion of the cycle, from impurity to purity and back again, recasts the linearity of the vertical terrestrial axis as a recursive loop—specifically, as the recursive loop of filiation and regeneration. Thus, in Simion's second version of the story, the spirit woman says that "men who would carry children would come through her," and she explained that she "wanted to stay behind to be the source of all adult, reproductive men" (*akali*).

These two schemes—the linear scheme of irreversible time and the individual life cycle and the cyclical scheme of reversible time—are related. When the boy returns to the middle tier, marries, and fathers children, he promotes his own death; the descent from the upper forest to the middle tier will culminate in his death—associated, as it is, with the lower forest and its waterways. He dies, then, but as propagator and eventual ancestor. The temporality of the individual life cycle is inextricable from transgenerational processes; the particular life and the life of the line are thoroughly intertwined (Biersack 1999). Hence, the *omatisia* ritual, an intervention in the male life cycle, belongs to particular lines of descendants.

The relationship between the particular life and regeneration-based transgenerational processes that is Ipili filiation was in fact a subtle subtext of the *omatisia* ritual. The ritual's magic promoted the physical growth of the participant, but the botanical symbols of this physical growth were also symbols of fertility. Bog iris and bamboo are said to grow quickly. In growing quickly, they mature *and* multiply; they "make a big *yame*," I was told, the expression "to make *yame*" referring to the multiplier effect in all fertility and suggesting transgenerational continuities and the physical connections thereof.[12] The passage of time was thematized in and through the ritual's distinctive sociology. Participants were distinguished as old-timers versus newcomers, and paraphernalia, knowledge, payments, and the spirit wife herself flowed from older to younger in the course of the ritual. Bog iris plants were transmitted from one cohort to another as seniors taught and equipped juniors.

The fertility symbolism was apparent in the overarching ritual design, which placed the marriage between the boy-husband and the spirit wife and the work of that marriage, the preparation of the boy for actual marriage and reproduction, at the ritual's heart. In every way the ritual emphasized heterosexual pairings: that of the boy with his spirit wife, that of the boy with his fiancées (these being offstage, in the residential area below). The sage Kualata told me that the ritual hinged on a coupling of male and female elements. The plants and the ground in which they are planted were masculine; the bamboo tubes and the swamp in which they are placed were feminine. He made these observations as we discussed the charcoal spell (*pongoma kamo*) that he said as he decorated and prepared to return to the residential area. In Kualata's charcoal spell, the "root" (*tene*) of the spell—the spell's key symbol and also the cause of its efficacy—is the *pelesole* bird (variant of *peletole*, "a flower pecker (*Melanocharis nigra*) and a tree runner (*Neositta albifrons*)"; Ingemann 1997: 58). This bird has pitch black feathers, and the boy's hair should be as black as those bird feathers. The boy prepared the charcoal paste by burning *yambauwa* wood (a.k.a *tato* wood—Fagaceae, *Nothofagus*; Ingemann 1997: 68) and mixing the resulting soot with the eggs of certain birds. A big, strong tree, the *yambauwa* tree is a masculine symbol, but the eggs, Kualata told me, are a feminine symbol. What the boy smeared on his face was more than mere "self-decoration," then; it was a symbol of a heterosexually based fertility (Biersack 1995). A similar symbol occurs in women's menstrual blood magic, for women traditionally stashed their menstrual blood at the base of the same masculine symbol, the *yambauwa* or *tato* tree (Biersack 1987).

Transcendance and Immanence

We are now in a position to understand the cosmological dimensions of the *omatisia* ritual. The key to the interpretation lies in the spirit woman's status as a "sky woman" and in her refusal to ascend to the sky, which is her manifest destiny as a sky person.

The traditional cosmos was divided between the sky and the earth. Earth was the where and when of spatiotemporalized objects—specifically of bodies of various sorts and especially the human body. These bodies waxed and waned, grew and declined, altered over time. They had, in short, a life cycle. Those beings who lived "on the earth" (*yu nga*)—and quintessentially human beings—lived a life span; they were born and then died. In between, they "replaced" themselves (Weiner 1980), both solving and compounding the problem of their own mortality. Death and regeneration, the particular life and the life of the line, are inextricably linked—*on earth*, that is. The sky, meanwhile, was free of objects and bodies (Biersack 1996, 1999). Its quintessential being was the sun, associated with light and thought or mind rather than body. The sun "had no body"; he (as the sun was gendered) "was not born, nor would he die." He was one, immortal and irreplaceable.

To the extent that spatiotemporalized objects and in particular bodies are cosmologized, located on earth rather than in the sky, they, their cycles, and the link between the particular life and the life of the line are accorded significance. The *omatisia* ritual was a determinate moment in the male life cycle, and coming to terms with the ritual requires coming to terms with the *meaning* of the life cycle itself—in fact, with the meaning of space and time or spatiotemporalized realities.

The category of people referred to as "sky people" (*tawe wanda akali*) appear to be immortal, like the sun. Their ascent into the sky at the close of some Ipili myths suggests their escape from the earth and its regime: a "reproductive regime," as I have called it (2001), in which death and regeneration are linked, reproduction is the core necessity and activity, and marriage is the crucial device for organizing and perpetuating society (Biersack 1995). The *omatisia* ritual meanwhile, and the parallel magical practices adolescent girls performed (Biersack 1998a), are fully implicated in that reproductive regime, as facilitators of marriage and its expected fertility.

As a sky woman, the manifest destiny of the *omatisia* woman was to ascend to the sky, thus transcending the landscape of fertility lying below (see Dlugosz 1995: 15). But we know from the various versions of the myth that she chose not to ascend to the sky but instead to cast her lot with the earth and its mortal but regenerative human beings. Refusing ascent, she became the "seed" and "source" of manhood. She did so with "seeds"—with bog iris plants and her body and blood, which were produced out of her own body. Like all women, she died to regenerate. The realm that the spirit woman thus represents is a realm of various domestications, organic processes and their spatiotemporality, and body-related life-for-death exchanges—in a word, a realm of worldliness and immanence and the work of worldliness and immanence. The spirit woman lives amid water, which Ipili speakers consider the substratum of organic life (Biersack 1998b; see Goldman and Ballard 1998); amid cultigens and houses; amid seniors and juniors; amid heterosexual arrangements and transgenerational processes. Through her martyrdom, commitment, and intervention, through her installation spatially in the upper forest and temporally between childhood and adulthood, the female spirit drives human biology and its regenerative cycles (see Biersack 1999, 2001). In that she becomes more than a symbol of fertility; she becomes a fatalistic yet heroic symbol of the human condition.[13] As an entirely voluntary participant in the life of the earth, the spirit woman represents the human condition as a *necessary* condition, as a "fact of life." That human life is spatiotemporalized, and so earthbound and limited; that death and regeneration are two sides of the same coin; that human life is mortal and regenerative, a matter of filiation, descent, and transgenerational temporal horizons; that human beings participate in a "reproductive regime" that is marriage based and that is at once social organizational and meaningful—these are the various texts and subtexts of the traditional Ipili ritual in which boys stole away under cover of night to the upper forest to rendezvous with their spirit wife and in the process to grow into sexually alluring males.

Chapter 6
Cults, Closures, Collaborations

Andrew Strathern and Pamela J. Stewart

In this chapter we review some of the ideas which have fed into the project of rethinking the category of "male cults" in terms of "female participation" in them. The chapter specifically builds on a model we have proposed called the Collaborative Model of cult activities, which replaces a preexisting model in the corpus of Melanesian literature that we may call the Male Exclusivity Model (Stewart and Strathern 1999a). We do not intend by this model to lump together all instances of cult activities as equally reflecting it or to ignore the obvious differences between societies that can be discerned, partly along an east-west axis in the Papua New Guinea Highlands. We do intend to foster an altered analytical orientation to these cults as a whole. We have attempted an analogous reorientation of comparative perspectives in an earlier publication dealing with eastern Indonesia and New Guinea (Strathern and Stewart 2000b) and a further comparative expansion, including reference to Amazonia (Stewart and Strathern 2002). We also look at the implications of such a reanalysis on how gender relations are perceived and described. "Male cults" within the Highlands of Papua New Guinea have been taken as indicative of a prevailing ethos and distribution of power between the sexes, expressing and reflecting everyday relations or representing heightened and dramatized ideological versions of relations. Before examining further how "male cults" have been represented, it is necessary to ask what is encompassed by the category of "male cults" itself. In general, our analysis belongs to a corpus of anthropological works that have tried to scrutinize ethnographic materials in an attempt to better understand gender relations in Melanesia.[1]

What Are Male Cults?

The term "male cult" has been applied to a congeries of gendered ritual performances in which the categorical performative units may be of a single sex. Yet these performances may have at certain levels quite different aims and performative parameters, including both genders as well as fused or partial representations of them. The criterion for discussing this mix of different ritual practices under a single rubric has been the stipulation that the immediate performers are males and that women do not participate on the same basis as these males. The criterion therefore privileges "being there": the entry into and exit from cult areas by men and the apparent exclusion of women, seen as creating an exclusive community of interest among male participants. The physical exclusion of women from ritual enclosures has sometimes been linked in the anthropological literature with "pollution fears": notions that women's bodily powers and exuviae can be antithetical to the ritual purposes the men sought to encompass in these cults and corresponding notions about the necessity for blood-letting (Allen 1967: 30–32, discussing Read 1952 on the Gahuku-Gama). To this criterion and its justificatory ideology, ethnographers added that the cults involved purposes that were quintessentially "male": the making of boys into men, and the expectation that men should be warriors (see generally Allen 1967). However, these factors, we would argue, do not exclude the female realm but rather include the entire social cosmos of gendered persons and in some instances clearly celebrate female as well as male power and recognize female contributions to social continuity. Indeed, Kenneth Read's own (1952) study acknowledged that men's rituals among the Gahuku-Gama imitated female physiological processes.

The earlier view of male cults was in many ways predicated on studies made from the 1950s through to the 1970s by ethnographers such as Read (1952), Langness (1967), Newman (1965), Watson (1967, 1983), and others in the Eastern Highlands Province of Papua New Guinea. The apparent stress on warfare in these Eastern Highlands societies supported the view that the creation of warriors was a prime purpose of their cults (A. Strathern 1970a: 373, commenting on Watson 1967). Further studies that followed in this vein of analysis included work with people from the Anga complex of languages on the fringes of the Eastern Highlands, such as by Maurice Godelier (1982), and Gilbert Herdt (1981, 1987b). A feature that was worked into this picture of male cults for the Sambia studied by Herdt, as well as other Eastern Highlands cases, was the idea that "female blood" had to be expelled from initiands in order to create their bodies as fully male. The implications here were said to be twofold: first, prior to this ritual expurgation, the initiands' bodies contained both male and female substances, and second, female blood was conceptualized as harmful and inimical to male growth. This last idea was connected with notions that menstrual blood is powerful and can be harmful to men—this being seen as menstrual "contamination" or "pollution" (Allen 1967: 37, 53 referring to the Eastern Highlands and Enga cases).

The certainties of this picture of male cults began to be challenged for societies farther west in the Highlands. There was a gradation in male initiation practices, from obligatory and universal to partial and patchy, as Michael Allen himself noted (1967: 35–47). In the Hagen area of the Western Highlands there were no extant male initiations at all, although traditions of them existed and vestiges appeared in cult practices directed toward other ends (A. Strathern 1970a: 374). Bachelors' cults in the Southern Highlands among the Huli and Duna (Ballard 1998; Glasse 1968; Modjeska 1977; Strathern and Stewart 1999a, b) as well as in the Enga Province (Biersack 1982; Meggitt 1964; Wiessner and Tumu 1998) appeared to be directed toward ensuring the growth of young men into maturity so that they could appropriately enter into all adult activities including marriage and sexual activity, rather than being exclusively directed toward preparing the youths for warfare (see also Allen 1967: 40). "Purification" rituals shared the aim of stimulating or ensuring growth through the removal of bodily impurities and the ingestion of substances such as "pure" water. A temporary physical separation of females from males would be involved here as well.

More notably, it has gradually become apparent that, in some of these areas, the putative male cults actually had as their focus the central figure of a female spirit, who was thought to bring benefits to both men and women through stimulating the fertility of the ground, helping crops and animals to grow well, enhancing the reproductive capacities of women and men, and bringing wellness in general. These were not initiation cults but fertility cults, triggered by adverse circumstances such as drought, sickness, or political misfortunes. One such cult was the *amb kor*, a female spirit cult in Hagen (Strathern and Stewart 1997, 1998a). In this cult, male performers entered into a collaborative relationship with the female spirit as her human husbands. They represented her in their cult dance as well as representing their own clans. Their male strength was seen as deriving from her ritual protection and the capacities that she gave to their whole community. Moreover, although the human wives of these men, as well as other women, could not physically enter into the inner parts of the cult enclosure, they actively collaborated with the men to ensure that the cult performance was a success. They observed sexual taboos, raised pigs for slaughter, and provided liberal supplies of domestic foodstuffs to complement the forest materials that the men secretly brought in. The collaboration here was not trivial, but essential, creating the flows of interdependency on which the cosmos was held to depend for its self-energizing capacities (see Stewart and Strathern 1999a for a further exegesis of our Collaborative Model). In return, the human women expected the spirit to grant them fertility, as was communicated in the cult's origin myth (Vicedom and Tischner 1943–48, 3, no. 16; see also Strathern and Stewart 1997).

The theme of the female spirit as a partner to human men turns out to be replicated in a whole set of regions in addition to Hagen: Pangia, Enga, Huli, Paiela, and Duna (Stewart and Strathern 1999a; Wiessner and Tumu 1998; Frankel 1986; Biersack 1982). Vivid traditions link such female spirits to sky beings, who appear as significant background figures in the mythologies of all these people (Strathern and Stewart 2000b; Biersack, this volume). Such female spirit figures stand in complementary counterpoint to male spirit figures on whom other cults are centered. There is a link between such sky beings and water, seen as rain or as the source of rivers and lakes (Strathern and Stewart 1999a, b).

In Hagen, a cult that has for descriptive reasons been labeled as the male spirit (*kor wöp*) cult, overlapping in its aims with the *amb kor* (female spirit), carries within its ritual structure and practices elements that recognize and celebrate sexual activity, women's participation, and a central symbolism of spring water that contains male and female components. This male cult, as an example of the category of "male cults," contains within it significant "female" elements. The *wöp* is also paired notionally with the *eimb* cult, which is centered on spring water and explicitly described as "female" (Strauss and Tischner 1962: 404–24). We illustrate this further by selecting some aspects of the cult (A. Strathern 1970b; Stewart and Strathern 2001; Strathern and Stewart 1999c).

The *wöp* cult expressed in the widest sense the regenerative powers of spring water (Strathern and Stewart 1999c). In this regard we see a remarkable conjuncture between Hagen, Duna, and Paiela modes of thought. If a clansman came across the site of a previously undiscovered spring, he would tell his kin, and eventually they would call in a ritual expert from a different area who would set up a cult area in which they could take care of the spring and make sacrifices in its vicinity.

A *wöp* performance took place among the Epkla-Elya people in September 1965 in a corner of the Nebilyer valley south of Mount Hagen known to Melpa-speakers as Kulir-Kona. Merlan and Rumsey conducted fieldwork in this area, but they have not written about the *wöp* cult, which probably was no longer practiced when they first worked there in 1981–83 (Merlan and Rumsey 1991). For the performance that we describe, ritual experts were called in from the Mundika group, who live in a high mountain area on the way to Tambul, the location from which the *amb kor* was thought to have come, southwest of the present Hagen town. One of these experts was Mundika Kaemb, or Raklpa, the other was called Kundil. These two men divided the ritual work between themselves, disagreeing on some procedural matters (see A. Strathern 1970b; Strathern and Stewart 1999c).

In this performance the main ritual contexts and sequences were as follows. Kaemb explained that he had been forced to remodel the site of the spring since an expert hired previously had spoiled it by opening it up and letting it flow too much, so that it lost its purity through becoming mixed with dirt. He himself reestablished it in two places, an upper spot called the *kor mong peng*, "the head (or source) of the eye of the spirit," and a lower one where the water flowed out and was collected for drinking called the *kor mong por*, "the bottom (or lower part) of the eye of the spirit." Kaemb said that when he drank the source water *nanga muntmong-e pral nemba wangndorom*, "my heart feels fresh and is comforted." He and Kundill explained that the cult participants sent a pair of boys into the area to collect water in bamboo tubes. The men would drink this water to sustain their virility so that they could impregnate their wives and produce sons, who were particularly needed during times of warfare in the past. One informant said, "We take our pigs and our yams and other good vegetables and cook these for *kor wöp*. Our wives will carry male children only if we cook the *wöp*—*wöp* gives them the children." Here we see that one of the aims of the cult was to replenish the number of males in the population via the power of the *wöp* spirit; for the small groups such as the Epkla-Elya, bordering on more powerful ones, this was of vital concern. The Hagen people have a clear ideology that both male and female children are the product of the mixture of human male and female substances (Strathern and Stewart 1998b), and cults other than the *wöp* were performed in Hagen that aimed at increasing fertility in general, for example, the *amb kor* (Strathern and Stewart 1999a, Stewart 1998).

The water of the *wöp* was supposed to make the men virile, potent, fertile, and sexually able. It thus resembles the "water of life" theme found among the Huli (Ballard 1998: 75).[2] At the end of the ritual sequence in 1965, the experts closed up the "upper eye" of the spirit, which had been decorated elegantly with ferns, and poured expensive sweet-smelling *Campnosperma* tree oil into it as an offering to make it quiet and still and yield its fertility gradually to the area.

This cult performance was triggered by hard times among the Epkla, with poor crops, sickness, and a declining population. The rituals included three elements of particular significance here. First, portions of pork were cooked inside the enclosure of a high tower house, *manga tamand*, where group ancestors were being called upon for assistance as well as the *Wöp* spirit itself. Near the tower house stood the *kor porembil*, an upright wooden post symbolizing the *wöp* spirit. There were also *wöp* stones, which had already been buried to recreate fertility, as is done in the *amb kor* cult. Older men, who had performed in the *wöp* previously and who were still alive, sacrificed at a smaller post capped with moss, known as the *tumb*. The old men said that if young men entered this particular enclosure set aside for their use, the youths' penises would become slack and limp. In the *wöp* dance the men's penises were supposed to shake vigorously up and down (*prökökl-mrökökl*) simulating a sexual movement of the organ—not unlike the cassowary dancers' movement among the Umeda described by Gell (1975).

Second, near the *porembil* pole, the two ritual experts organized the Epkla men late one evening to bring in special planting materials of sugar cane, taro, *Setaria palmifolia*, and *Rungia* (all ancient and special crops). These they planted in a systematic way in a "garden square" marked out by trenching. Then, at a signal from the experts, the men were told to rush at the "magic garden" that had been set up and snatch the sugar cane, consume pieces of it, and throw the remains as an offering into the spirit's eye, which Kaemb then covered over, pouring the tree oil on top of the plant remains.

Third, on another day at dawn the men gathered in the same area, holding a very thick liana, *kan keunga*, and danced near to the *wöp porembil* in a sequence known as *peng mumuk*, "holding together the head," a dance of both unity and persistence or survival, since unity is equated with health and life. After this, at the final dance, known as the *kor poke*, both men and women decorated themselves elaborately, paraded in the outer parts of the cult area as a whole, and broke out of its fenced entranceway in an exuberant display of strength and power. Women participated in the sacrifices, receiving parts of pork including liver from the two experts at a spot near to the tower house. The cult rituals thus made an explicit inclusion of women, and the sacred water of the spring was destined to invigorate their husbands and help them to produce sons (compare Bamford, this volume, on women's participation along with men in Kamea rituals). The spring water itself was compared by the ritual expert Kaemb to amniotic fluid in a woman's womb, which gushes forth at birth. An earlier expert, in opening up the spring prematurely, had broken it as a woman's amniotic sac is broken, causing the fluid to gush out, he said, implying that the water had lost some of its power when not properly contained (compare Ballard 1998: 74). "Water," then, seems to have both male and female connotations of fertility in the *wöp* cult. It is also clearly a marker of health in general.

A number of details in the *wöp* stand out in contrast to the *amb kor* or female spirit cult in Hagen. The latter is concerned with fertility but also purification, and its male performers enact rites of gendered alliance. In the former, both collaboration between the sexes and also male sexual capacities, helping men to satisfy female desires and vice versa, are brought openly into play. As a variant of "male cults," the *wöp* celebrates maleness, while also openly celebrating the congress of the sexes as a source of cosmic renewal.

All these ethnographic findings suggest that there are regional differences in the Highlands, as noted by Allen (1967) and Feil (1987), among others (see below), and also that we might wish to reanalyze some of the Eastern Highlands cases. Indeed, it was Bonnemère and Lemonnier's corpus of work on the Ankave-Anga, including that on male initiations (e.g., Bonnemère 1996: 293–308) and on several other themes that first drew attention to variation among the Anga themselves, and Bamford's materials on the Kamea Anga-speakers have added strength to this impression of variation (see papers in this volume, Bamford 1997, Lemonnier 1981, Bonnemère 1996). Comparisons between the Anga and other Eastern Highlanders such as the Gahuku-Gama (Read 1952) or Bena-Bena (Langness 1967) cannot, however, be undertaken here.

Ideas of Collaboration

The basic idea in the earlier literature, founded on notions of sexual separa-tion, sexual antagonism, and relatively unmediated male domination, was that male cults instantiated a world brought into being by males for their own pur-poses, based on the exclusion of women and of the female world associated with them. While this picture may hold for some of the Anga and Eastern Highlands societies of a certain historical period (precolonial and early colo-nial times, from the 1930s to the 1960s), it does not convincingly hold for the rest of the Highlands. It is possible to pick out elements of practice that cor-respond to the older model in some respects, for example, notions regarding the powers of menstrual blood, exclusive male commensality of pork or game, and exclusive distribution of the genders in spatial contexts (for example, among Huli and Duna). However, these are contradicted by the more recently established pieces of evidence (or by evidence that, if available then, was not highlighted or granted significance). From these pieces, it is feasible to develop, as we have done earlier (Stewart and Strathern 1999a), a model of gender re-lations, as imaged in cult contexts, that is based at least partly on collaboration rather than simply on antagonism, separation, or inferiority.

A model of this kind does not deny the existence of conflict and antago-nism, either as expressed in cult symbols or as occurring in contexts outside cult practices. The picture of complementarity it proposes also does not deny the presence of inequalities of power or the possibility of male domination or instances of female domination/manipulation; or at least the kind of prestige hierarchy originally proposed by Ortner and Whitehead (1981) and reworked as a hierarchy of virtue by Kelly (1993). What the model does effect is a po-tential reordering of perspectives in relation to existing ethnographic accounts. We illustrate this here in three different ways: through the mutual observance of taboos, material preparations, and expected outcomes of practices.

Mutual Observance of Taboos

As we have pointed out elsewhere (Stewart and Strathern 1999a), the way in which cult taboos have been represented has been influenced by the Male Ex-clusivity Model, but the Collaborative Model represents the fact both women and men must follow set taboos in order for the cult to be successfully com-pleted. Women are said to be excluded from entering cult areas, on pain of punishment. In the case of the *amb kor*, this punishment is thought to come di-rectly from the female spirit who is central to the cult. Men who participate in the cults are said to observe taboos on sexual intercourse with women, but this taboo of course extends to women, who are also required to observe it. Equally, the men are secluded and must observe ritual precautions when en-tering or exiting cult enclosures. In Hagen, women and men alike expressed the taboo on women entering the cult area as being an effect of the female spirit herself: both sexes were thus passive in relation to the orders of the spirit and both sexes had to observe the taboos in order to please the spirit. If men transgressed any of her taboos, the cult's aims would not be realized. If women entered her area, the spirit would reverse them, turn their genital aprons round to their backs, and expose their genitals to view, causing them shame. Likewise, if a man went into or left out of the cult area without being accompanied by his male partner from the opposite gendered house (men's house or women's house) to his own, he would be struck down by the female spirit. This, then, we might say, was female spirit dominance, not male domination. Women actively respected both taboos (on entering the cult area and on sexual intercourse) as one of their contributions to the cult's overall success.

Material Preparations

In terms of the material preparations for rituals, we often find that women do a great deal of work in furnishing food supplies for cult activities. These provisioning activities are *not*, we would emphasize, trivial. They do not belong to any putative domestic domain, lower in value than the public domain. They are of the same relative worth as the men's actions in gathering forest leaves, woods, bark, and plants that are needed for the cult actions. Pigs, the prime instruments of sacrifice in the cults, are the products of the joint labor of the sexes. We have to see all the activities as parts of an overall complementarity (compare Biersack 1995 on the concept of the "service economy"). This does not deny that a ritual hierarchy exists, since the male ritual experts, who come in from other areas, control items not available either to the local men or the women and male participants are taught by these experts proper procedures that give them ritual power. There is a gradation in participation, in fact, for both men and women.

Expected Outcomes of Practices

Perhaps one of the most significant points is that cult outcomes are said to benefit the entire cosmos. These cults are crucial transformers or switchers in the cosmos as a whole. Hence they benefit not only males but everyone, as well as the local environment itself. Given this, we question whether the male realm is really seen as encompassing the female. Rather, we argue that it is the cosmos itself, which runs through the collaboration of the sexes, that transcends each sex and binds them together. We are not arguing this, of course, in a literal sense here, but are suggesting that this is what cult symbols evoke rather than representing unisexual interests or unisexual powers that operate without reference to or recognition of each other as implied in a model of Male Exclusivity. In addition, it is important to stress that cults are as much about preparation as about separation: preparation, that is, for the everyday contexts to which they are a prelude (compare Biersack 1982: 257, n.10).

It is relevant to adduce here an idea of the gendered division of ritual labor. If we accept the idea, widely expressed by Pacific Islanders themselves, that ritual is a kind of work done to accomplish aims, it is reasonable to use the expression in this context. Ethnographers have long been accustomed to write of the everyday division of labor or forms of work on the basis of gender, always implying that a level of complementarity, and therefore collaboration, is involved. This perspective holds both when the sexes contribute jointly to the production of the same crop or item of culture and when they separately produce items but use these jointly or in pursuit of agreed-upon overall aims. What we have proposed in our Collaborative Model is that ritual work should be seen in the same terms. Essentially, what is important here is the notion that both sexes are needed to produce results, even if certain activities are undertaken, in a given sequence, by one sex. Women carry children during pregnancy and they alone give birth to human life but that does not deny the role of men in the process even though they are excluded from the immediate performance. Implicit here is the need to rethink the trope of exclusion. Rather than thinking of these cults as simply effecting a separation and a closure between the sexes/genders, we should think of them equally as effecting junctures and openings, and alliances. Indeed the separations made are also the opening points for new alliances.

Gender and Gendered Practices

This view of gender relations, which stresses alliance as a basis for these relations implies the relativity of gender itself: that which is female is always seen in relation to that which is male and that which is male is always seen in relation to that which is female. In part this proposition corresponds to the observations made by Anna Meigs in her work on the Hua, to the effect that male and female qualities can be acquired and lost over time, that gender in this sense is incremental or decremental, influenced by food, transactions, and the processes of maturation and change that go on over time (Meigs 1984). This proposition corresponds to the familiar point that males may represent female values and vice versa. In this way men in the *amb kor* could "mark" the spirit herself. Women, in relation to the *wöp* cult, could similarly "mark" male values since they received the spirit's source water via men's semen and converted it into male children. These points, in turn, further problematize a category such as "male cults" and suggest that we look instead for the intertwining and substitutability of the male and the female in all cults that have as their prime aim fertility. Since the production of persons is also part of the work of fertility, we can look also for elements of gender alliance in male initiation cults as well.

To this context also belongs an important aspect of the Collaborative

Model: that it incorporates the schema of potentiality versus actuality. This potentiality is expressed in a host of ways, one of which is the positive recognition of female reproductive capacities marked by the onset of menarche. An example of this can be seen among the Abelam of the East Sepik Province in their yam cult, where a secret stone, described as female, is central to the men's yam-growing rituals. The yam stone is said to be like "a beautiful girl during menarche" (Hauser-Schäublin 1995: 47). Hauser-Schäublin describes this as a "fundamental complementarity," in which the male yam growers sing at displays of the longest yams songs that detail the importance of menstruation to fertility (46–47). Here we see the affirmation of the positive (i.e. fertility-giving) powers of menstrual blood. A similar affirmation appeared in the *amb kor* cult in Hagen, where the spirit was said to sometimes present herself to the leader and to initiate the cult by showing to him a display of menstrual blood, signaling that her cult needed to be performed in order to restore fertility to the community. Also, the origin story of how reproductively able female humans were generated in Hagen describes how female sky beings were tricked into opening themselves when they rubbed against a banana tree in which human men had placed flints or pieces of pearl shell, causing the women to bleed (Strathern and Stewart 1997, 1999a).

Highlanders of New Guinea are very concerned about sources and origins. Sources are sites of the potential. To be realized, the potential has to be altered or developed through ritual. So in the *wöp* and *eimb* cults, the expert had to locate the sacred water source, contain it, channel it, decorate it, and finally close it over. He had to open it up and then close it. Indeed in one account of an *eimb* site (Strauss and Tischner 1962: 414), the two "eyes" of the spirit are called "open" and "closed." Men had to drink the water and transform it into semen, which their wives then transformed into children. The verb *kökli*, to "straighten," "fix," or "cook" is used for all these kinds of actions. At each stage, an element of potentiality is preserved as the precursor of an ensuing realization. In the cult contexts, this is often expressed in rules that the sexes should not have sexual intercourse, since the stage of growth is antithetical to the stage of the use of bodily substances. We find this temporary restriction on sexual intercourse in the *amb kor* and the Duna *palena nane* cults (although, interestingly, the taboo was absent in the *wöp*).

The Duna *palena nane* was a boy's growth and maturation ritual that was practiced in the *palena anda* (*palena* huts) situated in the high forested areas above the dwelling houses of the community. The boys would be secluded from married men and human women while staying in the *palena anda*, but were dependent on the guidance of a female spirit, who worked in collaboration with a male bachelor to grow the boys, making them handsome and ready for marriage. This female spirit (*payame ima*) represented a category of female spirits who possessed considerable power. She entered into the lives of chosen people, bringing them special knowledge (Strathern and Stewart 1999a; Stewart and Strathern 1999a). She was believed to give curing and healing powers to select people as well as giving to men the power to divine for witches using a divining stick, *ndele rowa* (Strathern and Stewart 1999b; Stewart and Strathern 1997, 1999b).

The female spirit was said to come to a man who was destined to become a ritual expert for the *palena nane*. This expert became the spouse to the female spirit and did not take a human wife during the time that the female spirit remained with him as his help-mate and companion. He instructed the boys during the ritual time when they were enclosed in the *palena anda* in the ways to make them grow. The power that the *payame ima* gave to men was one that protected them from witchcraft, seen as originally derived from a male ancestral spirit and subsequently passed on to humans through mothers or fathers (Stewart and Strathern 1999b). This female spirit's prime role was to share her knowledge. She was pervasive in imagination and folktales as the source of special powers for men provided they adhered to the terms of the relational contract established between them. She presented a potential source of wealth and power to those that she deemed worthy.

There is a further element involved here, related to the potential/actual schema. For the cults that we have been describing, the cult's symbolic actions are not "instead of" human ones. They are not "mystifications" of human relations, either. Rather, they are "models for," displays of potentiality that can be seen as relating to an ideal world. When the men in the *amb kor* cult learned about the spirit and her powers by listening to the narrative of how she appeared, how she came to cult leaders and what she offered, they were learning about or reaffirming an image of the female which could be carried over, if only partially, into their own social world outside of the cult itself. They were creating a model for the social world by their own imagination. Gender, we may say, is just as much imagined as community. And this reaffirms the importance of the potential, which is what the various cult taboos signify. These taboos play their part in the work of reframing or contextualizing experience that Philip Guddemi, following a number of writers including Roy Rappaport, has advanced as central to ritual action (Guddemi 1993: 8–9).

Regional Comparisons

Comparisons in anthropology have been both championed and denigrated. As ethnography advances deeper into realms of interpretation and symbolism and as critics question the basis of the forms of "knowledge" that ethnographers produce, the comparative enterprise becomes more difficult and the impetus to undertake it becomes lessened by these pressures. Nevertheless, we think that comparisons are important and illuminating for a number of reasons (see also Strathern and Stewart 1998b, 1999d, 2000b). First, comparison-making forces us to re-examine our own ethnographies. Ethnographic data can be made to speak to one another within comparative frameworks. In this regard, we may ask what the materials on "fertility" cults have to tell us about "initiation" cults, and vice versa. Perhaps the chief point here is that, at a certain level, these cults are all about fertility and all partake of similar views of the cosmos. At a more specific level, if we find "gender alliance" to be a significant theme in the western part of the Highlands, and note the differences that have been pointed to in earlier ethnographic materials (A. Strathern 1970b; Stewart and Strathern 1999a), can we also find it in the Anga and Eastern Highlands cases? Similarly, while the theme of initiation has been stressed by ethnographers writing on the Eastern Highlands and backgrounded in writings on the Western Highlands, what do we make of its latent presence in the Western Highlands (compare A. Strathern 1970a: 375)?

Second, comparison-making can lead to a new perception of the distribution of phenomena. The Collaborative Model we have developed has grown out of a perception that ideas about powerful female spirits are not an oddity in Highlands societies but are important across a geographical span from Hagen through to the Ok area. They are found also in the Strickland-Bosavi area. For example Edward Schieffelin (1976: 126–27) describes a set of such notions existing at the very heart of the Kaluli *bau a* (or *bau aa*) bachelors' cult in the past. This author points out that the aim of the *bau a* rituals was to make boys grow to manhood, an aim partly achieved by the secret insemination of boys by healthy older men. Men keep secret from women magic for hunting, gardening, fighting and "the beauty of ceremonies" (1976: 124). Decorated men, on the other hand, are supposed to fill women as spectators "with admiration and desire" (1976: 126; see also Jeudy-Ballini 1999 on attraction). This parallels the ways in which the *palena nane* cult in Duna grew boys so that they would be beautiful and thus selected by women for marriage (Strathern and Stewart 1999a). The *bau a* rituals celebrated productive manliness in a way that benefited everyone, quietening the greed of witches, preventing sickness, and in general "promoting prosperity" (Schieffelin 1976: 126). Schieffelin argues as follows in relation to these data: "It is in the opposition between male and female that Kaluli locate those qualities and powers that are necessary to the success or failure of their most ordinary concerns" (125). On the other hand, he also writes on the next page: "To cap it off, a *mamul* (spirit) woman from Mt. Bosavi, in the guise of an oddly shaped stone, was married to the leader of the *bau a* at a ceremony before the climactic distribution of smoked game to male relatives and friends from all over the plateau" (126).

In Schieffelin's usage, "opposition" has a particular meaning, referring to a situation of conflict or difference that calls for resolution. Opposition is therefore a dialectical, processual term. Opposition is supposed to lead not just to a conflict but to its resolution in a continuing scenario. In our view, however, this formulation does not go quite far enough. If "productive maleness" is supposed to encompass the female element among the Kaluli, what is the need for this marriage between human male and female spirit of the montane forests, a marriage that parallels, in abstract form, the structure of the Hagen *amb kor* and the Duna *palena* cults? The ethnographic detail that Schieffelin himself presents allows us to assimilate the Kaluli case into these Highlands cases and to argue that a notion of alliance and collaboration is needed in addition to his notion of opposition. Schieffelin's stylistic transition to the dénouement of the *bau a* in the spirit marriage ritual, draws attention to this point: "to cap it off," implying that this is an important element, in a way that his analysis does not itself reveal. It is in fact the prelude to the exit from the cult area of the handsome, grown bachelors. The spirit marriage is an integral precursor to the display of the boys' successful growth and *their* potential marriages. And it is important further to note here that it was the Kaluli girls who were expected to *choose* men they liked, that is, found attractive. Schieffelin refers to the "ultimate triumph of the male image" when a girl is so attracted to an emerging bachelor or to a visitor at a ceremony that she elopes to his place (1976: 126). But there is another side to this. The male is in a sense powerless. He is on display but he cannot choose, whereas the girl can. This indicates the likely presence of male anxiety and competition over sexual matters. The portrayal of a successful marriage by the cult leader to a powerful female spirit might be seen as overcoming or resolving this anxiety and thus acting as a good omen. Most generally, we cannot truly speak only of male agency here. Rather agency is dialectical and rebounding (to paraphrase Bloch's idea of rebounding violence as expressed in Bloch 1992). Gell (1998: 16–17) also provides a way of thinking this matter. He proposes a model of alternating agency. At a given moment one side is the agent and the other the "patient." But at the next moment the direction is reversed. The emerging bachelor is the agent when he attracts a girl, but the girl is the agent when she chooses him. And the boy's "beauty" is perhaps a gift of the female *mamul* spirit as well as a product of male insemination (on agency and substance relations see also A. Strathern 1996; Strathern and Stewart 1999b.)

The picture we have gained from this discussion of Schieffelin's materials, of a female stone figure at the heart of an apparently "male cult," is paralleled both from the Abelam area (see above) and by a detail in a paper on the Ipili (Paiela) *kepele* cult by Gibbs (1978). Gibbs describes the *kepele* cult as performed in times of environmental crisis or difficulty, to restimulate fertility. Performed by men who are guided by ritual experts, it centered on two stones. The *ewa*, a round black stone, was said to be the head of an original ancestor (perhaps the sun). An expert would bury this stone along with pork belly fat, so that it would "keep its eyes closed and sleep," that is, not make people sick (Gibbs 1978: 439). The second stone was the *kepele* stone itself, in one narrative supposedly the bone of another ancestor but described by Gibbs as "a large white vulva shaped stone" (439). The experts brought to this stone the *yupini*, a male figure constructed out of wood and cane. The *yupini* was made to dance up and down, showing its genitalia. When the *kepele* stone was uncovered at the back of a cult house the *yupini* was made to simulate sexual intercourse with this stone. After this action the *kepele* was buried with pig fat, leaves, and tree oil. This was said to make it feel comfortable.[3] Subsequent ritual sequences linked the *kepele* to ideas about sky beings and a snake (python) identified with the rainbow (see Strathern and Stewart 2000b for further discussion of this topic). Men made paintings on bark of this snake, two sky men and "a woman." The "woman" here, we suggest, is a female spirit and is the same as the *kepele* stone itself. The *kepele* cult, then, belongs to the widespread class of "fertility-crisis" cults, rather than male initiation or bachelor growth cults, but shares with both of these an overall concern for social reproduction and the use of the symbolic sexual union to stimulate fertility for the community as a whole. The *yupini*, we suggest, is like a human male, and the *kepele* is the female spirit; hence the ritual structure here corresponds to the same elementary form that is at the heart of the collaborative scenario (see Dosedla 1984 and Wiessner and Tumu 1998, chap. 7 for further discussions of the *yupini* and *kepele*).

Details of this sort are clearly relevant to the theme of what has been described as the male appropriation of female powers, which has formed a significant part of the literature on male cults. While ethnographers have reported on the presence and significance of "female" elements in "male" contexts and "myths of matriarchy" and male trickery as a basis for domination, perhaps these same writers have not taken seriously enough the *continuing, acknowledged, and explicit presence* of female sources of symbolism in these contexts. A complete domination and trickery might have been expected rather to obliterate such signs from the ritual enactment. Andrew Lattas, for example, stresses male trickery as at the heart of the Varku cult among the Kaliai of West New Britain. But he acknowledges that "nearly all the major male mythic heroes of this culture belong to the female gendered moiety," and therefore they partake of "symbolic femaleness" (Lattas 1989: 456). For the Kaliai also the original creator is the cassowary, a figure symbolically encompassing both male and female, and the male ancestor who took the *tambaran* cult originally from the women is said to have originated from the cassowary's left—or female—side wing (456). Lattas continues that this ancestor was "physically male" but "symbolically female, his very person representing a unity of gender opposites." The cassowary is said to have taken the bullroarer from its inventor, his sister/wife, and to have taken women's beards and given them to men, and removed men's breasts and given them to women (Lattas 1989: 457). These forcible mythic exchanges of identity are matched in actual ritual processes by the collaborative actions of the sexes in dealing with Varku, and by the fact that Varku's mask is referred to as female. Lattas concludes that "the tambaran embodies and reifies the social power of female procreation" (466). We would go a little farther than this, in fact. Lattas struggles here with the meaning of trickery or lies, lies that represent the moment of imaginary creation. Yet the myth that he narrated does not speak of trickery or secrecy. It speaks of anger, shame, and role reversals involving switches of power: perhaps the actual dynamics of human gender relations as these are practiced in day to day life. In the rituals of Varku the sexes do *actually collaborate*. The celebration of "the social power of female procreation" is perhaps quite immediate, even if it is overlain by Kaliai men's own rhetorics of deception. Their practices belie their own mythology of "lies." Indeed, the meaning of the term "lie" itself in this context is somewhat moot. Given the explicit prevalence of female imagery in the ritual, we may wonder whether this is a "culture of lies" after all. Perhaps it is the ritualized recognition of negotiated gender relations.

Lattas makes further observations regarding female fertility powers. He argues that, for the Kaliai, "female sexuality represents both the mythical source of male power and yet that which threatens male strength in the present" (Lattas 1989: 466). This observation, which can be taken to hold for parts of the Highlands of New Guinea also, resonates with the significance of the "scheme of potentiality" in Highlands rituals that is designed to resolve the contradiction involved. It resonates also with the "double gendered" character of mythical creator figures such as the cassowary (Strathern and Stewart 2000b) or in the Ok region with its immensely elaborated practices centered on Afek, who combines male and female capacities but is herself primarily female, as is shown by her marriage to her brother Umoim and her production of children, crops, and animals through her reproductive organs.

What we have done here is to insert the category of female spirits into a descriptive context that was identified before by the rather vague category of "male cults." It is evident that this reorganization of the ethnographic map goes hand in hand with the realization that cult practices have historically been constantly moving from place to place. The Highlands was the scene of a great deal of cultural importation, and such imports carried within them the traces of other imports, making for very complex cultural assemblages. In this way comparison turns up elements that reveal their own movements and helps greatly to complicate our pictures of cultural patterns. While we can still use ethnographic baselines in terms of language designations, these become devices of convenience rather than essential indicators of separation. This in turn may lead us again to question any reified distinctions between areas themselves, even though tendencies can be observed or hypothesized (e.g., Feil 1987). Aletta Biersack's chapter (this volume) amply testifies to this point. In reading it, we were struck seriatim by the cumulative similarities between the Paiela and the Duna (where we work and have collected a rich ethnographic record), although certainly there are differences too. The similarities, or commonalities, include the following: the association of the female spirit cult with lakes and rivers; the general importance of water as life-giving; the upper forest zone as the area associated with sky beings, the zone of *tawe* (in Hagen this term appears as *tae* or *tei*); the spirit's invisibility to those not linked to her in marriage; her role as a source of wealth; the spatialization of the temporal life cycle between forest and domestic areas; the aim of bachelor cults to make boys attractive and the role of smoke in magic that blows into girls' eyes and arouses desire in them; and the symbolic use of items such as the bog iris and bamboo that are known for their speedy powers of growth.

With regard to the Ankave and the Kamea, the work of Bonnemère, Lemonnier, and Bamford has already shown clearly two things: one, that the mothers of male initiates, through their observance of taboos, crucially and collaboratively participate in the boys' successful passage through initiation rituals; and two, that substances imbued with female powers, such as fruit-pandanus juice, may also be held to be important in fostering male growth (Bamford 1997: 148–67; Bonnemère 1996: 293–307). Elements of our Collaborative Model certainly apply in these contexts. There seems to be a general agreement that there are marked differences between the Ankave/Kamea cases, on the one hand, and the Baruya and Sambia, on the other. These are matters that the Anga experts are themselves best able to sort out empirically and explain, in terms of history, demography, and warfare. However, even for the Baruya and the Sambia, some comparative issues arise. Among the Baruya, for example, shamans may be female as well as male, and this suggests a positive recognition that female powers as well as male powers may be needed to encompass certain ends. Godelier writes that "the most hidden secret" of the shamanic initiatory practice is that the power to heal which shamans of both sexes possess "is supposed to originate from the light of Venus, a Baruya woman, formerly sacrificed to the thunder god, and metamorphosed into a star" (Godelier 1982: 24). He comments further that "the power of men has its origin in the appropriation, the capture, the conversion of a female power" (24) This is not, as his account makes clear, the kind of appropriation that takes the power involved away from women, since women do become shamans, and Godelier in fact notes that "certain shaman women are considered to be much greater than a large number of their male colleagues" (24). These are remarkable observations for a culture otherwise described in much of the literature as being orchestrated by male domination.

For the Sambia, Herdt notes another image of female power, the Mother Cassowary, connected with the force of thunder and lightning (1981: 135–37). This old female cassowary, the Mother, is said to stay behind in the forest when the rest of the birds disappear on foraging trips. She holds on to the cassowaries' territory as its "boss" and eludes capture by male human hunters (1981: 137). She sends one set of cassowaries (male) into the sky and another (female) into the earth, and summons them back by goring wild fruit and pandanus trees and making their produce fall down, following this with a "trumpet-bark" that is the sound of thunder. She commands the lightning to make a bright path for the male sky-dwelling cassowaries to return to the high forests and make themselves available again to male human hunters (Herdt

1981: 137). Given this reference to the cassowary's bark as thunder, it is possible to ask if the Baruya also think of thunder in the same way. Is the thunder-god, then, in fact the cassowary? Putting together Baruya and Sambia ethnography in this way might be illuminating. The Sambia image of the cassowary seems compellingly analogous to the idea of the female spirit as a sky being that we have found in the Western and Southern Highlands provinces. Sambia also say that cassowaries are "identical to women," and men "sometimes metaphorically refer to women as cassowaries" (1981: 136; this volume).

Further, we learn that there are female hamlet spirits who may be said to cohabit with the forest-dwelling spirits of deceased male leaders and give birth to cassowaries. These female hamlet spirits are also typically the familiars, first seen in a dream, who enable men to become cassowary-hunters. The "spirit marriage" theme shows clearly here (Herdt 1981: 86, 143).[4]

This point suggests that Sambia men are not oblivious to female powers of a generative or cosmic kind that might profitably be *combined* with male powers in procreation, for example. Herdt himself stresses the originary power of semen, in this context, arguing that breast milk is seen by Sambia as a transform of semen and that it is semen that is at the heart of procreative reproduction.[5] Girls are said to have a blood organ (*tingu*) that hastens their physical development, whereas boys are said not to produce their own semen and instead require oral insemination and magical treatments (Herdt in Herdt and Stoller 1990: 56), but Herdt also states that pandanus tree sap, which is equated with women's breast milk, replaced semen in male bodies (1981: 111). These ethnographic details allow the reader to make further interpretations. Herdt writes that the "magical power" of semen "does things to people, changing and rearranging them, as if it were a generator." They can do little to affect "this semen principle," which passes through their bodies "as an electrical current through a wire" (Herdt in Herdt and Stoller 1990: 58). Elsewhere, however, Herdt writes that "semen (maleness) and blood (femaleness) are vital . . . blood must also combine with semen to create the embryo" (Herdt 1981: 195). This sounds more like a chemical reaction than an electrical current passing through a wire. Clearly, both semen ("maleness") and blood ("femaleness") are actively involved in the process which produces a new product—an embryo. Again, the ethnographic materials provide clues to further analysis.

Breast milk and semen are certainly considered comparable by Sambia. Males can also obtain replenishment of semen from pandanus nuts (Herdt 1981: 110). The aerial roots of pandanus trees are tapped for their sap, which is compared to breast milk, and one informant said "It [the root] is the same as the breast of a woman . . . from which milk is taken. The tip is cut, the milk is drunk. I drank it when I was a bachelor to replace my semen" (Herdt 1981: 111). Herdt provides an elaborate table of gender associations of the nut pandanus, showing how it combines male and female attributes (114–15). In terms of nourishment only pandanus sap is said to be truly like milk and therefore able to replace semen. This in turn suggests that, if from one point of view milk is a transform of semen, the reverse also holds, and thus semen is gendered both female and male. Something quintessentially male can therefore emerge out of something female and vice versa. If the two are opposites, they are also in another way the same (cf. Herdt 1981: 110 on the intricacies of translation problems here). Given this, it is not surprising that the act of heterosexual procreation also involved transformations. Herdt, in one passage, reports the idea that a fetus is formed from semen that displaces female blood from the womb (195). Yet, both male semen and female blood "are vital" to this process, which involves a mixing of blood and semen, and we are told that blood, in the newborn, comes from the mother, bone and skin from the father (195–96). Elsewhere, and later, Herdt expresses it as follows: "The womb is the container and transformer of semen" (Herdt in Herdt and Stoller 1990: 63). He implies an inertia on the part of the female womb in this process, but the idea that "transformation" occurs suggests the opposite—an active reaction or rearrangement of semen substance into fetal substance. From this transformation, then, we learn that, even if bone and skin come from semen, the womb is the transformative agent. If semen is a generator, blood in the womb is a transformer, and clearly blood and semen do work, that is, expend energy, in forming and feeding the fetus. Both semen and blood are important, and both may therefore be said to have "magical power," especially since magic is a transformer of substances and situations in general.[6]

These brief observations may suggest that it is worthwhile to look at the Anga materials from the standpoint of the Western Highlands. We find a complementarity in the theories of procreation and a recognition of female powers linked to notions of the Mother Cassowary and of sky beings (Strathern and Stewart 2000b) that places a certain "signature" on the Sambia and Baruya, making them less "different" from other parts of the Highlands than we might have thought. Maternal influence persists through milk, and "milk" can be equated with semen, so here is another element in which male and female are not antithetical opposites but a complementary and in some ways interchangeable pair, illustrating again a basic feature of the Collaborative Model.

We have one final comparative point: the female spirits we have tracked here mostly turn out to be sky beings as well as beings linked with water. Sky beings are an important category in mythologies that can be traced all over eastern Indonesia and the broader areas of Melanesia beyond Papua New Guinea (Stewart and Strathern 1999c). A whole cosmology is implied here, and it is far more important than is allowed for in the idea that such notions are "vague" or "in the background" of more salient ones (Strathern and Stewart 2000b). Given this broad background, it would be interesting to explore further the byways of ethnography throughout the Highlands of New Guinea and beyond, and examine how sky beings, female spirits, and features of our model fit together on a wider scale.

In light of the analyses presented in the contributions to this volume, it would also be interesting to revisit and perhaps recontextualize the earlier psychoanalytically oriented discussions regarding initiations, identity conflicts, male and female sexual anxieties and desires, and the power of bodily fluids such as menstrual blood and semen. The Collaborative Model as well as that of what we call "Gendered Relationality" (the cosmological inclusion of a spectrum of sexually valenced entities) can assist us to explore the range of emotions involved in these rituals, which structure their performative aspects.

Chapter 7
The Variability of Women's "Involvement" in Anga Male Initiations

Pierre Lemonnier

Anga societies occupy a special place in the ethnographic and theoretical context of gender studies in New Guinea. The northern Angans, who live in the
Eastern Highlands of Papua New Guinea, a region for which Lewis Langness,
Kenneth Read, and others stressed the crucial role of gender relations in local
social organization, are the object of one of the most detailed accounts of
male initiation ceremonies in the island, for which we must thank Maurice
Godelier (1986) and Gilbert Herdt (1981, 1987b). Following these studies, devoted respectively to the mechanisms of male domination and to the development of boys in a highly ritualized context, Bonnemère (1996) and Bamford
(1997), writing on the Ankave and the Kamea (also known as Kapau), introduced the presence of women into a picture that they have thus profoundly
modified. Not only have they shown that apparently very similar societies har-
bor deep-seated differences, they have also underscored the differences concerning the very points that have made the Anga so famous: the sites and the
violence of male domination and the existence of boy-inseminating rites
(Herdt 1984b: ix), as well as the marginality of women in male ritual, which
both Bamford and Bonnemère show to be partly an artifact of male-biased
ethnography.

The Anga, we were told in the anthropology of the 1980s, and notably in
Godelier's model of Great-Men societies (1982, 1986), display a crucial link
between male solidarity and superiority over women, boy-inseminating practices, and sister exchange. With his description of one Anga society (the
Iqwaye) in which some of the men knew nothing about boy-inseminating rites
(following a temporary mission-imposed ban), Mimica (1981) had already implicitly cast doubt on the purportedly central role of male homosexual relations in these societies. In addition, the Ankave and Kamea ethnographies

have shown that there were incontestably "great men" in Anga societies with neither marriage by sister exchange nor boy-inseminating practices. Finally, proof of an important role played by wealth in the framework of sister exchange in the Baruya society was yet another blow to Godelier's model (Lemonnier 2002).

As for gender relations properly speaking, the chapters in this volume by Bamford and Bonnemère show that, far from being absent from male rites, women on the contrary play a fundamental role.

Anga comparative ethnography is not a pure (and tedious) exercise in erudition; it is a not only useful but indispensable means of validating and even reformulating theoretical propositions constructed from the analysis of one or another of these societies—or other Melanesian groups. At least this is the case for those who, like me, consider comparative ethnography to be at the core of anthropology (this is a key methodological point with clear theoretical consequences).

As is widely known, there are at least two ways of articulating anthropological theory with comparative ethnography. One is to pick information here and there in view of consolidating a theoretical proposition, with the obvious risk of retaining only the data that fit the theory. The other, which I propose to illustrate here, is to test the theory against possible counter-examples and to contextualize these in order to ascertain whether the hypothesis at hand should be accepted, modified, or thrown out altogether. Context in this case does not refer only to the noticeable differences in social organization, gender relations, and male rituals reported between northern Angans (Baruya, Sambia, Iqwaye, Watchakes) and southern and southwestern Anga groups (Ankave, Kapau, Menye). It has also to do with the time and historical context of the ethnographies in question, in other words, with the influence of the Pax Australiana, missions, and local involvement in the market economy.

Needless to say, to argue for comparison is not simply a methodological proposition. It is also a theoretical statement about the need to consider women's involvement as a variable in itself, as a social phenomenon prone to vary, with important anthropological consequences. It is not so much a matter of actually demonstrating that women play a role in male ritual as of characterizing their participation, its underlying principles, and its correlates (if not consequences). The general questions raised and statements made here are an attempt to define what we mean by the "participation" of women in male ritual, and what "complementary" or "equal" participation of the two sexes in ritual signifies. Not only must such expressions be handled with care, it may also be the case that they conceal precisely what we want to study: the full details of women's presence/absence in male ritual. Not only do we seek to discover what women do or don't do in Anga ritual, we also hope to discover in what respect their role in making men echoes their status in a given society.

Running counter to many theories defended in this volume, the present contribution maintains that it is theoretically untenable and irrelevant to consider a priori that male rituals in Melanesia have one dominant function or meaning, such as to make warriors, to break the mother-son bond or to reproduce social hierarchies. All these aspects are always present in this sort of ritual, but the emphasis placed on each aspect differs. The question therefore is not what is the "key" to the analysis of women's role in New Guinea male rituals, but what domain or set of social relations are stressed by a given Anga society, and how is this done. Once again, the first step in dealing with this question is to undertake a detailed comparative ethnography of Anga rituals.

Anga societies call for an anthropology of nuances, and the amount and quality of the ethnography recorded since the days of Beatrice Blackwood in the mid-1930s has long led us to reformulate our views about the area. Ten years ago, the general picture of these societies, drawn after accounts by Herdt (1981), Mimica (1981) and Godelier (1986), focused on boy-inseminating practices, sister exchange, and very strong male domination. Now, thanks to the analyses and models developed in the early 1980s, it has become fairly easy for people like Bamford, Bonnemère, and myself to see that the situation among southern and southwestern Angans was often strikingly different from this model. Indeed, all Anga groups are definitely great men societies that fit into the general model elaborated by Godelier: societies in which the group is (or was) focused primarily on warfare and male initiations. Around these two events are articulated the three principal hierarchies that structure the life of the society—the ranking of great men (masters of the initiations, great warriors, sometimes great shamans); the subordination of all women to the men as a group; and the authority of the older men over the first-stage initiates. In all Anga groups, at the heart of this system of institutions and social relations lies, to a variable degree, the idea that women's sexual physiology is detrimental to men, that it saps their bellicosity and thereby jeopardizes the group. The initiations are a source of physical and moral strength for the men and are the framework for transmitting the practical knowledge that enables men to mitigate this dangerous state of affairs.

Some key features of the previous models now appear, however, to be peculiar to northern Angans (Baruya, Sambia, Iqwaye, Watchakes). In particular, most Anga societies do not practice sister exchange, but give a brideprice instead, and they do not have boy-inseminating practices, but "grow boys" through the use of various substitutes for blood, which is seen primarily as a female component of the person. In several southwestern societies, male domination is far less strong, though still present and crucial. Other key and spectacular cultural features of northern Anga peoples, such as suicide (probably one of the highest rates in the world) or compulsory cooperative behavior in everyday life, are simply absent in some or most other Anga groups.

As far as we can tell from oral history, linguistics, and genetics, today's Anga cultures and social organizations derive from those of a people established somewhere around Menyamya (Morobe Province) some thousand years ago. There have probably been numerous borrowings from non-Anga peoples, yet the relative homogeneity of Anga cultures is impressive. By many standards, Anga people, like their languages, are "different" (Healey 1981), at least when compared to their immediate neighbors. The various ethnographies available on these social organizations and cultures provide a rare opportunity to follow the various stages in the process of transformation, deformation, and differentiation of a previous structure that has led to the contemporary situations.[1]

Anga male rituals show at the same time very strong similarities and a series of peculiarities and contrasts that are meaningful with respect to the roles and status of women and of femaleness in these societies. Seen from afar, for example with reference to New Guinea as a whole, these dissimilarities dwindle into mere nuances, local variations on a general theme, but within the Anga framework they constitute such strong contrasts that it is sometimes more appropriate to speak of significant differences. Using a comparative approach to the ethnography of Anga male rituals, this chapter will examine possible co-variations or correlates of the different patterns of women's direct or indirect participation in male initiations, which in turn says much about the role and status of Anga women in general.

When we look at Anga male initiations, we see that we are clearly dealing with a single, overarching model. The general characteristics described by Herdt (1981, 1987b), Godelier (1986), and Bonnemère (1993, 1996, 1998a) for particular Anga societies apply in all Anga groups: the rituals that are mandatory for all boys are presented as procedures necessary to make them grow and turn into strong warriors and to counteract the debilitating influence of women. Less explicit but still crucial functions of the initiations are the reproduction of hierarchies (men versus women, ritual experts versus ordinary men, older initiates versus young men) and the boys' separation from their mothers. Whoever has witnessed this separation among the Baruya and Sambia (Herdt 1981: 135, 216, 289–90) or the mothers wailing when the initiates parade in front of the women at the end of the final stage of the rituals will agree that the severing of the mother-son link is essential here (Bamford, Bonnemère, this volume), and harrowing for the protagonists. Male rituals are also generally the time for detection or confirmation of individual "supernatural" powers.[2] Following a remark made by Herdt (1987b: 25–27) and my own observation of the Ankave male rituals,[3] I would like to underscore the acquisition of bravery—or how not to run away when you are scared to death by the irruption of enemies in your hamlet—as another important component of Anga male ceremonies.

Although the Angan discourse stresses acquisition of strength and bravery by the initiates and the building of a collective force, there is a tandem group of features common to these rituals—the scenery and the staging, both of which always comprise implicit references to the human birth process (with the possible exception of the Iqwaye ritual), at least in the first and second stages of the ritual, which must be regarded as a single, two-step ritual event.[4] For the outside observer, the process at the end of which the boys appear as transfigured, "completed" males and warriors is patterned on the human physiological process of conception, intrauterine growth, and feeding (Bonnemère, this volume). From one Anga society to another, the variations on male rituals appear above all in the way the phase of the novice's "rebirth" is thought and enacted, and in the role ascribed to female powers—or to women themselves—in this process. The rebirth is either reenacted or completed (I should say reenacted *and* completed) using images of the woman's procreative capacities and of the growth of the fetus and infant (Godelier 1986: 52, 1999: 114; Bonnemère 1996: 345–52).[5] Furthermore, the key substances put on or in the novices' bodies are more or less explicit surrogates of body fluids (Bonnemère 1994).

For the most part, the scenery and staging are the same in all Anga groups. In particular, alongside huge and crucial differences—semen here, blood there, absence of "female initiation" in several groups—there is almost incredible regularity in several sets of elements that figure in these rituals, and, even more, in the sequencing and external appearance of the various "acts" of the ritual.

In some cases, the "event" seen or undergone by the novices looks the same, but its explicit meaning varies enormously. For instance, I have observed strikingly similar stagings among the Baruya and Ankave, in which a body lying on the ground was associated with a display of wealth and abruptly revealed to the novices. In both cases, this is the time when the initiates are shown the shell money that would compensate their being killed by the elder men in the event they revealed secrets to the women. But, whereas the Baruya use the pseudo-corpse to illustrate the fate of men who misbehave in life ("steal" another man's wife, etc.), the Ankave man lying on the ground starts humming the story of an ancestor whose murder stands at the origin of the male ritual.[6] Several aspects of these playlets have hardly anything in common, and yet they give the anthropologist a keen feeling of déjà vu. Likewise, although the Sambia are the only ones to comment on the bloodletting supposed to "remove female contaminants from the body" of the novice (Herdt 1987b: 140), a similar bleeding occurs during Baruya male initiations, precisely at the same "moment" as among the Sambia (i.e., after going through a tunnel, prior to the actual piercing of the septum). At one stage, a Baruya warrior bites his own tongue so that it bleeds; this is also the moment when an enemy used to shoot an arrow into the novice's thigh, making it bleed. At the same point in the nose-piercing ceremony, Ankave boys are beaten with cassowary quills and are supposed to bleed. During this same step again, Kapau-Kamea were described in a patrol report as having the bridge of their nose, their shoulders, and their ribs rubbed with a bullroarer until they bled.[7] But, as far as we know, there is no explicit reference to eliminating female blood among the Baruya, Ankave, or Kapau. In other words, a sequence in the ritual may have totally different meanings in different Anga societies (e.g., the display of shell money) or be totally forgotten (expulsion of maternal blood). Herdt (this volume) recalls that "the meaning of any object is always contingent upon the setting and the type of linguistic praxis which accompanies it."[8] Furthermore, it is obvious that some of the elements present in all Anga groups may have no meaning at all and may be considered simple "remnants" of a previous ritual organization (Lemonnier n.d.).

Conversely, the different Anga cultures may "act out" the same function of the ritual in various ways. For instance, among the Baruya, Menye, and Sambia, the materialization of the unity of the society or the solidarity of the men is expressed by simultaneously planting the posts of the ceremonial house (Godelier 1986: 34). The Ankave do not do that; instead, each warrior brings one of his own war arrows, and the master of the initiations makes them into a magic bundle that is held by a dancer during the nights just before the actual beginning of the secret part of the ceremonies, in other words, at the "moment" when northern Angans also prepare their dancing ground and communal ceremonial house.

In addition to variations in the staging and performance of the ritual, which would require entire books to compare step by step for every Anga society having been documented with respect to male initiations, these rituals show often pronounced differences in their overall organization as well as in many key elements.

The nature of the substances and objects featured in the male rituals is probably the main difference between two sets of Anga societies: those that stress semen as the key substance versus those that emphasize blood.[9] Bonnemère has demonstrated that the nature of the body fluids or substitutes used to strengthen the boys clearly parallels that of the bodily substances to which each group attributes the making of a human being in the mother's womb (1994: 28, 31). This is not surprising if the general framework of Anga male rituals is that of procreation and growth.

Boy-insemination practices are conspicuously absent in all those groups where eating and rubbing red pandanus juice/seeds is recognized as an independent stage—the Ankave and Kapau.[10] Conversely, marita (Tok Pisin for *Pandanus conoideus*) is absent (Baruya, Watchakes) or merely mentioned (Sambia) in northern Angan rituals.[11] Possible "intermediary cases" would be the Menye (who are said to have rubbed semen on the novices' bodies; Mimica 1981: 60), and the Sambia (where pandanus juice is used during the second stage; Herdt 1987b: 125–27).[12]

The use of flutes and bullroarers parallels the opposition between the kind of body fluids featured in the rituals. Although flutes and bullroarers are played in all groups, the former are emphasized only where the boys are inseminated, which is not surprising if the flutes happen to be used to teach fellatio to the novices, as is the case among the Sambia (Herdt 1987b: 148ff); the flutes are kept secret under pain of death among the Baruya, Sambia, and Watchakes. By contrast, Menye or Ankave boys can be seen amusing themselves publicly with the flutes. Flutes are played during Ankave male initiations, but there is nothing secret or sacred in this playing, which is done by young men, and the flutes may also be played by children at any time. Conversely, the bullroarers (which are always supposedly a secret from the women) are dramatically revealed to the novices only in those groups with no boy-inseminating practices. The Iqwaye (Mimica 1981: 61) and Menye similarly keep only the bullroarers secret.[13]

The number of stages (from three among the Ankave to seven among the Sambia), length of ceremonies, and behavior in the interval between ceremonies comprise another big difference, regarding in particular what I would call the "practical details" of the separation of the novice from his mother and, more generally, from the female world. By "behavior between ceremonies" I mean, for instance, the long separation of a Sambia, Baruya, or Iqwaye (Mimica 1991b: 100), boy from the women (notably from his mother), which lasts for years, compared to the Ankave (or Menye) initiates, who are allowed to stay close to the women (and sleep in their parents' house if they wish) as soon as they leave the forest hut in which they have been secluded. Ankave boys normally slept in a bachelors' house (*not* a men's house) and they would all gather in a men's house in times of war, but they could approach women freely, which is simply incredible by Baruya or Sambia standards.

The other Anga specialists participating in this volume (Bamford, Bonnemère, and Herdt) have written much about the length and brutality of the boys' separation from the female world and about the active involvement of the mothers in breaking the link with their child. Here comparison reveals an opposition between the Baruya, Iqwaye (Mimica 1981: 52, 1991b: 100), Sambia, or Watchakes, on the one hand, and the Ankave, Menye, or Kapau-Kamea, on the other.[14] In particular, the separation of the novices from their mothers is considerably shorter and less abrupt in those groups where boy-insemination does not take place.

In passing, I would point out that we have here another nice example of what I would call a simple "nuance" that carries salient anthropological implications: yes, Ankave men should keep their distance from women in times of war, and because of the same fear of women as among northern Angans, but this fear, which is a sort of everyday terror in the Baruya case, is a serious matter only in times of active warfare among the Ankave. Intermediary cases can be found: Watchakes did have bachelors' houses and probably ingestion of semen, but they stopped avoiding women as soon as they reached the second stage of the rituals, that is, after three years or so in the bachelors' house.[15]

The extent, terms, and meaning of the "participation" of the initiates' mothers (and sisters, and mothers' brothers) in the bodily and mental transformation of the Anga boys has been discussed at length by Bamford, Bonnemère, and Herdt. Their ethnography and analyses clearly show that the participation of women in the ritual is not in question (this as well as Herdt 1987b: 114); what need to be assessed are the modalities of this participation and its importance for the success of the rituals.

With respect to women's "positionality" (Herdt, this volume) in male rituals, I would contrast maximum distance between the women and the initiates, say among the Baruya or Sambia, where the mothers are secluded individually,[16] with the case of the Ankave or Kamea, where the mothers' participation in the transformation of their son's body is direct and active, expresses a sort of symbiosis between mother and son, and is considered necessary to the success of the whole ritual process. Baruya or Sambia mothers are, along with other women—and often the most active ones—involved in the collective building of the ceremonial house, and they play a role of their own (notably in resisting their boys' removal by the men) in the public rituals that unfold on the dance-ground (Godelier 1986: 34; Herdt, this volume).

As soon as the novices enter the ceremonial house or are led deep into the bush, northern Anga women virtually cease playing any visible role.[17] By contrast, both Bonnemère and Bamford underline the active involvement of the mothers of the novices in the first stage of the ritual, which goes far beyond merely being present as an audience. Ankave and Kapau mothers are collectively secluded and their activities restricted. They share the same food taboos and some of the body treatments applied to their sons. They have no sexual activity during the initiations, which is very rightly interpreted by Bamford as a way to avoid being pregnant during the initiations.[18] Their welcome of the new initiates parallels the ritual applied to a newborn baby. And so on. Should the mothers not behave properly, the boys' sores would not "dry," and the "rope of their nose" (*se'me' ngwa'* in Ankave) would break. At stake here is the very success of the transformation taking place in the bodies of the novices assembled and sheltered in the forest.

Again, what distinguishes southern Angans is not the fact that women play a role in male initiation, but the emphasis on the particular behaviors of the initiates' mothers, which take the form of active and positive actions. Aside from their participation in the preparation of the first public steps of the ceremonies (bringing material, dancing, etc.), which is common to all groups, northern Anga mothers play a role that could be qualified as passive (seclusion, taboo on scratching one's skin), or, when active, as negative: they protect their boys and try to retain them; they "kill" their names (Baruya). Although Ankave mothers adopt these passive or negative behaviors, they also share the same food taboos as their sons, they soak their bark capes every day in cold water, as their sons do, and so on (Bonnemère, this volume). In so doing, they play an active and *positive* role in the transformation of their sons' bodies. They help them surmount the close encounter with death that is part of the initiation process; they actively participate in the healing of the sore in their septum so that it does not become infected, fester, and prove fatal. The scope of the mothers' actions is broader among the Ankave or Kamea, and it also affects the "new" body of the boys. Southern Anga mothers are not only part of the ritual that helps end a relationship with their sons, they also participate, from their own collective shelter, in the metamorphosis and transfiguration of the novice with whom they were in symbiosis.

Similar and even more active participation of women may be found at a crucial step of the ritual described by Blackwood in 1937 among the "Nauti" (Kapau; 1978: 131–32). During the red pandanus ceremony, she saw the men seize four women and take them to a place she could not see. The explanation she received was that the women "went because part of the archway under which the boys had to be taken was loose and they brought others [?], but, she adds, this account was not clear here" (1978: 131). This happened a moment before the novices were beaten with cassowary quills (to make them bleed) and then smeared with red pandanus. I would suggest that, plausibly, these women were themselves part of the tunnel through which the initiates passed just prior to being smeared with the red marita juice. In this case, this is the shortest distance between women and initiates found among the Anga, the women being at the actual scene of a rite.

Another key "variable" is the existence and complexity of *female* rites, which also vary widely from one Anga group to another (from individual cleansing and decoration to collective rituals, nose-piercing, etc.). Collective female rituals are found among the Baruya, Sambia, and Watchakes (Godelier 1986: 46–51; Herdt 1987b: 108).[19] Another absolute correlation is that collective female rituals exist only where the boys are ritually inseminated, among the Baruya, Sambia, and probably Watchakes.[20] Drawing on the Ankave case, Bonnemère (1996: 381) has shown that collective female rituals do not exist in those Anga societies where women are not systematically denigrated. The Ankave would (and actually do) say: "Women are dangerous for our weapons and fighting ardor." The Baruya (and Sambia) say something like "Women are dangerous," but they add "and this is their fault!"[21] As Godelier has described, northern Anga female rituals are a time when the women themselves drum into girls the sad news that they are responsible for the men's difficulties in life (Godelier 1986: 46–51). Consequently, in those societies where the belief that men are the only ones who can transform boys into warriors is the strongest, female rituals function as a reinforcement of the ideological male discourse and therefore as a means of imposing male domination. And, whereas male domination is an obvious part of the men's discourse during northern Angans' male initiations, it is less clear cut in the Ankave ceremonies; moreover, Bamford (this volume) doesn't "see" it in the present form of Kamea rituals.

The participation of women (mothers and sisters of the novices) in Anga male rituals is only one element of the representations of the young boys' transformation into full warriors. In every group, the very necessity of these rituals derives from this invariant of Anga thought, the belief in the debilitating power of women and, more precisely, of their sexual fluids. In the Anga context, the general theme of "rebirth," which characterizes all initiation rites, takes the form of a tour de force: enacting a process that is female by nature but at the same time minimizing the part women take in it in order to compensate for the imaginary damaging effects of female sexuality on male bodies. This contradictory goal is achieved through a series of ambiguities aimed at dissimulating or disguising the female factors involved in male initiations. But while all societies repress the necessity of female factors, some repress it more successfully than others.

In this respect, the covariations of the ways women or female powers are involved in the rituals often exhibit a specific internal logic. For instance, the secrecy of the rituals and the length and severity of the boys' physical distancing and concealment from the women, shown by Godelier and Herdt to be key aspects of Anga rituals, are much more highly developed where boy-insemination is central to the rituals, that is, among northern Angans. However, following Bonnemère, we must add that this set of characteristics is accompanied by the denigration of women, the explicit negation of their procreative powers, and the women's own acknowledgment of their responsibility in debilitating the men. Northern Angans admit the necessary complementarity of female and male principles in making boys grow, but the female elements are acquired by ruse, theft, and violence (Godelier 1999: 125–33). To semen, which gives strength, the Sambia or Baruya add various (and often vague) principles of female origin.

Northern Anga women are kept in a marginal position during the ritual— and in a much more marginal and less visible one than the mothers and sisters of southern Anga initiates (Bonnemère, this volume). For instance, Baruya mothers remain secluded, each in her own house, during the ceremonies, whereas the Ankave gather all the mothers and sisters of the initiates into a special shelter near the fathers' own shelter, where they live for weeks until the boys come back from the forest. Unlike northern Angans, Ankave men say explicitly that the seclusion and appropriate behavior of the mothers is a sine qua non of the success of the rituals. In other words, a Baruya mother plays no direct role in the ritual metamorphosis of her son, she can only be a hindrance to—not an essential element in—the initiation process (Bonnemère, this volume).

The recourse to semen for building the body of the young warriors that characterizes northern Angans has its own logical implications. First, it may be postulated that "relying" on male body fluids alone to make the boys strong and fierce considerably slows the process of changing their bodies, whereas the "use" of female substances gives the boys the benefit of the girls' innately rapid maturation. This would also explain why the separation of the boys *has* to be very long in those groups where their growth relies explicitly on semen. Not only does it take something like ten years or more to grow into a fully mature man, but the complexity and the sequencing of the process are underlined by the number of stages: five among the Baruya, Iqwaye, and Watchakes and even six among the Sambia (Herdt 1987b: 107). It is also noteworthy that the ingestion of semen is one of the men's principal secrets. Conversely, the use of red pandanus juice is not kept secret among southern Angans; only the fact that it is eaten and that the boys' skin is beaten and bruised prior to their being smeared with the seeds is hidden from the women.[22]

In other Anga groups, those that openly feature female principles in the ritual—blood, seen as a maternal element—the complementarity between the sexes remains. Among the Ankave, to the male powers conveyed by the awl used to pierce the nose of the novices are added the female powers contained in the nose ornament immediately slipped into the septum. The awl is believed to be made of the humerus (or tibia) of the primordial ancestor, who according to the myth explained to the Ankave how to initiate the boys. The nose ornaments are cut from cassowary quills explicitly associated with the woman who went into the forest and changed into a cassowary, while a cassowary left the forest to become the woman who is the ancestor of all women. After this dual-gendered regenerative impetus provided by the piercing, the growth of the novice is obtained by the secret anointing with red pandanus seeds and juice. What is symbolically concealed is the masculinization of the blood substitute, which, according to the myth, is the blood of the ancestor who distributed the languages and body decorations to the first members of all Anga cultural groups and of all humankind. As the first man to emerge on the surface of the earth, this ancestor had no mother. His blood was not of female origin, and it was this blood that engendered the red pandanus and red cordylines that even now are the vegetal agents of Ankave male rituals. Although female by essence, the blood that makes the boys grow is largely masculinized. As already mentioned, the dilemma of how "to make men as women do, but without women" can be circumvented only through some ambiguity: a partly female *kwaimatnie* for the Baruya (Godelier 1986: 94); masculinized maternal blood for the Ankave.

Unlike the northern Angans' violent acquisition of female powers, the Ankave do not "capture" any of the female principles (flutes) used during the male rituals. These principles are simply present in the sacred *oxemexe'* bundle, in the form of cassowary quills. This absence of violence and the acknowledgment of positive female roles can also be read in the relationship of the women with these objects. Not only are they not taken by force from the women, Kapau mothers are the temporary guardians of the bullroarers (Bamford, this volume). As for the Ankave, they know that, twice in their recent history, women endangered their own lives to recover and hide the *oxemexe'*, which otherwise would have been destroyed or stolen by enemies. One has only to suggest to a Sambia or Baruya man that a woman might touch a flute or a *kwaimatnie* to realize what this mere possibility of contact between women and sacred objects means for an Anga. Although acknowledged to be dangerous, Ankave (or Kamea) women are not denigrated or held responsible for their dangerousness, and they actively participate in the transformation of their sons.

It is important to note—and here is another meaningful nuance—that "acknowledged complementarity" of the sexes does not mean "equality." In this respect, I am not too sure that "both sexes are equally involved" in Kamea (or Ankave) initiations (Bamford, this volume). In effect, Kamea women are not directly involved in the actions performed over days and weeks in the secrecy of the forest. To take just one example, during the nose-piercing ceremony women play no role whatsoever in the beating of the boys, the revelation of the bullroarers, or the actual piercing of the septum, which is the action that defines this stage for the Kamea-Kapau (Blackwood 1978: 123–27; Simpson 1954: 102–5; Hastings 1961–62: 2–4; my 1980 notes). Nor are Kamea or Ankave mothers directly involved in the beating, actual rubbing of pandanus juice, and heating of the body of the boys, which take place in the ceremonial shelter away from the women and out of their sight (Blackwood 1978: 129–32; Simpson 1954: 105–6; Hastings 1961–62: 4–5; my 1980 notes).

The meaning of what the Kamea men act out in the secrecy of the bush is probably lost for ever.[23] But whatever this meaning may have been, it is certain that women take no direct or active part in these secret actions on the body and mind of the novices, which take place in the ceremonial enclosure out of their presence. This introduces an absolute bias and asymmetry into the respective involvement of men and women in the rituals. Even in the Kapau case described by Blackwood, in which women are brought to the very scene of the "marita ritual"—which I suggest above is the most active participation we have of women in an Anga male ritual—the women are "seized" and "pulled" by the men and they intervene for only "a few minutes." They do not control anything. Southern Anga women are much more present and active during the male rituals, but this does not mean they play a part "equal" to the men's in organizing or performing the ceremonies. This in turn means that the reproduction of political hierarchies is also at issue in these rituals. In passing, although it is important to stress the generality of the "complementarity" between men and women that may be found in all sorts of male rituals in New Guinea (Strathern and Stewart, this volume), it appears in the Anga case that such a catch-all formula would tend to dissolve more anthropological questions than it solves.

Indeed, another salient feature of northern Anga cultures is the way beliefs in male preeminence in the making of a baby or an initiate pervade almost all aspects of life. For instance, the range of the ritual specialists' activities is fairly wide in the societies where they intervene in the installation of the supplementary spirit of various other specialists, notably shamans. Whereas Baruya or Sambia men spectacularly and solemnly assert their ability to control the making of the specialists (great warriors, shamans) who are crucial to the very survival of the group, the Ankave great men simply confirm the presence of these spirits, which have already been discovered by the mother of the specialist-to-be.

In the same vein, for anyone who goes from one Anga group to another, the contrast is conspicuous between the bustle that characterizes most male activities among, say, the Baruya, and the solitary, quiet work of an Ankave or Menye man; the latter will work on his own house or garden fence for weeks, whereas northern Angans will get together and try to complete the work as fast as they can: another exciting way for the men to compete within the team of coworkers and to show off their strength and skills to the women. The male solidarity acquired and stressed during life in a Baruya or Sambia men's house extends spectacularly into the realm of cooperative activity in everyday life and clearly goes with the omnipresent and explicit reference to the exclusiveness of men's powers and substances in the physical and mental transformation of the boys. Not only do the men gather around or inside the men's house every day to do all sorts of things out of the women's sight, they also display, in numerous public activities, the "collective force" (Godelier 1992: 19–20) they build and acquire during the male ceremonies and in the men's house. Conversely, collective work is almost totally absent in those groups where the rituals rely primarily on surrogate (although remasculinized) female substances: the Ankave, of course, but also the Menye (Lemonnier 1984b: 116; 1998a). In the latter cases, male solidarity is limited strictly to warfare and the organization of male rituals.

The Anga case is a reminder that we should keep in view the idea of an anthropology of nuances when addressing the question of women's involvement in male rituals. I think it highly improbable—or undecidable—that some of the current approaches to the question are better than others. Our aim is certainly not to propose an either/or view on this question; rather, we offer complementary ones. It is not possible to decide whether Anga male rituals are primarily (if not only) a matter of reproducing male domination or resocializing the boys' desires (Herdt, this volume), or that they deal above all with the severing of the mother-son link, or that they are mainly a way to build social identities (Bamford, this volume), and so forth.[24] All these phenomena clearly operate simultaneously, and what has to be done is to try to see how and to understand why they are articulated in a particular way in a given Anga society. As Herdt rightly puts it (this volume), an approach that favors male domination is not wrong or obsolete, it is "incomplete."

In all Anga societies, men are indisputably the stronger; they are the shouting and dominating sex. Among the Ankave or Kamea as elsewhere, it is the women (and girls) who return in the evening to the hamlets, dripping with sweat and rain, and bent under forty kilos or more of sweet potatoes, firewood, and children. They are the ones who hasten to prepare the family evening meal, while their husbands, brothers, and sons lounge and gossip around a good fire. The exploitation of female work is no less intensive among the Ankave (and Kamea) than among the Baruya or Sambia. It is just less violent.[25]

Similarly, another functional aspect of the initiations—to make strong warriors, according to what all the Anga say—cannot be dismissed on the pretext that it may be out of intellectual fashion: in June 1998, among the Ankave, I could still hear tens of statements like "Now [that you have received the pigs' teeth that mark your belonging to the third and last stage of the male initiations/hierarchy], should the Okaye invade our valley and hamlets, you won't run away and leave your kids and wife behind!" Warfare ended in this area in the early 1970s, and the fear of the state and its police is present in every mind (Lemonnier 1998b). Yet on the other side of the mountain wall that separates the Ankave territory from the valleys in and around Menyamya are thousands of grassland peoples. Members of these long-standing enemy tribes know perfectly well that a few hundred Ankave live in the middle of thousands of acres of almost empty tropical forest. And the Ankave know they know. And this is quite enough to make them conduct male initiations, to make fearless warriors. Just in case.

Finally, as demonstrated by Bonnemère (this volume) the details of the implication of female powers and abilities in Anga male rituals reveal a contrast between two sets of societies. Northern Angans (Baruya, Sambia, Watchakes) emphasize an entirely male-controlled transformation of the boys into warriors: masculine flutes, semen-ingestion in the secrecy of the men's house, minimum active role of the mothers, long separation from the women, emphasis on cooperative actions, and so on. All this helps to affirm the imaginary and omnipresent superiority of men, in ritual life and in any valorized activity. This massive and redundant accumulation of maleness in the case of the northern Angans contrasts with an ambiguous mixture of male/female powers among a southwestern Anga group like the Ankave. There, too, everything contributes to make and complete the boys without the women, but this time with the (often explicit) recognition of women's procreative and nourishing powers, as well as with their active and positive participation in the rituals. It would be hard not to link this crucial characteristic of southern Angans with another finding already noted by Bonnemère (1996: 387–88), that tension in the everyday life of couples is less where women's powers are at least partly recognized. This recognition also goes hand in hand with a settlement pattern of couples living on their own in the forest rather than in male bands, marked by a type of cooperation that, in the course of everyday life, takes place within the couple, by the absence of hysterical demonstrations at the sight of menstrual blood, and by men's spectacularly less brutal behavior toward women. Male domination is present among the Ankave, but it is far less strong.

Women's involvement in male rituals appears to be only one of the social domains in which Anga societies define the status of women. Questions like "why do some New Guinea societies have male initiations and others not?" or "why do some Anga societies grow babies and boys with semen while others choose a female blood substitute?" probably cannot be answered yet. But what the Anga case shows is that, once such a cultural choice is made, it has immense consequences—or at least very strong correlates—which anthropology needs to investigate and theorize.

The Anga comparison invites us to look carefully into what is entailed in the participation of women in rituals that go far beyond the domain of male ritual alone. It also points to the need to deconstruct such misleadingly obvious notions as "participation," "domination," "equality," or "complementarity," which can conceal highly meaningful social aspects and nuances of gender relations that only a fine-grained comparison will reveal. Women's participation in male ritual is certainly not something that can be accounted for by a presence/absence type of analysis. It is at the very core of that set of ideas, behaviors, and social practices by which men more or less impose their rule on the female portion of society.

Chapter 8
Of Human and Spirit Women: From Mother to Seductress to Second Wife

Polly Wiessner

I am taking away his heart.
I am pulling up his cordyline plant.
I am taking out his essence.

Let his heart droop,
Let his essence droop
Let his cordyline droop.

I am putting his heart into the fire.
I am putting his essence into the fire,
I am purring his cordyline into the fire.

Heart burn to ash,
Essence burn to ash,
Cordyline burn to ash.

(Traditional Enga magical spell from the upper Lai valley, to take possession of a young man's heart and soul recited while breaking off fern tips
and throwing them into the fire)

The peripheral position of women in the exotic religious ritual of Highland New
Guinea has captured the attention of anthropologists for the past three decades.
For parts of the eastern Highlands and Highland fringe areas, men are seen as
manipulating cosmology and relations with the spirit world so as to appropriate
female powers of reproduction with the ultimate goal of domination (Allen
1967; Godelier 1986; Herdt 1981, 1984a). Underlying these interpretations is an
implicit assumption that a major axis of competition exists between men and
women, and that ritual is part of the struggle through which men control, repress, or dominate the opposite sex. There is also the sense that cosmology in the

hands of males is immutable. In western areas of the Highlands, however, the situation is different. Here the realms of male and female are held distinctly separate on the basis of body ideology and gender roles, one the one hand, and yet defined as complementary, on the other, so that the strongest currents of competition flow within the sexes, not between them. Such complementarity offers both men and women a hand in altering ritual and aspects of cosmology.

An ideology of separation and yet essential complementarity for production and reproduction (A. Strathern 1979) stretches back in time far beyond the reach of historical traditions. Among the Enga, two myths establish a good part of the cosmological framework structuring male-female relations. According to the first, there was a time when the world was inhabited only by the immortal sky people, who lived a life similar to that of humans but in a perfect world. One day a sky woman gave birth to a son on the slopes of Mount Mongalo in western Enga. When the baby cried, her husband told her not to breastfeed the child but to wait until he fetched the water of eternal life (*yalipa endake*) from the sacred spring high on the mountainside. The woman waited and waited, growing impatient as the baby cried. The husband reached the spring and filled the gourd, but before he could return home, the mother had fed the child with breast milk. As a result, they descended from paradise to earth and were burdened with the realities of life, including hard work and mortality. The humans who descended from sky to earth organized themselves in a segmentary lineage system that mirrored that of the sky people (Meggitt 1965b).

Mortal men, unlike the immortal sky people, were endangered by the procreative power of women, a heat that could burn out the physical and intellectual power of men. A second myth tells of what man did to tame these female fires and make male-female relations possible once more. It begins with a pair of "hot" women, mother and daughter, who crossed a certain bridge regularly to go to their gardens. A man undermined the bridge, and when the two crossed, the bridge collapsed and the two women plunged into the river and were carried downstream. The mother, who was fished out before she became sufficiently cooled, became the forebear of western Enga women, while the daughter, carried further down stream and rescued in eastern Enga, was better cooled and less dangerous to men. Had the plan worked entirely, women would pose no threat to men, but as it was the procreative powers and substances of women were imperfectly cooled. Women remained hot enough to require separation from men, but were cooled enough so that cooperation and reproduction could take place with the aid of ritual protection. The map of rigidity of male-female Enga contamination beliefs and taboos conforms to how long the ancestress of a particular area was submerged.[1]

Variants of such myths to legitimate separation between the sexes are found throughout the western Highlands (Frankel 1986; Goldman 1983). Given their prevalence and yet diversity of expressions and meanings, their origins are most likely ancient, and the conditions under which such notions developed beyond our reach today. Nonetheless, they laid down an ideology that structured virtually every area of life in Enga and in surrounding Highland societies. They allocated private roles and biological reproduction to women, and public roles and responsibility for production and reproduction of the social order to men. Women were regarded as naturally complete for fulfilling their reproductive roles; by contrast, men were regarded as incomplete. To mature into handsome and effective adults, young men had to be endowed with the power to withstand the effects of sexual contact with human women and reborn or initiated into a corporate group of men (see also Bonnemère, this volume; Godelier 1986). In these endeavors, they sought the company of peers and the transformative charms of an immortal sky woman.

In this chapter, I will use material from Enga historical traditions to trace patterns of cooperation and competition, from the time of the introduction of the sweet potato until the present, as well as to identify obstacles confronting men and women as they sought to accomplish their respective tasks (see Table 1). I then discuss the role of the immortal sky woman (spirit woman) in assisting men via three major circulating cults. In chronological order, these are (1) the *mote* male initiation in the *kepele* cult, where the spirit woman came as surrogate mother to the boys; (2) the *sangai/sandalu* bachelors' cults, in which the spirit woman came to the bachelors as seductress and bride, and (3) the female spirit cult, in which the spirit woman came to mature, married men as co-wife. These cults were practiced in Enga consecutively but with overlap, the *sangai* being added to the ritual repertoire after the introduction of the sweet potato and the female spirit cult in the early twentieth century. I will propose that the changing role of the spirit woman was the result of triadic interaction during a period of rapid social and economic change, interaction between men and other men via the spirit woman, men and women in daily life, and women and other women, including the spirit woman. Interaction in each of these spheres was affected differently by economic change and contributed differently to alteration of ritual and cosmology.

A historical perspective on female participation in male cults makes it possible to address a number of issues central to this volume from an angle that complements papers grounded in the ethnographic present. The first concerns the differences between initiation, bachelors' cults, and female spirit cults. These three types of male ritual are usually described for different societies, but are they mutually exclusive? Do they have diverse cosmological underpinnings, or can they draw on a common fund of cosmology, coexist, and be aimed at developing different relational configurations important in various phases of the life cycle of men? Second, is male ritual and female participation as described in the ethnographic present "tradition" aimed at reproducing the status quo of gender relations, or might such ritual be part and parcel of a process of change? If so what is the role of women in bringing about such change? Third, when do women play a purely symbolic role in male ritual and when do they appear in flesh and blood?

TABLE 1. Chronological Scheme of Events Discussed in Text

Prehistory (b.p.)	
12,000	Earliest archaeological evidence for Enga: Yuku cave in eastern Enga, hunting and gathering site at ca. 1,300m
10,000	Kutepa rockshelter western Enga, hunting and gathering at 2,300m
2000–4000	Pollen evidence indicates forest clearance for horticulture in eastern Enga
250–400	Introduction of sweet potato to Enga and beginning of Enga historical traditions

Historical traditions (generation before present)	
8+	Population shift from high altitudes to lower valleys Beginning of early *Tee* cycle
7	*Kepele* cult first practiced by horticulturalists of western Enga *Sangai* bachelors' cults arise in central Enga
6	Beginning of Great Ceremonial Wars *Sangai* spreads to western Enga
5 (ca.1855–85?)	*Kepele* cult imported into central Enga, called *aeatee* *Mote* rites dropped from *aeatee* Emergence festivals added to bachelors' cults
4 (ca.1885–1915)	*Tee* cycle expanded to finance Great Ceremonial Wars *Sangai* spreads to the eastern Enga, called *sandalu*, courtship enters *sangai* *Aeatee* cult expanded to coordinate *Tee* cycle and Great Ceremonial Wars Female spirit cult imported into eastern Enga, used to plan *Tee* cycle
3 (ca.1915–45)	*Tee* cycle begins to subsume Great Ceremonial Wars *Enda akoko nyingi* becomes part of *sangai* First contact with Europeans, 1934 Last Great Ceremonial War fought, 1938–41 *Tee* cycle subsumes Great War exchange routes
2 (ca.1945–75)	Female spirit cult spreads
1 (ca. 1975–2005)	Papua New Guinea independence, 1975

The Enga and Their History

The Enga are horticulturalists who inhabit the western Highlands of Papua New Guinea (Brennan 1977; Feil 1984; Lacey 1975; Meggitt 1965a, 1972, 1974, 1977; Talyaga 1982; Wohlt 1978; Waddell 1972). They number over 200,000 today. Their position as the largest single linguistic group in Papua New Guinea, neatly nestled in the heart of the western Highlands, gives a misleading impression of homogeneity. In fact, Enga territory is highly varied, ranging from the high, steep, rugged valleys in the west to the wide, low, fertile valleys of the east.

The material on which I will draw is taken from two sources. The first is a series of interviews with over a hundred elderly Enga women conducted by Alome Kyakas (Kyakas and Wiessner 1992). In these interviews, women were asked to tell their life stories. No leading questions were asked, no topics of interest were suggested, no interruptions were made. The objective was to elicit perspectives the narrator herself felt to be important; the results yielded a well-rounded picture of women's goals and profiles of cooperation and competition from approximately 1930 to 1980.[2] The second is a body of historical traditions collected by Akii Tumu and myself between 1985 and 1995 in 108 tribes of Enga (Wiessner and Tumu 1998). Historical traditions extend from just prior to the introduction of the sweet potato some 250–400 years ago, until first contact with Europeans in the 1930s, and on into the present. Each tribe (phratry)[3] and clan of Enga has its own historical traditions, said to have originated in eyewitness accounts, that have been passed on in men's houses over generations (Lacey 1975; Wiessner and Tumu 1998). They contain information on such matters as tribal "origins" some 300 years ago, tribal founders, former areas of residence and past lifestyle, relations with neighboring groups, wars and migrations, the origin and diffusion of cults, trade, ceremonial exchange, agricultural techniques, environmental failure, and developments in song and dress. All clan histories include a genealogy that links each member to the tribal founder by patrilineal descent (or through marriage and adoption when applicable). This can be subdivided into two phases: (1) the founding generations, which include the nonhuman ancestors, tribal, and clan founders who constitute the model for corporate group structure and (2) a genealogy extending from the generation of subclan founders until the present that appears to record actual people and events. The second phase of genealogies provides a framework within which to date or sequence events. Working with the histories of over a hundred tribes allowed us to look for internal consistency, to check narratives at both ends, and to evaluate specific traditions within a regional perspective.

From information contained in historical traditions, I will sketch changes through time in patterns of cooperation and competition between men and women for production, exchange, politics, and ritual. All ritual discussed in this chapter was performed until at least the 1950s, so historical accounts are enriched with eyewitness experience. For further information on methods see Wiessner and Tumu (1998).

Cooperation and Competition: Production

Just prior to or after the arrival of the sweet potato, production schemes differed greatly from those of subsequent generations.[4] Men appeared to have shouldered the better part of the work load; they hunted, made war, and did a good part of the garden work and all the wood work—chopping firewood, fencing, and house building. Women cultivated taro together with men, planted other crops, gathered forest products, and were responsible for the time-consuming work of producing bark twine and net goods. Pig husbandry receives little mention in male or female work routines. Such a division of labor would have given men a heavier work load. Dependence on taro agriculture was heavy in the fertile valleys of eastern Enga, while hunting and gathering played a more important role in the west. The western population was divided by niche, with shifting horticulturalists who led a precarious existence in the valleys and groups who claim to be primarily hunter-gatherers in the higher altitudes. Relations between the two were characterized by intermarriage and exchange of forest products for agricultural ones, on the one hand, and tension and misunderstanding, on the other. It was in areas where hunters and horticulturalists met that contamination beliefs and taboos were the most rigid.

After the sweet potato was accepted as a staple, the productive base of eastern and western Enga became more homogeneous. Expanding networks of ceremonial exchange increased demands for pig production and with it, women's work loads. Still, division of labor nurtured a strong complementarity between men and women: men had to clear gardens before women could plant; men had to fence gardens securely or women's efforts would be lost to the pigs. Women cared for children under five to six years of age; men took the boys into the men's house when they reached seven or eight and looked after them until adulthood. Responsibility was further clarified by the fact that men and women held magic formulae to accomplish their respective tasks.

Women's life stories of the twentieth century do not describe their increasing work loads as appropriation of female labor for male name. Rather, they express family ambitions for production comparable to those of their husbands, detailing their plans and strategies for building a pig herd to increase the wealth of their families and forge networks of exchange. Women say that it is their efforts in production and exchange that make ordinary husbands into big men. Competition between husband and wife only enters the picture when the question of the husband marrying a second wife arises. Only after years of marriage does women's sexual jealousy succumb to their economic ambitions to increase the family workforce. At that time mature wives of successful men take the initiative to select co-wives and raise the pigs to help pay the bridewealth.

Exchange

After the introduction of the sweet potato, exchange flourished as vast networks linking different valley systems were constructed in response to population redistribution (Wiessner and Tumu 1998). In eastern Enga, a cycle of ceremonial wealth distribution, the *Tee* cycle, grew out of the efforts of big men to expand their spheres of influence in order to keep control of the trade. The early *Tee* cycle was conducted on a small scale among clans along trade routes; however, it introduced a powerful new system of finance: concatenation of relationships so as to allow families to gain access to wealth beyond the bounds of kinship reckoning (see map).

In central Enga, a very different system of exchange was constructed via the Great Ceremonial Wars. Here, tribes and clans who had been displaced in wars that occurred after the introduction of the sweet potato engaged in tournaments to display force, forge alliances, and brew the exchanges of massive proportions that followed. These tournament wars, fought periodically over three to four generations (ca. 1860–1940), built networks that linked four major valley systems and put displaced groups back on the map of trade and exchange).

In western Enga, similar integration was achieved through the *kepele* cult, which unified entire tribes or pairs of tribes for communication with the ancestors. *Kepele* cult performances of western Enga tribes were linked into a cult network extending from the Porgera valley, down the Lagaip valley, and on into Kandep. Within this network, ritual experts, rites, participants, and invited guests circulated widely.

In the last half of the nineteenth century, the costs of the Great Ceremonial Wars in terms of organization, wealth, and time spent in fighting rather than production became formidable and thousands participated (see Table 1). Big men of central Enga then drew on the *Tee* cycle to provide finance for the Great Wars and to reinvest the wealth flowing out of them. Rapid growth took place in both networks, and organization became formidable. In response, big men turned to ritual for support. The *kepele* cult, which had formerly been imported and performed on a small scale in central Enga, was expanded into a performance that could be used to unify tribes at the western terminus of the *Tee* cycle, coordinate the *Tee* cycle with the Great Wars, and display readiness for exchange to other clans. Despite these efforts the Great Wars were difficult to sustain. As participants in the Great Wars gained more experience with the *Tee* cycle, they opted to discontinue the wars and replace their networks of exchange by the extensive *Tee* cycle routes. By first contact, some 30,000–50,000 participants engaged in the *Tee* cycle, circulating tens of thousands of pigs and valuables. Successful manipulation of these vast exchange networks by big men created economic inequalities of a magnitude hitherto unknown in Enga history.

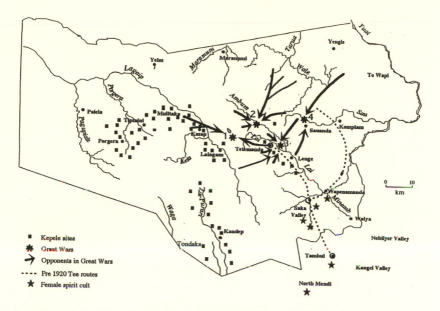

Locations of the *Tee* cycle, the Great Ceremonial Wars, the *kepele* cult, and the female spirit cult.

Exchange was thus at the heart of interest in Enga society, engaging the attention of men and women alike. Like other realms of life, it was structured by a division of labor. Women produced pigs and net items for exchange and wove the networks along which wealth flowed. Men assisted with aspects of gardening and pig production, produced or procured other items for exchange, and engaged in the complex politics of coalescing individual contributions from outside and within the clan for clanwide ceremonial exchange events. Men dominated the public domain of ceremonial exchange and reaped name and fame for themselves and their clans. However, wives of successful men stood to gain from the influx of wealth to the family, private admiration of their efforts, possibilities to arrange advantageous marriages for their children, and, above all, an abundance of wealth to channel to their own kin.

The focus of competition in exchange was largely between men and their rivals, both fellow clansmen striving for the status of big man and big men in other clans who had their own designs for the flow of wealth in the region. Nonetheless, exchange did generate some contention between the sexes. Women were expected to direct wealth to and from kin in their natal clans, while men had to juggle pigs to meet requests from their own clansmen, wife's kin, mother's kin, and other affines.

Accounts from shortly after the introduction of the sweet potato indicate that a good portion of the wealth exchanged came from home production, with supplementary wealth raised from a small circle of close affinal or agnatic relatives. As exchange networks grew, the limited labor forces of households could not meet growing demands. Families had to rely increasingly on wealth obtained on credit from a wide range of affinal and maternal kin. Under these circumstances, men entrusted more and more of the private arrangements to their wives and other close female relatives. Negative connotations of females stemming from contamination beliefs were thereby eroded by the supportive action of women as wives, sisters, daughters, and aunts as diplomats in exchange. By the 1930s, some women in eastern Enga were able to assume public roles in the *Tee* cycle in their own right after the death of their husband.[5] Among these was a woman named Takime, a *Tee* leader of renown who traveled with men from one end of the network to another to organize the *Tee*, presenting the wealth reaped from her efforts in her own name on the ceremonial grounds with the full support of her clanspeople (Kyakas and Wiessner 1992).

Tribal Politics

Just as cosmology stipulates separation and inequality between the sexes, the descent of the sky people to earth lays down the fundamental divisions for the organization of men—tribes (phratries), clans, subclans, lineages, and men's houses. While the separation between men and women created unequal, incomparable, and complementary units, the division of men by the segmentary lineage system produced equal, comparable, and competitive units. Men, as potential equals, competed with other men for spouses, men of different household units competed for lineage leadership, men of different lineages for subclan leadership, and men of different subclans for clan leadership. Clans competed with other clans over exchange, land, and other matters, and tribes competed with other tribes in the Great Ceremonial Wars. Men had much to negotiate in order to hold together corporate units in the face of internal competition and to mediate conflicts between different corporate groups.[6]

Women, who often married in from enemy clans, were excluded from segmentary lineage politics. They did not attend clan meetings where matters of security were discussed, nor did they speak at public forums where other clanwide decisions were made. Women often despised initiatives of men to incite warfare, but their objections were not even heard at home. When wars escalated, women retreated to live with relatives in other clans, taking the children and pigs with them. In domestic politics women had no formal "legal" path through which to air complaints, but they did have a strong recourse via protest action (M. Strathern 1972). Protest action involved anything from burning the house to stabbing a co-wife to running home, leaving the husband to tend pigs, gardens, and children. Women's protest action was accepted as women's nature, and runaway women were coaxed home or eventually coerced to go home by their own relatives, but were not expected to pay compensation to cancel the effects of their protests. Protest action had the potential to bring about change precisely on these grounds—it was attributed to women's nature, and therefore the protagonist was "not guilty" and her action not canceled by compensation.

Throughout the span of Enga historical traditions, politics thickened in a way that affected men to a much greater extent than women. With the redistribution of population after the introduction of the sweet potato, corporate groups had to seek new ways to reestablish the balance of power. An increase in population growth rates caused groups to grow to an unmanageable size and split more frequently than they had in the past. As exchange networks expanded, conflicts of loyalty between obligations to fellow clansmen and obligations to exchange partners in other clans were accentuated. Differential success in manipulating networks ruptured the equality of men, brewing jealousy and social tension. It was no wonder that men sought the help of the spirit woman.

Enga Religious Ritual

At the center of the Enga spirit world were two sets of supernatural beings: the immortal sky people (*yalyakali*) and their mortal descendants, the ancestors (*yumbange*) (see Brennan 1977; Meggitt 1965b). The sky people were regarded as keepers of the cosmos, responsible for natural events like weather, thunderbolts, and landslides, as well as protectors of individuals. Should men or women fail to conform to moral codes, the sky people would abandon them, laying them open to death. By contrast to the sky beings, who were not directly attached to specific human corporate groups, the ancestors (*yumbange*) were composed of all deceased male (and perhaps female) tribal members.[7] They were believed to directly affect the welfare and prosperity of their descendants if appropriate communication was maintained through ritual. The Enga ritual repertoire to communicate with the sky people and the ancestors was not static; throughout the course of history, cults were imported and exported within Enga and between Enga and neighboring groups in attempts to emulate the successful, confront new problems, set the course of change, or mediate its effects.

As in other realms of life, male and female participation in ritual followed the division between private/public and domestic/corporate. Women practiced love magic to secure husbands, carried out joint rituals with their husbands upon marriage to assure family fertility and prosperity, conducted menstrual rites to further their husbands' success in hunting, warfare, and exchange, participated in healing ceremonies for their children and close relatives, and conducted individual fertility rites to promote the growth of gardens and pigs.

When ritual moved from such private concerns to group prosperity and reproduction, men took over on two accounts. First, with a norm of patrilocal residence, only men had a direct connection to their ancestors.[8] Women were removed from their natal ancestors and yet had no immediate link with ancestors of their husbands' groups. Second, the pool of ancestors was composed of potentially dangerous ghosts of deceased tribesmen. Contact with such male forces was believed to be able to contaminate pregnancy and produce deformed offspring.

Men assembled periodically for public ritual to placate and please the ancestors and enact essential relations of unity and cooperation, thereby counteracting the disruptive forces of competition. Women were excluded from cult space and cult rites, though they worked together with men to provision the cults, hosted affinal kin and other invited spectators, and, very important, participated in the festivities to celebrate the completion of a successful rite. In the majority of ancestral cults, female procreative power was represented by female ancestral stones. In addition to ancestral cults, a variety of cults for the sky people were also in the hands of men. Most notable among these were cults for the spirit women, who were believed to hold the power to transform men : the *mote*, the *sangai*, and the female spirit cult. These cults will be the focus of this chapter.

Spirit Women in Male Cults: The *Mote* Rites for Boys

Enga women were considered to be naturally equipped for their roles in life,[9] but men needed further processing in order to (1) grow, mature, and withstand the debilitating effects of sexual contact with woman, and (2) be integrated ritually into a cohort of "brothers" in order to manage a social order fraught with complexity and conflict. Prior to the introduction of the sweet potato, male ritual appears to have been much less elaborate in most parts of Enga. Boys of central and eastern Enga were taken from the women's house to the men's house with little fanfare, where they were educated by their elders. Small individual rites were practiced in the seclusion of the forest to promote the growth of hair, bodies, and clear skin. Only in the high country of western Enga, among groups that claim a tradition as hunters, did spirit women visit young men in the context of male corporate ritual: the *mote* rites or boys' initiation in the *kepele* cult. Here two sky women, Yongulame, the morning star, and Kulume, the evening star, came to the boys as second mothers, giving them the water of life to symbolically wean them from mother's milk, reverse adverse effects of breastfeeding, and initiate the stage of physical, social, and spiritual growth that turned boys into men.

Historical information on the pre-sweet potato *kepele* cult is sparse; it can be deduced only from descriptions in cult-origin myths and the content of rites performed in the twentieth century. The *kepele* had its roots in a cult to assemble dispersed "hunting and gathering" tribes of the high country in western Enga and initiate young men into the secrets of the spirit world. Whether it had other objectives in earlier times is unknown. After the arrival of the new crop, when groups inhabiting the high country acquired land from relatives and settled in the lower valleys, they brought the *kepele* with them. Subsequently it was restructured. Rites directed at the sacred ancestral stones were added and emphasis was placed on agricultural fertility (Wiessner and Tumu 1998). In the course of the *kepele*'s development, much of the original meaning of *mote* rites seems to have been forgotten.[10]

By the eve of first contact with Europeans, the *kepele* cult was an impressive event (Gibbs 1975). It was called when poor environmental conditions prevailed, indicating that the ancestors were discontented. Word was sent out to each clan to bring specific materials and foods from their own areas for the construction of the tribal cult house. On the appointed day, the clans converged on the cult site in full ceremonial dress, singing and dancing. Men from each clan or subclan bore designated material for building the cult house, a perimeter post representing their group, and special foods for the feast. The cult house was jointly constructed by all tribesmen. Upon completion of the house, a large feast was held for contributors and their families. The house was then left to "age" for a few months to a few years until the main phase of the *kepele* was called.

Before the main phase, word was sent out to celebrants and guests to plant gardens, fatten pigs, gather materials, and to assemble boys for *mote* rites. Requirements stipulated that every male provide one pig, and one pig only, to express the potential equality of all men. The sacred area for the cult was fenced off to separate male celebrants and sacred rites from the gaze of women, children, and invited guests from near and far. The *kepele* ancestral cult house was repaired and decorated, and additional houses were built. When the celebrants and spectators had arrived, the majority of the pigs that had been brought for the ceremony were staked out and clubbed in public view. For the larger ceremonies of the twentieth century 300–500 pigs were provided. Pork for sacred and secular consumption was carefully separated and sacred pork was prepared very differently for each category of celebrant—boys, adult males who had attended the *mote*, ritual experts, and old men who would soon join the ancestors, endorsing social divisions within Enga society.

The large pig kill marked the onset of five days of ceremonies. Men took pigs or the specified pieces of pork inside the sacred area and steamed them in pits for the various rites. One pig was specially slaughtered for a ritual expert, who retired to a small hut, the *tapaita anda*, and filled a gourd with the "water of life" to be given to the boys. This fluid was composed of the condensed breath of the ritual expert who blew on a cool stone ax blade and let the droplets roll into a gourd container where it was supplemented by pork fat and sugar cane juice. The boys were told that this gourd was filled by the spirit woman who sat lactating and feeding a baby in the *tapaita anda*. Meanwhile women, children, and visitors remained outside the sacred area singing, dancing, feasting, trading, arranging marriages, or engaging in other social activities.

At the same time that tribespeople assembled, boys between the ages of approximately eight and fourteen were brought by their fathers to special *mote* shelters built within the sacred enclosure. They were not permitted to go out during the three-day rites even to urinate or defecate, a restriction designating an infantile state. Their diet was limited to the juice of sugar cane and a few sweet potatoes given to them by their mothers beforehand. When all the preparations had been made, the *mote* boys were lined up by clan/tribe and height/age. Age groups were indicated by features of dress: wig styles, feathers, and so on. A ritual expert then appeared on the scene to lead them to the *mote* house. His face was concealed by a mask fashioned from a dried gourd with two holes cut out for the eyes and one for the mouth, his head was covered by a foul, disheveled wig, and his neck was bedecked with strings of dried bones. As he flicked his tongue in and out of the mouth hole of his mask, the young men were separated from the little boys: quite a few candidates fled in terror, returning to attend the *mote* when they were considerably older. Cane belts were then tied around the waists of the boys while the ritual experts recited spells.

In the evening, the boys were led to the cult house. Before entering the house, or once seated within it, they were given the "water of life" from the gourd prepared by the ritual experts. The names used in some *kepele* houses to describe the stages of filling the gourd and drinking from it depict symbolic weaning from the mother. The filling was called *wane manjanya pilyamo*, "the pregnant woman is expecting"; the completion of this process *wane mandipalamo*, "the baby is born"; and the drinking of the sacred liquid by the boys *wane andu tuu nelyamo*, "the mother's breast milk is drying up." The spell recited while the boys drank is intriguing in that it mentions different body fluids—blood, menstrual blood, and semen—recalling similar themes in initiation of many Highland fringe societies. Whether semen ever played a role in the *mote* of the past is not known. In partaking of this water of life given to men by the spirit women, boys were cleansed of the effects "human" breast milk and close contact with women, factors that nurtured in early childhood but stunted later in boyhood. Some of the harm that had occurred when humans became mortal was reversed.

Inside the ritual house, the boys sat in total darkness, fearfully anticipating the formidable events to come when they made contact with the spirit world. Outside the cult house, experts whistled to signal the presence of ghosts and augment their fear. Sacred words of wisdom were chanted to herald the arrival of the sky women: "You two girls, dawn and night, evening and morning, would you bring the everlasting fire, bright as gold, would you bring it home please" (Lacey 1975: 134). After some time, two beautiful sky women entered the cult house. By the light of their torches, they briefly revealed to the young men the sacred bark paintings—sun, moon, man, woman, rainbow, cassowary, dog, and specific sky beings—and a woven image of a rainbow python coiled around the ceiling of the *mote* house. The boys' hearts were said to jump and tremble in fear at the sight of such strange objects. In all testimonies that we collected the fact that these were really men dressed as women is only mentioned as an aside at the end.

During some performances, the boys exited by a back door, where they passed by a man of wisdom and knowledge holding the following symbols: a piece of ginger (*alamo* or *kokali*) so that their enemies would taste them like ginger and suffer a long time before they died; a green plant (*ema*) so that the young men would own the most fertile part of the land; a piece of pork liver (*mena pungi*) so that they would be rich men; and a piece of possum meat (*saa wapisa*) so that they would be skillful hunters. They were to take a deep breath and smell each object (Lacey 1975: 133–34). Boys were then sworn to secrecy concerning everything they had seen and done during the ceremony. After the boys emerged from the *mote*, their cane belts were cut off by the ritual expert and planted beneath the roots of other trees, so that, as the roots grew, they would become firmly fastened in the ground. Such measures were believed to protect the boys from untimely death from illness, "since trees usually only die when chopped down or uprooted, not from disease." As far as we could determine, the symbolism of *mote* rites was known to ritual experts and some elders; the boys only experienced awe and fear at the revelations.

After the *mote*, some ritual experts allowed the boys to witness the feeding and mating of the ancestral objects; others only permitted those who had attended to *mote* several times to do so. The sacred objects representing the ancestors consisted of stones in shapes reminiscent of male or female genitals and a basketwork figure fashioned to look like a man (*yupini*).[11] The *yupini* was paraded to the *kepele* site and placed in the cult house, while the sacred stones were unearthed from their resting place in the ground. Next the *yupini* (or the male ancestral stone) was made to simulate copulation with the female stones, while spells to promote fertility were recited. After copulation, the *yupini* was fed with pork fat and the sacred stones were greased in it.

These rites were repeated during the following days until the ancestors were believed to be content to sleep, leaving human affairs to proceed unhampered and with prosperity. At some cult sites, skulls of deceased male tribal members were deposited in a tribal skull house within the *kepele* site. Later, during the *kepele* ceremonies, the skulls that had accumulated were placed in a pyre between layers of edible plant foods, pig fat, and firewood, to be ceremonially cremated. When cult rites were concluded, some of the cult houses were destroyed; it was believed that the good will of the ancestors had been evoked and fertility would prevail. Young men who had undergone *mote* rites, elated by the power of the *kepele*, danced on tree branches and performed a number of stunts before the crowds of spectators.

Ideally then, *mote* rites separated boys from their mothers around the time when they would have moved from the women's to the men's house. Once given the water of life and introduced to the secrets of the spirit world, they could enter a second stage of growth to become productive members of society who participated in communal ritual for the reproduction of the tribe or clan. Nonetheless, the bond with the mother was not severed, just altered. Nurturant mothers continued to protect their sons from often harsh fathers until adulthood (Kumbon 1998, Meggitt 1965a) and assured that boys developed close bonds with their maternal kin. Later in life maternal kin provided what were perhaps a man's most supportive exchange partners.

The *mote* was continued until approximately the 1960s, when contact with missionaries led to the discontinuation of the entire *kepele* cult.[12] However, the importance of the *mote* seems to have gradually waned with a ritual shift away from the theme of separation from the mother to one of constructing appropriate paths to marriage and the complementarity of male-female relationships that were so essential to the success of men. It was in this context that a female spirit was called on, as seductress and bride in *sangai* bachelors' cults, to assist men in quite a different role.

Sangai and *Sandalu* Bachelors' Cults

Prior to the introduction of the sweet potato and for many generations after in some areas, young men conducted private rites of growth, *sauipi*, and *yomondi*, but no communal rites were held outside the limited sphere of the *mote*. The early history of *sangai* bachelors' cults is vague, though claims that they were instituted over the past seven to eight generations are supported by records in detailed historical poetry, which tell when and from where each clan purchased the *sangai*. When information from *sangai* poetry of clans from different areas of Enga is compiled, a very coherent picture of its diffusion through Enga over the past seven generations emerges. It appears that *sangai* bachelors' cults may have first been crafted in central Enga, though one cannot rule out the possibility that elements were imported from the south or west (see Wiessner and Tumu 1998). The purpose of the *sangai*, to promote the growth and maturity of young men, is one and the same as that of former private rites; however, several crucial elements were added. *Sangai* rites were communal, not individual, involving all young men of a clan or subclan. *Sangai* bachelors' cults were hierarchically organized: boys moved up the age hierarchy by attending several cult performances held at one- to two-year intervals until they were considered ready for marriage. Physical, mental, and social transformation was believed to be achieved via first marriage to a spirit woman, who seduced them from bachelorhood into adulthood. Both female powers and male community were deemed necessary to fashion successful men. Thus, hand in hand with increasing emphasis on agricultural cultivation came the careful cultivation of men.

Enga *sangai* origin myths are variants of the following. A despised, ugly bachelor is scorned by his peers, who are on the way to perform rites of growth. When he arrives home dejected and sad, an elder in the clan advises him to go to a certain place in the forest. During his journey he comes across a perfectly kept house, and realizing that nobody is home, he enters and waits to see what will come. As he sits there, he suddenly feels something like an earthquake and hears footsteps of somebody walking around at the back of the house. He remains very still with eyes wide, wondering what will happen next. Suddenly the most beautiful woman he has ever seen appears in the doorway and looks straight into his eyes. Clues, such as the quake of the earth at her footsteps and flashes of lightning with her smile, indicate that she is a sky being (*yalyakali*).[13] She goes to the courtyard, cuts a cluster of pandanus nuts, steams them for him together with sweet potato, and tries to seduce him.[14] The sexual details of this scene are graphic. Overcoming his pollution anxieties, he gives in with pleasure. In the morning she is gone. The same thing happens the following two nights, except that after the third night she remains. In the morning, she dresses him with the finest paraphernalia and transforms him into a being as magnificent as she. He then joins his clan brothers, who marvel. From here on he is called Lyaiakali Lelya, a name commonly given to sky people who are protagonists in myth.

Meanwhile, another miserable, rejected bachelor with a long neck and ugly face notes Lelya's transformation and follows him day and night to learn his secret. Overcome with pity, Lelya tells him to follow the same bush track. The same thing happens, but this bachelor refuses her, saying that he had come to be transformed, not seduced. She runs out of the house and stays away all night. The next night the same thing happens, and on the third, angered by her advances, the bachelor shoots the spirit woman. The drama sets off a violent storm and Lelya realizes that something is amiss.

He rushes to her house and weeps over her body in despair. She instructs him to cut some bamboo containers and arrange them in two clusters of four, one male and one female, separated by a cluster of two, one male and one female. When this is done she tells him to pull out the arrow and fill the containers with her blood, plug them with clay and leaves, and bury them in a swampy area. Then she instructs him to bury her and return later to harvest *lepe* plants from her grave, one of which will grow by her head and the other by her feet. She teaches him the procedures and spells for caring for these sacred objects and for passing them on so that future generations of young men can be similarly transformed. With a faint smile, she dies. The narrator of one version ended with these words: "So the *sangai* [sacred objects used in the *sangai*] originated from a woman, and therefore they are regarded as persons. Because the [spirit] woman made men, they [the sacred objects] always helped all men, the ugly and the handsome alike, so that they would be healthy and good-looking."

Following the instructions of the spirit woman, the sacred objects and accompanying poetry were transferred from clan to clan via sale and purchase, permitting the transformation of all men.[15] The purchase of *sangai* rites was an intentional move on the part of clan elders to emulate clans whom they perceived as prosperous and having a particularly promising cohort of young men. On the assumption that their success stemmed in part from bachelors' cults, they encouraged senior bachelors to assemble pigs and other valuables and undertake the journeys to execute the purchase. Once the payment was made for the sacred objects, either the senior bachelors attended a performance of the seller's clan to learn the rites and accompanying poetry or senior bachelors from the seller's clan traveled to the buyer's clan to teach the same. With each transfer, verses were added to *sangai* poetry to record the transaction and tell of the transformative effects that the sacred objects had on those who acquired them.

Sangai bachelors' cults essentially represented seduction into marriage and adulthood by the spirit woman through which all men could become transformed into physically, mentally, and socially competent adults. Through the power of the spirit woman, biological inequalities and those of family standing were erased, and all men were recreated as equals. Analyses of *sangai* poetry indicate that ideals of transformation vary with time and place. Poetry of groups removed from the major exchange networks focuses on physical transformation, while that of clans within the sphere of the *Tee* cycle and Great Wars emphasizes ability to produce and manage wealth (Wiessner and Tumu 1998).

The *sangai* spread from central into western Enga, where boys attended *mote* rites in their childhood and the *sangai* during adolescence. Around the time of first contact the *sangai* was remarkably similar across central and western Enga, and even into Ipili regions (see Biersack, this volume). Before coming into close contact with the spirit woman via the sacred objects, young men of the appropriate age in a clan or large subclan[16] were separated from both mother and father. They retired to a secret place in the forest where they cleansed their eyes under a waterfall and purged their bodies and senses of all that was considered impure—prior contact with women, female fluids such as breast milk and menstrual blood, sights of pig or human feces, and so on. Only then were they permitted to enter the cult house, where they were disciplined by a strict dietary and behavioral regime and required speaking in measured, symbolic language. Senior bachelors presided over all events.

In the four days that followed, the bachelors tended their plots of *lepe* plants and conducted rites for the communally owned fluid, both of which represented the spirit woman.[17] Mental capacities were developed during evening sessions to comprehend and memorize the *sangai titi pingi*, a lengthy praise poem for the sacred objects recited in obscure metaphor that taxed the very keenest of minds. Nights were spent by lapsing into short periods of sleep followed by discussion and dream interpretation, where young men placed visions from the subconscious into political frameworks of warfare and exchange. Verbal skills were trained by turning interpretations to metaphor and song. During the day, attention was turned to physical transformation—cleansing the body with the aid of leaves from the sacred *lepe* plant, wig-making, and preparing ceremonial attire for emergence. The young men of a clan or subclan who endured the rites, hardships, and dreams together left from the cult house with bonds of brotherhood and solidarity that would last throughout their lifetimes. They were assessed by elders as to whether they were ready for marriage and then retired to spend a few days in the seclusion of the men's house.[18]

If bachelors remained faithful to the spirit woman through a series of cult performances extending over a period of five to ten years, they acquired the strength to withstand the effects of contact with women and the skills to accumulate enough pigs to pay bridewealth for a human wife. The *sangai* thereby provided a formalized and safe road to marriage among groups who held strong contamination beliefs, fear of sexual intercourse, and tense relations between the sexes. Possibly the themes of sexuality and explicit details of seduction are not repressed in the *sangai* origin traditions as they were in the female spirit cults of surrounding areas (Strathern and Stewart, this volume) as a means to alleviate sexual anxiety. Furthermore, through the *sangai*, every young man was defined as potentially equal to his peers, assured of the support of his fellow clansmen in raising bridewealth, and endowed with the capacity to excel and eventually become a big man. For elders, the *sangai* was as beneficial as for the participants themselves. It gave them a chance to instill clan loyalty, cultivate values appropriate to changing times, and exert control over the younger generation. It kept young men out of the marriage market until the age of twenty-five or thirty, freeing more women for polygynous marriages with ambitious older men.

The *sangai* was also appreciated by old and young women alike, though they kept their distances from the secretive rites. Life stories indicate that women were proud to see their sons or boyfriends transformed into healthy capable adults during the *sangai* and to have them defined as equal to all other men. As mentioned earlier, women felt that they were the ones who made big men of their husbands through their productive efforts and private initiatives in exchange. Equality provided a blank slate on which women could make their marks; had men been defined as unequal to other men from the outset, it would have been more difficult for women's work to leave a signature. With the approval of bachelors, elder men, and women alike, the *sangai* was acquired rapidly by most but not all clans of central and western Enga.

Around the end of the nineteenth century, an addition was made to previously secretive bachelors' cults. In the atmosphere of the Great Ceremonial Wars, where public display of power and wealth was the order of the day, an emergence festival was added to mark the completion of the cult and display the upcoming generation to the public. Young men spent the final morning of the cult donning ceremonial attire that made even the skinniest of lads impressive. Dressed to perfection, they proceeded in a dignified parade to the ceremonial ground, where they performed a dance and presented dream interpretations in song. Elder clansmen watched with pride, men from neighboring clans evaluated the strength of their neighbors, and young women were love-struck. When the emergence festival was over, people gathered to discuss upcoming exchange events.

By the fourth generation before the present, the *sangai* furnished an important occasion to gather people to discuss *Tee* exchange. Clans of eastern Enga eagerly purchased the sacred objects and spells, experimented, and altered the cult substantially to fit the social and ideological landscape of their area. In eastern Enga, it was renamed *sandalu*. As the history of acquisition of the *sangai* by eastern clans is relatively recent, the intent behind purchasing the *sangai*—emulation of the successful acquisition of an event to assemble crowds to plan exchange—are well documented in historical traditions.

With the addition of public emergence festivals to the *sangai*, a formerly secretive cult used to negotiate relations within male corporate groups touched on domains in which females also had vested interests—courtship and exchange. Young women became more and more intrepid under the pressure of female competition to be first to claim their desired men from the *sangai*. They awoke at dawn on the day of emergence and crept through the forest to the seclusion hut where the bachelors were preparing food. Quietly hiding themselves in the bushes, they eavesdropped on the conversation and giggled at the half-naked bachelors. When the bachelors retired into the hut, the girls burst out of the bushes and sang songs at the outer gate of the fenced seclusion hut. After some time they entered the cooking area, where they began to sing and dance. The bachelors asked the senior bachelor to drive away the girls, so they could come out and get dressed, but the girls stood fast until they were given a burning stick to indicate they were favored ones and then sent home with a request to bring ornaments for the bachelors to wear upon their emergence. On their way home, the girls lit a large fire to let other girls know that they had been the first to arrive and that their advances had been accepted.

The bachelors, in response to the overtures of the girls, shifted their attention from the spirit woman to human women. On the night before their emergence, they performed love magic to attract the girls of their choice to the cult house. Senior bachelors who presided were not ones to blow the whistle on such activities, since they would be some of the next to come up for marriage. Love magic and courtship became a preoccupation of those participating in the *sangai*; some men said that during their seclusion they spent most of their time worrying whether any girls would come to court them, whether the ones they loved would come, or whether too many would come and thereby draw the disapproval of senior bachelors.

Once kindled, competition among women was hard to quell. Sometime between 1915 and 1920, a decade or so before first contact, two Layapo women in eastern Enga, Pyasowana and Luatae, overcome by jealousy, broke the solemnity of an emergence festival, pulled a man named Tuingi out of the dance line, and fought ferociously over him. Their actions were regarded as protest action, the product of female nature, and so little could be done. Poor Tuingi was obliged to marry both. Over subsequent years, others followed suit and, before long, disruptive courtship during emergence festivals (*enda akoko nyingi*) became the norm. In these, girlfriends attending emergence sing-sings (*tok pinn kom*) respectfully watched the performance until they felt that the bachelors had had sufficient time to present themselves. Then they rushed forward, abruptly breaking the sanctity of the dance, dragging their boyfriends out of the line, and stripping them of some of their finery, which the bachelors had to reclaim privately at a later date if interested in the girl. Girlfriends and their supporters encircled the chosen man and danced around him, singing bawdy songs complaining that their boyfriends had been taken away from them for the *sangai*, or boasting of prior sexual relationships, for example:

Lyumbuwana from Aipinimanda,
I make love to her son at the back of the house,
I released him to attend the *sangai*.
Poko's penis is not on the ground.
I am proud and happy because it is in me.

Competing groups composed of girls and their supporters fought over the bachelors, sometimes leaving them totally naked. Elders looked on with grudging disapproval, but allowed this disruptive courtship to become an integral ending to *sangai* performances for a number of reasons. One was that the juxtaposition of rites that separated the sexes, on the one hand, and ones that blatantly touched on sexuality, on the other, was not foreign to Enga bachelors' or ancestral ritual. For example, the *sangai* origin myth involved graphic sexual seduction, and in fertility rites sacred stones were made to physically copulate. Another was the fact that women were playing an increasingly active role in exchange and so tolerance for their expression of preferences in marriage was considered. Finally and significantly, were the practical considerations: such drama drew large crowds for subsequent discussions to plan upcoming *Tee* exchange.[19]

The *enda akoko nyingi* moved westward to make inroads into the strict pollution beliefs and taboos of western Enga. Most men of western Enga report that it reached their clans in the 1960s, some forty to fifty years after the first incident, though a few clans in the far west never adopted female courtship or emergence ceremonies into their *kepele* performances (see also Wohlt 1978; Gibbs 1975).

As human women assumed a greater role in the *sangai*, the spirit woman withdrew, and only fragments of her presence remained in *sandalu* lore of eastern clans. For example, on the basis of his interviews with knowledgeable men of eastern Enga in the 1950s and 1960s, Schwab (1995: 27) cites fragments of *sangai* tradition given to him by elders stating that the *sangai* originated from a woman. However, these elders were unable to elaborate and knew nothing of the spirit woman. Meggitt's informants (1964) were apparently also not aware that the *sangai* centered around celestial seduction.

It should be noted that changes in *kepele*-cult cosmology occurred as the *sangai* spread throughout central and western Enga, linking women to fertility and prosperity. While the diffusion of the pre-sweet potato *kepele* cult was linked to the journey of a mythical rainbow python, the spread of the post-sweet potato *kepele* cult was attributed to two wandering women, mother and daughter. These women seduced or were seduced by men they encountered, taught the men the magic spells of fertility, and later turned into sacred cult stones. With these alterations in *kepele* cosmology and the spread of the *sangai*, the spirit woman withdrew from her role as mother in the *mote* of tribes adjacent to the major exchange networks. For example, at the *kepele* cult house near Laiagam, where the wandering women delivered the cult, the *mote* was used only to train future ritual experts. At other cult houses in the Lai valley, founded by the wandering women, the *kepele* cult (called *aeatee* in central Enga) was substantially altered, and the *mote* initiation totally discontinued. In the initial stage of *aeatee* cult-house construction, two human women, one representing the mother and the other the daughter, rode the kingpost for the cult house as it was carried in great ceremony from the forest to the sacred site. Human women had penetrated what was formerly male ritual; the "hot" vaginas of women rode atop the central symbol of male corporate groups.

The Female Spirit Cult

The spirit woman did not abandon men in adulthood, nor did they cease to seek her transformative charms. Around the end of the last century, when the *Tee* cycle had just become linked to the Great Ceremonial Wars, big men in pivotal clans at the western terminus of the *Tee* cycle were making elaborations in the *kepele/aeatee* cult, using its performances as occasions to plan and time the *Tee* cycle (Wiessner and Tumu 1998). Big men from clans at the eastern end of the *Tee* cycle then sought similar ritual means to enhance the prosperity and reproduction of their groups and to stage public events that would gather people to "talk *Tee*." Hearing of new developments in the southeast in the form of the female spirit cult, big men of the Saka valley were eager to try it.

According to historical tradition, the spells for the cult were first brought by a woman named Kangala from the Mendi area, who married a big man of the Saka in the fifth generation before the present. However, the cult was first performed when the sacred stones, which served as a reservoir of the female spirit's power, were imported by Kangala's fellow Pauakaka clansmen. Shortly after, the female spirit cult was acquired from the Tambul area by the Yambatane Watenge clan under the initiative of Pakiala, a prominent organizer of the *Tee* cycle. When sacred plants sprang up in the spot where he had defecated after a large feast, and sacred cult stones appeared in the earth, Pakiala summoned ritual experts from Tambul to perform the cult. Subsequently, big men from other clans in eastern Enga followed suit. In an extreme case, men from a Yakumani clan at Wapenamanda made a night journey to steal the sacred stones of a nearby Waimini clan in the late 1950s or early 1960s. They proclaimed that the stones had appeared at their place and summoned ritual experts from the Tambul area to orchestrate their first performance. As it was common belief that such stones could wander, nobody suspected theft.

The female spirit cult presented the immortal sky woman to men neither as mother nor as seductress and first wife, but as second wife, who came to men as a bride, but remained a virgin with a closed vagina, giving men protection against the menstrual fluids of human females. She brought health, fertility, and wealth to them and their families. Two cult houses were constructed for the rites and fenced in, one male and one female, and adult male celebrants divided into two opposing but complementary moieties representing males and females. Its central theme was that "male and female must be both separated and indissolubly linked" (A. Strathern 1970b: 49).

Superb descriptions of cult performances and analyses are given in the publications of Strathern and Stewart (A. Strathern 1970b, 1979; Strathern and Stewart 1998a, this volume); it is not necessary to elaborate here. Enga appear to have simply imported the cult opportunistically and followed the instructions of ritual experts; only a few knew the meaning of specific actions performed, though the role of the female spirit was acknowledged. In some cases the female spirit cult appears to have been conceptually merged with cults for the ancestors. What does draw many remarks in descriptions of performances, however, is the emergence parade at the end of the cult, when men broke out of the cult enclosure's outer gate and danced to the ceremonial grounds in full dress, each holding a magnificent pearl shell before his eyes. Not only physical attractiveness was displayed by these married men, but also power and wealth. Subsequently the men returned to the enclosure and reemerged carrying bags of pork for the feast. Great crowds gathered for this event, knowing that the host clan had performed the cult with two goals: to ensure the health and prosperity of its members and to provide a public forum to plan the *Tee* cycle that would follow.

Through the female spirit cult, an immortal sky woman brought all the benefits of a second wife to families without generating sexual jealousy. She also reinstated potential equality to all married men at a time when inequalities had become prominent. Women approved of her efforts and raised the pigs to help men purchase her powers, just as they raised pigs to pay bridewealth for second wives. They also readily accepted her wealth—the pearl shells that first entered the *Tee* cycle about the time the female spirit cult was imported. It is said that some women fell in love at the mere sight of a beautiful pearl shell, and so these new valuables became an essential component of bridewealth by female demand. Unfortunately, European patrols entered Enga before the female spirit cult had spread widely, and so it is difficult to know what the future would have held for the immortal sky woman in her new role as second wife.

Historical Perspectives on Female Participation in Male Ritual

Returning to the question posed at the beginning of this chapter: what does a historical perspective add to our understanding of female participation in male ritual as discussed by Pascale Bonnemère in the introduction to this volume? First, it shows that types of male rituals—initiation, bachelors' cults, and female spirit cults—may not be as different as they first appear to be, but can be expressions drawn from the same fund of cosmology to build relational configurations critical to men in certain life stages or in specific socioeconomic contexts. In the Enga case, all three types of male ritual drew on Enga belief that the original progenitors of humans, the mythical sky people and sky women in particular, could come to the aid of individuals. When they appeared depended heavily on the needs of a variety of relationships. Prior to the introduction of the sweet potato, it apparently sufficed to have the assistance of celestial women in separating boys from their parents and integrating them into a community of men who cooperated in reproducing relations with the spirit world. After the introduction of the sweet potato, when the center of the economy shifted toward intensive agricultural production and ceremonial exchange, men's needs were altered. A spirit woman was then called on to facilitate the transition from bachelor life to adulthood by bonding men into a cooperative cohort and recreating order at a time when competition was threatening relations between men. The spirit woman also eased the path to marriage in a society that was fraught with fears of female contamination, on the one hand, and yet required cooperation between the sexes to forge exchange networks, on the other. When the complexities of exchange networks became so great that they could only be mastered with the help of female kin, a spirit woman was called on in adulthood to reinforce cooperation within and between the sexes. And so, driven by the needs of men and the actions of women, spirit women moved from the role of mother to seductress and bride to cowife for married men. Their presence in rituals at any one stage in the life of men did not preclude their return to assist in another. Had contact with Europeans not occurred, it is likely that all three types of male rituals involving female spirits would have been practiced contemporaneously in some parts of western Enga.

Second, a historical perspective cautions against assuming that male ritual as experienced in the ethnographic present is "tradition" aimed at reproducing the status quo. It underlines the importance of asking the question whether ritual might also be part and parcel of the process of change. While some studies (Barth 1987) indicate a conservative role for male ritual, Enga male ritual was used to preserve the status quo in some areas of life and to bring about change in others. Females were instrumental in both processes. On the conservative side, male ritual was used to reproduce the potential equality of men, even after blatant social inequalities had emerged. Women supported these efforts. Mothers were proud to see their sons transformed into equals to all other men via initiation and bachelors' cults. Young women felt that, if their prospective husbands were equal to other men, then their own hard work in building family wealth and reputation would show. On the progressive side, male ritual was important in ushering in new norms, values, and attitudes. Items such as pigs and pearl shells gained prominence, value, and meaning as exchange items owing in part to their prominent positioning in male cults. Women cooperated in efforts to value items by producing or acquiring outstanding pigs and other items for ceremonies or demanding them as part of bridewealth (Wiessner 2001). Through qualities praised in bachelor cult poetry, ideals were shifted from equality of all men to initial equality of men to be broken later in life through economic and political achievement. In twentieth-century bachelors' cults, young women assisted their boyfriends in their quests to excel by gathering the finest decorations they could find for them and bringing them to the bachelors' cult house so that they would stand out from the others in the emergence ceremonies. Last but not least, women's aggressive and entertaining courtship within the context of bachelors' cults and exchange did much to soften barriers between the sexes.

Looking at Enga ritual through time makes it possible to see in which contexts women enter male ritual symbolically and when they participate in actuality. Throughout the course of history, women were represented symbolically in all Enga male ritual and participated indirectly by provisioning cults and celebrating their outcome. However, direct female participation in male ritual did not occur until the Great Ceremonial Wars and the *Tee* cycle became so complex that men had to work together regularly with their wives and agnatic female relatives to manage family exchange ties. This cooperation did not erode the essential separation between the sexes, which was grounded in contamination beliefs. Nonetheless, it did strengthen appreciation of the contribution of females to the fertility and prosperity of men, giving men confidence in the good will of women. Subsequently, as a result of female initiative and indirect male consent, women entered male ritual in flesh and blood. The most assertive role of human women in penetrating male ritual occurred through integrating courtship into bachelors' cults. Nonetheless, even in the most sacred and conservative ancestral cults of central Enga, women made an impact. For example, in the *aeatee* cult (Central Enga), two women in ceremonial dress were at the center of the procession that brought the kingpost for the cult house from the forest to the building site, where it would be erected as a male symbol of tribal cohesion and identity.

The female spirit cult was a relatively new introduction to Enga at the time of first contact and involved no direct female participation. Had it persisted long enough to be readjusted for the Enga context, it is very likely that females would also have claimed more direct participation as they had for the *aeatee* and bachelors' cults. And so through time human women, with their earthly efforts to make big men of their husbands, increasingly joined the spirit woman in transforming men.

The Fate and Future of Female Spirit Cults

The *kepele* and *mote* were discontinued with Christian influence. Though the idea of the immortal rainbow python, so prominent in *kepele* mythology, has reappeared in some modern religious movements, all aspects of *mote* rites seem to have disappeared. By contrast, the *sangai*, which did not conflict with Christian principles, had a much slower decline. Some clans of Enga continue to hold the *sangai* today, usually in the context of an event to gather crowds for election campaigns. In these, it is probably fair to say that the fundamental concept of marriage to a spirit woman has vanished. As far as we could determine, key concepts from the female spirit cult never really penetrated eastern Enga before missions entered the area, and so few traces remain today.

Though specific female spirits of the past may have vanished, the recognition of a female force in Enga religious beliefs continues today. Philip Gibbs (personal communication, April 1999) has noted a strong move in Catholic church circles toward a devotion to the "Blessed Mother," with many connecting her to the spirit woman of the *sangai* or other female sky people. He has also sensed a revival of female "spirit" in a more secular sense of women's creativity in taking control of their own lives. With local churches making more effort to integrate Enga tradition and Christianity, new permutations of the female spirit and female spirituality will appear just as they have in the past.

Chapter 9
Relating to Women: Female Presence in Melanesian "Male Cults"

Bruce M. Knauft

It seems so obvious that one has to wonder why it hasn't been done sooner. In highly selected ways, of course, previous writings *have* considered the presence and spiritual imagery of women in the so-called male cults of Melanesia. But not in the same way as in the present contributions. This chapter attempts to assess the distinctive contributions of the current volume, to contextualize them in larger historical and theoretical terms, to specify some comparative insights raised by the contributors, and to apply these insights—critically and reflexively—to the male rituals and initiations that I documented in 1980–82 and again in 1998 among the Gebusi of Papua New Guinea's Western Province.

Appropriation of Women

During the first three decades of writing about ostensibly "male" cults in interior New Guinea—from the early 1950s to the mid-1980s—images of femaleness figured prominently in the objects, myths, and beliefs that attended these rites.[1] Nevertheless, primary emphasis was placed on the ways that men usurped, manipulated, and trumped femaleness for their own ritual and social interests. In the process, Melanesian men were seen to appropriate and transform female capabilities for their own reproduction, solidarity, and political control. In received wisdom, Melanesian male cults entailed the exclusion, disparagement, and domination of women by men. This oppositional view of female exclusion and gendered antagonism did illuminate selected and important aspects of ritual and gender relations in Melanesia. But it also contained biases that can now be put in their own cultural and historical context.

Classic perspectives on ritual and gender in Melanesian anthropology were highly consistent with Western sensibilities during the era following World War II, from the 1950s to 1970s. During this period, Western competitive individualism was galvanized by gendered opportunities in domestic and labor organization that had been enabled by the war. Western men increasingly found themselves vying with women who aspired to greater prominence in economic, social, political, and domestic arenas. In the Melanesian context, this was consistent with the discovery of "sexual antagonism" between men and women, especially those who (coincidentally) did not enjoy being confined to the so-called domestic sphere. Correspondingly, the "jural" and "political" domain attributed to Melanesian men was connected analytically to the absence of higher-order Melanesian institutions and hierarchies that, in a structural and functionalist perspective, would presumably have provided a firmer foundation for male control. This lack of stability paralleled what Harvey (1989) has identified as a key problematic of Western modernity during the latter half of the twentieth century, namely, the difficulty of maintaining efficacy in higher-order institutions of economic and political control. In Melanesian anthropology, reciprocally, the concern with structural instability became a key point of comparison and contrast between Melanesian political systems and the ostensibly more ordered and coherent forms of social control that were not associated with "sexual antagonism" but with rank and lineage organization in Polynesia, Africa, and many parts of Asia. Melanesian men, by contrast, were seen as having unstable coalitions based on competitive egalitarianism, shallow genealogies, and shifting coresidence.

Refracted through the lens of high modernist anthropology, Melanesian men were seen as sandwiched between higher-order political constraints and lower-order domestic ones. As such, they were inhibited from forging enduring institutions of political organization and stable domestic control. The seemingly natural result of this decentralized condition was Melanesian men's self-definition through polarization against women, on the one hand, and their polarization against other men through warfare and competitive exchange, on the other.

Though certainly dotted by countertrends and exceptions, this view concerning Melanesia was anthropologically common during the 1950s, '60s, and '70s. It was certainly not grounded in feminism, and it tended to suggest that male domination was functional and ultimately adaptive for Melanesian societies as wholes. But it did hold in common with feminism—particularly the second wave feminism of the 1960s and '70s—notions of collective social and political opposition between women and men. During this period, the corresponding "anthropology of women" was strongly dedicated in document the cross-cultural inequality and "status" of women vis-à-vis men (Rosaldo and Lamphere 1974; Reiter 1975; Leacock 1981; Sanday 1981). The larger goal was to uncover the whys, wherefores, and widespread distribution—perhaps even universality—of male dominance in human societies and cultures. Beneath this agenda was the common assumption—implicit if not explicit—that culture functioned as an ideology that prevented women as individuals and as a collective group from achieving equality with men. From the viewpoint of masculinist political anthropology, this ideology was functionally valuable and socially adaptive. For second wave feminists and Marxists, on the other hand, it was seen as oppressive and ultimately inhumane. Both vantage points, however, agreed that women and men were structurally opposed and that the deep social and political cleavages of this opposition were reflected in cultural beliefs and values buttressed by male symbolic appropriation of female power.

Regardless in which direction it was pushed, the structural analysis of male-female opposition, at least through the 1970s, was ultimately at odds with anthropology's longstanding emphasis on Boasian relativism and Maussian relationality. This echoed in the tension between feminism and cultural anthropology, as effectively highlighted by Marilyn Strathern (1987). Whereas feminism—especially second wave feminism—stressed the commonality if not potential universality of women's rights and interests, relativist strains of cultural anthropology stressed diversity and relativity. More generally, Marxism, structural-functionalism, and feminism all looked for structural similarities and differences across cultures. By contrast, a more relativistic view looked for irreducible differences.

Arguments or Complements?

The tension between intrinsic and externalist views of society and culture is nothing new in anthropology. Moments and perspectives that stress the distinctiveness of alternative life-ways and cosmologies (including fundamentally non-Western ways in which people relate to each other) have often clashed with generalizing theories and postulated models. Over the decades, such tensions have driven many of anthropology's major debates, and they continue to do so, for instance, in recent discussions of modernity or globalization.

Since the mid-1980s, a relativist moment has been especially prominent in the anthropology of gender relations and in third wave or postmodern feminism.[2] By itself, however, unmitigated emphasis on local or regional distinctiveness (or, for that matter, on discursive deconstruction and alternative voicing) promotes the view that peoples and cultures are not just irreducibly different, but, by logical extension, almost incomparable or unknowable to us. Unbridled relativism can also make it difficult to understand the dynamics of contemporary change, including our ability to see emergent patterns of inequality and ideology.

It was just these difficulties, in earlier guises, that structural Marxism and Marxist feminism objected to during the 1970s and mid-1980s. Concerning male cults in Melanesia, for instance, it seemed that taking the beliefs and ideologies of male cults at face value ignored the ideological work they did in legitimating men's domination of women and in making this domination seem culturally "natural" (see Josephides 1985; Godelier 1986; A. Strathern 1982). Invariably, however, this more critical view compromised the subjective diversity and relational distinctiveness of cultural formations. Reductionism, however qualified or partial, is practically intrinsic to critical and comparative perspectives.

In my own opinion, it is vital to maintain a robust dialogue between moments of analysis that are relativist, on the one hand, and those that are critically comparativist, on the other (see Knauft 1996, 1997a). Appreciative relativism puts us in touch with alternative sensibilities and subjectivities. It is also provides anthropology one of the field's strongest cards in combating ethnocentrism. At the same time, however, relativism also carries excesses of particularism and uncritical acceptance of cultural ideologies. As a complement to these excesses, more comparative and critical moments of analysis can be particularly important. Conversely, comparative perspectives tend to proliferate structures and models that compromise our understanding of nuances. As a reciprocating dialogue, however, each of these vantage points can provide a useful check and balance on the other.

Where does this leave us concerning male cults and the chapters of the present book? Against the simple genealogy portrayed above, the increasing consideration of gender as a cultural and relational system during the 1980s served, in part, as a relativizing move against the structural and structural-functionalist perspectives prominent during the 1950s, '60s, and '70s. Marilyn Strathern's work has been particularly important and influential in this respect. On the one hand, her use of Melanesian case material problematized and relativized assumptions about gender systems in relation to nature and culture (M. Strathern 1980, 1981a, b). On the other, in *The Gender of the Gift* (1988), Strathern deconstructed and threw into question Western assumptions about sex-role identity and individualism by emphasizing how Melanesian social affiliations were fundamentally relational in nature. In the process, she undercut the problematic of individual autonomy versus collective solidarity that had long underpinned structural and functional arguments in Melanesian anthropology, including in the analysis of male cults and initiations.

It is consistent with Strathern's sensibilities that, as she herself has noted, her formulations work through "indirection" rather than by programmatic statement or systematic application. Though she treats a wide range of comparative material from the anthropology of Melanesia, Marilyn Strathern ultimately seems more interested in relational forms than in the relative distribution of sociocultural forms in Melanesia, their changes over time, or their articulation with socioeconomic and political inequalities.

It is just here that the chapters of the present book make significant contributions, and they do so with distinction on several levels. As a topical contribution, this volume puts the comparative analysis of female actors and idioms of femaleness at center stage in our understanding of so-called male cults in Melanesia. Though the treatments address femaleness as a cultural form or cosmological construction, they also address women's practical presence, contextual agency, and embodied experience in relation to male cults and initiations. At some junctures, the chapters in this volume are sociological or comparative in ways Marilyn Strathern would herself be wary of. But in the process, our larger notion of how and in what ways these cults are "male" is further reframed. In the process, we can see with greater nuance exactly how and in what ways the designation of male-exclusive cults or initiations has effaced the relational and agentive dimensions of female action and symbolization.

Pregnant Themes

In light of the preceding discussion, the focus of the present volume is ripe for expansion. Given that boys, bachelors, and men in many Melanesian societies have undergone fundamental changes through ritual activity, and given that these changes are part and parcel of gendered transactions and redefinitions in the community as a whole, how could we consider women—as mothers, sisters, or maidens—to be somehow outside of or independent from this process? How could women as actors be left analytically in a social void or vacuum by the presumed ritual agency of men? From the vantage point of current sensibilities, and from our understanding of Melanesian cultural orientations, they certainly cannot. This in no way denies the striking degree to which women may be subjected to social exclusion, secrecy, denigration, disparagement, or onerous labor in and as a result of male cults and their legacy in Melanesia. But women are not just "subjected to," they are subjects in their own right. Their subjectivity is not just as "women" but transactionally configured in and through their relationship to sons, husbands, and other male relatives, as well as with other women. How could it be otherwise?

This said, putting women and femaleness at center stage in the present analysis of Melanesian male cults is only a point of departure; important and thorny issues are raised in the process. Exactly what *kinds* of "presence" have women had in various Melanesian "male" cults and initiations? In what ways has this presence been variable as opposed to being a reflexive or automatic product of a relational view of Melanesian ritual practice? To what extent is the "presence" of women in male cults and initiations social and agentive or beyond men's invocation of images of femaleness? At issue is how and to what extent women have been social actors and agents in Melanesian "male cults," and in what ways they experience their activities as meaningful and important. These are not questions that can be answered on prior grounds. Rather, they lead us to the specifics of the various chapters.

As an armature for discussion, a few distinctions may be helpful. In a sense, so-called "male rituals" in Melanesia are almost intrinsically "about women." Insofar as an even putative notion of masculinity is being configured, maleness is almost by definition fashioned against complementary constructions of what it means to be female. As a figure/ground relation, the two cannot be dissociated; a change to one is a change to the other. In semiotic terms, femaleness is intrinsic to male rituals and inherent in their signification.

At the same time, the degree to which female significations are explicitly elaborated in male cults can be highly variable. This is amply illustrated in the chapters of the present volume. As Strathern and Stewart indicate, spirit women or spirit brides are present in male cults in much of the Western Highlands of Papua New Guinea and westward across areas that include the Duna, Mountain Ok peoples, and the Strickland-Bosavi area. In the present chapters, male cults that focus on spirit women include the Duna *payame ima* cult, the Ipili *omatisia* bachelor cult, the Enga *sangai/sandalu* bachelor cults (as well as more recent Enga female spirit cults for adult Engan men), and the Mount Hageners' *amb kor* cult. Across the Strickland-Bosavi area, female spiritual presence is prominent in the marriage of male spirit mediums to spirit women, who become the link between the living and the unseen world in male spirit séances (Schieffelin 1977; Sørum 1980; Knauft 1985, chap. 11, 1989). Among Gebusi, the presence of spirit women at séances is crucial for the curing of sickness, divining sorcery, finding lost pigs, and helping forecast the success of hunting, fishing, and fighting expeditions.

Femaleness also has high face value in many male initiations in Melanesia. Though the dominant view has been that vestiges of femaleness are denigrated and purged from young initiates—for instance, through blood-letting and other forms of traumatic expulsion—there is in fact an ongoing cultural conversation or dialogue between idioms of masculinity and femininity in associated rites. In many respects, Melanesians may have been less absolute about the differences between maleness and females than has been ethnographically assumed. Even in societies where so-called "sexual antagonism" was pronounced, femaleness was typically not considered "bad" or loathsome in an overall or general sense. Rather, certain specific bodily practices and emanations, such as menstrual blood, were considered inimical to boys or men, particularly in contexts that epitomized or archetypalized masculinity. Even here, symbolic blood (or vegetal analogs of blood) was sometimes eaten by male initiands (as described in this volume by Bonnemère for the Ankave) or symbolically smeared on them, as in the smearing of initiate boys with red pandanus seeds or juice among both the Ankave and the Kamea, portrayed by Bamford. At one point in the Ömie initiation, described by Rohatynskyj, mothers run at the young boys with skirts flying loose, thus bluffing at exposing their genitals directly to the male novices.

More generally, relational transactions between masculine and feminine idioms were renegotiated or reinscribed at the critical junctures of most

Melanesian initiation rites. Indeed, as the chapters of the present volume stress, the purpose of male bachelor cults and later-stage initiations was not just to make male warriors but to make husbands. In this sense, the larger purpose of cultivating contextual masculinity in "male cults" occurs for the larger purpose of facilitating productive and reproductive relations *between* men and women (see M. Strathern 1988; Knauft 1999, chap. 2).

Women's "Presence": Cosmic or Social?

As has often been noted, the spiritual presence of women is not the same as their social presence in ritual activities. These aspects of gendered agency are importantly and sometimes dramatically different—and this difference can be key to pragmatic significance of rituals as well as to their cultural meaning.

Women are excluded from bachelor cult and male initiate cult houses in most of the societies described in this volume, including where images of femaleness or spirit women are cosmologically prominent. Among Gebusi during the early 1980s, there appeared to be a wide chasm between the centrality of Gebusi spirit women in men's spirit séances and the rigid social exclusion of real Gebusi women from these same events.[3] This also included the disparagement of married Gebusi women for embracing, in slightest hint, the lascivious flirtation and bold sexuality that was characteristic of spirit women and responded to so enthusiastically by men at the séance itself. The spirit woman was a married woman—spiritually married to the male spirit medium, through whom she spoke. But the ribaldry that escalated dramatically between her persona and that of the assembled male audience was, from a male point of view, anathema to married Gebusi women. In essence, men configured a fantastic image of feminine sexuality against which real married women were deemed to be at once deficient and worthy of brutalizing for attempting to emulate.[4] Spirit séances were also the most common occasion for sexual relations among Gebusi males. In these, the ostensibly heterosexual arousal occasioned by the spirit woman's singing was redirected by men onto uninitiated teenage boys, who served as their fellators (Knauft 1986, 1987). In one sense, sexual relations between males closed a circle of men's appropriation through which female sexuality itself became yet another index of male self-sufficiency and exclusion of women. That some Gebusi séances were accompanied by violent images or pantomimes of sexual violence against women seemed to underscore this point.

On the other hand, the discrepancy between spiritual image and social behavior can work to the benefit of women in other cultural contexts. In some societies, including the Etoro, not far from Gebusi, a highly debilitating and polluting image of femaleness pervades ritual life and sexual beliefs (Kelly 1976, 1993). And yet the actual tenor of Etoro gender relations was reported by Kelly (1993, personal communication) to be highly cooperative and largely devoid of antagonism or strife between men and women on a daily basis, including in domestic partnerships and between husbands and wives. Despite the fact that Etoro witchcraft was ideologically associated with women, a majority of Etoro witch-killings appear in fact to be targeted against males (Kelly 1993: 550n11, 181ff).

These patterns underscore the venerable observation that spiritual imagery and social behavior can be complexly and importantly divergent. It also emphasizes the importance of what Lemonnier, in his contribution to this volume, so felicitously calls "an anthropology of nuances." At present, this emphasis cautions against knee-jerk assumptions that women must have had a socially prominent or equal role in most of the male cults and initiations of Melanesia. It is important not to contravene a prior ethnographic image of female exclusion with an equally lopsided one in which women as well as femaleness are now seen as co-equal with men across the board of male cult variation. The sociological presence and social incorporation of women into initiation or bachelor cult proceedings seems greater, it may be noted, in southern than in northern Anga societies. Bonnemère in her chapter suggests that, in the latter area, emphasis on male reproduction through boy-insemination dovetails with a mythological and cosmological denial of female reproductive capacities, an apparently greater degree of male domination, and minimal presence of women during initiations. Concerning the substantial participation of women in the initiation rituals of southern Angan societies, Lemonnier suggests that "The exploitation of female work is no less intensive among Ankave (or Kamea) than among Baruya or Sambia. It is just less violent" (Lemonnier, this volume). Bonnemère likewise suggests that "male domination remains crucial in explaining Anga initiations, and there is not much to justify a total rejection of the existing analyses of this aspect" (Bonnemère, this volume).

Societal variations within the Anga-speaking region of Papua New Guinea dovetail with the larger-scale assertion of Strathern and Stewart (see also Stewart and Strathern 1999a), who suggest there was relatively greater collaboration between women and men in the cults of the Western Highlands—as opposed to a more exclusionary forms of gendered separation in the cults of the Eastern Highlands and adjacent areas (see Feil 1987; Herdt, 1982a). For Enga of the Western Highlands, Wiessner's contribution to the present volume richly documents a high degree of spatial and historical variation in female presence in men's spiritual and bachelor cults—spiritually, symbolically, and sociologically. The deep historical time frame unearthed by Wiessner reveals an important larger trend: that the sociological importance of Enga women in the *sangai* bachelor cults has increased over time. This cult shifted from the bachelors' cultivation of ties with the *spirit* woman to a concern—by both bachelors and unmarried women—with love magic and attracting a human wife in marriage. Women's own agency has increased to such an extent that the culminating presentation of the costumed bachelors occasioned highly aggressive action by young Engan women to claim the young man of their choice. In some cases, "competing groups composed of girls and their supporters fought over the bachelors, sometimes leaving them totally naked" (Wiessner, this volume). On the other hand, Enga cults such as the older *mote* male initiation cult and the more recent female spirit cult for married men involved much less active participation of women in the cult itself while appropriating female labor to supply food for their enactment.

Variation in women's cult participation is perhaps brought full circle by Lemonnier's intriguing observation that, at least for Anga groups, explicit rites for *females* occur in just those societies where women are most fully *excluded* from male-cult activity. This may also be the case for some Eastern Highlands societies, in which women were rigidly excluded from male cults but had their own initiation rites (Hays and Hays 1982; Newman and Boyd 1982; see in Lutkehaus and Roscoe 1995). In this respect, the effacement of women as social agents in male cults can sometimes be complemented by their social participation in rites of their own. At the same time, as suggested for the Baruya by Godelier (1986) and for the Ankave by Bonnemère (1996: 378), male and female initiations can themselves work in complementary ways to reinforce male domination.

Given such variation, enthusiasm for considering the role of women and femaleness in Melanesian male-cult activity should be tempered by the dangers of now projecting women equally and everywhere into Melanesian male cults. Within this mix is the drawback of defaulting to a generic notion of female "presence" that tacitly conflates the spiritual or symbolic presence of femaleness with the sociological participation and agency of women themselves. Even as we more fully consider the extent of female presence and participation in so-called male cults, it is important not to confuse the cosmological or symbolic presence of femaleness with the extent to which women actually participate in or are excluded from the proceedings. This caution underscores rather than undercuts the significance of female spiritual and cosmological imagery, including in the absence of women themselves. As my brief mention of Etoro suggests above, the very extremity of cosmological beliefs may in some instances articulate with a more interactive emphasis between men and women in daily social life. Deeper consideration of contextual identifications and their relational patterning over time points us toward a larger and more adequate understanding of gender relations.

Patterns of Social Participation

If women's participation in male cults has been highly variable, one side of this coin is the social exclusion of women and presumptions of their ignorance about ritual activities and associated meanings. Even in extreme cases, however, women's ignorance is never complete. And as women get older, they gain greater understanding of the preparations, patterning of male absences, and changes that occur among men of different ages and ritual cohorts. Over time, women's understanding of male rites invariably gets deeper. Though it may be a male ideology or formal dictum that everything is secret from women—that they "know nothing"—this is usually far from the truth. Often, there is tacit understanding that married and older women know the general contours of what goes on in the male cult house even if they do not know all the details. What is typically maintained, however, is the notion that women have no legitimate right to voice their knowledge or understanding publicly, especially in the presence of men. In this way, the cultural presumption that associated knowledge and activities are an exclusive male province can be maintained irrespective of women's more explicit knowledge in fact.

Even when women are socially "absent," they are in some respects still a sociological as well as a spiritual presence. As a Simmelian perspective would emphasize, the fact that women know that activities and important knowledge is being withheld from them itself creates a new kind of gendered social relationship. Often this relationship is a kind of meta-collaboration or collusion, in which women cooperate in maintaining the fiction of their own "ignorance." This collaboration is important if not essential to the successful completion of the rites. Moreover, a relationship of seeming exclusion cuts in two directions. If men are off by themselves excluding women, this easily gives women a freer hand to express their own sensibilities, stories, and fantasies apart from men. This is indeed what Eileen Cantrell found among Gebusi women while I was off in the rainforest with men conducting fish-poisoning rituals, from which women were stringently excluded.[5] It was during this period of "exclusion" that Gebusi women told special and secret stories among themselves and joked about and sometimes made fun of men's activities. At the same time, they actively cooperated with the men's desire for privacy and fervently wished for the successful completion of the men's fish-poisoning expedition. Of course, collective sociality and information-sharing among women it itself highly variable depending on societal context. One might anticipate collective sharing of female knowledge during male absences in societies with residence based on communal longhouse organization, as was the case among Gebusi and many indigenous south-coast cultures (see Knauft 1993). Patterns of female social bonding in the absence of men can be much less in societies where residence is dispersed residence in hamlets and family compounds or where domestic life is riven by competitive co-wife relationships.

The meta-collaboration of women and men in so-called exclusionary male cults is also evident in the labor that women typically undertake to supply the starch staple and selected other foods for the initiation feasts—and especially for the hosting of visitors that usually attends the large climactic initiation ceremonies. This point is emphasized in Strathern and Stewart's chapter (see also Stewart and Strathern 1999a). Women also often produce significant items of male bodily decoration, which attract attention and appreciative gazes when the new initiates are presented for public view. In the chapters of the present volume, this circumstance is evident among Baruya mothers, who, as Bonnemère describes (this volume), make the body decorations and loincloths for their sons' return from the bush. Among Gebusi, adult women as well as men become "sponsors" (*tor*) to the male initiates by crafting major costume elements that include scores of finely woven chestbands (*dakil*) that are a major item of costuming on the initiates' torsos.

Ankave mothers are remarkable in undergoing a kind of "initiation couvade" that parallels some of the same strictures that their sons endure simultaneously in the bush. These similarities include staying in seclusion in a large collective shelter, a ban on going outside except during a particular period of morning light (when they each soak their new bark cape in fresh water), and a taboo on various specific foods and on drinking liquid (Bonnemère, this volume, 1996). This fact turns on its head the notion that mothers' rigid separation from their sons indicates their "exclusion" from and ignorance of the ritual process. Among Kamea, discussed by Bamford, mothers of the initiates are even entrusted to keep the sacred, wrapped bullroarers that are central to the cult's secrecy. As Bonnemère discusses, Baruya mothers suggest that the pain boys undergo is similar to their own in childbirth, and woman wears an additional bark cape on her head during the same period at which her son in the forest wears the bark cape his mother has made for him. As such, as she puts it, "Baruya women consider themselves to be involved in the initiation of their sons and they link their participation to the fact that they gave birth to them" (Bonnemère, this volume).

The social involvement of women in Melanesian male cults and initiations is especially evident in final climactic rites. These typically involve public display of cult adepts or initiates in costumed finery for an assembled audience of women, children, and the community at large. Such display is common or usual at the conclusion of Melanesian male cults and initiations. Even in those cases where women stay on the periphery and remain largely undecorated at these final events, they participate crucially as a principal part of the audience. Indeed, the male accomplishment of growth, masculine transformation, and bodily adornment can hardly be complete without the appreciative if not adoring gaze of women, children, and others in the community. As Biersack emphasizes for the Ipili, it is very common for women as well as men to be seen as having invested and given up their life-energy for the sake of the initiates. For many women, the ritual recognition of this important and inexorable process would seem to mix a sense of accomplishment at the successful completion of their maternal labors with bittersweet sorrow in the acceptance of relinquishing maternal responsibility. The physical results of women's child-raising labors are foregrounded in the very act of their cultural transcendence. This is not just the physical apotheosis and relational transformation of the results of women's mothering but a change of life status and a kind of rite of passage for the mothers and other related women. On psychological and cultural as well as social grounds, then, the nonparticipation or absence of mothers and sisters, wives and maidens, is practically unthinkable in these final ceremonies.

Life Cycles of Female Representation

Beyond the various ways Melanesian women have participated socially in male cults and rituals, the chapters of this volume suggest key variations in the dimensions of femaleness that are symbolically emphasized in male cults and rituals. Bonnemère suggests that male initiation among Ankave symbolically emphasizes the birth process itself. This is dramatically indicated by Ankave practices such as the coating of the initiands with red pandanus juice about their head and shoulders after they emergence from a uterine-like tunnel of painful trauma. Bonnemère nicely contrasts this with the breast-feeding imagery of Sambia male initiation, including the explicit designation of insemination through fellatio as a Sambian analogue to boys' nursing. In this process, as Herdt has elsewhere shown (1981, 1987a, b, 1999b), men's secret flutes serve as "transitional objects" that the boys are trained to suck as they switch from the breast to the penis as the source of life-giving sustenance. One might note here that in the Ömie *ujawe* initiation described by Rohatynskyj (this volume), mothers actually come to the novices' garden house and take their sons in their arms as if to give them their breasts. Their initiated sons, meanwhile, close their eyes and call out "Mother, my breast."

Another variant emerges among the Kamea, whose initiation symbolism emphasizes the postpartum separation of boys from their mothers. The final severing of maternal connection is graphically indicated among Kamea when women encircle the initiands toward the conclusion of the rites. Men on the outside jostle and knock against the female enclosure and eventually break through it to force the initiates back climactically to the men's cult house. As Bamford suggests, the boys' ascension to a nonfemale status is thus enacted as a final decontainment from maternal encompassment. That this process is reciprocal between mother and initiand is underscored by the fact that a Kamea boy whose mother has died does not undergo initiation. He has already been "decontained" by his mother's death, which makes the reenactment of his maternal separation both impossible and redundant at the initiation itself. Instead, the boy accedes automatically to the prerogatives of male society.

A general sense of maternal investment in male spirit cults is indicated by Wiessner for the *mote* rites that used to accompany the Enga *kepele* cult. Though the historic details are difficult to recover, Wiessner shows that the spirit woman served as a surrogate mother to Enga boys at a time when they were shifting residence from the women's to the men's house. As part of the cult, boys were given "water of life" in ways that verbally and symbolically enacted their weaning from maternal sustenance.

By contrast, the Enga *sangai* and *sandalu* rites, also described by Wiessner, emphasized a maidenly rather than maternal agency. The focus here was on the cultivation of bachelors' sexual attractiveness and marriageability via the attentions of a beautiful young spirit woman. A similar emphasis is evident in the Ipili *omatisia* bachelor cult, described by Biersack. Mythically and ritually, the emphasis in both cults was ultimately on enabling rather than preventing sexual relations with women. In the Enga *sangai*, real women became the most important viewers in a social as well as theatrical sense at the culmination of the cult. At one level, the final presentation of bachelors provided a key occasion for women to evaluate the attractiveness of prospective husbands. Beyond this, Enga women could become quite aggressive and demand access to or even besiege the man of their choice. Boyfriends could be pulled out of line by girls singing bawdy songs, and, as mentioned above, competing groups of girls might strip the bachelors of their decorations (Wiessner, this volume). According to Wiessner, male elders tolerated this activity in part because Enga women played such an active and important role supporting men's initiatives in *tee* ceremonial exchanges.

Finally among the Enga is the wonderful contrast drawn by Wiessner between the bachelor cult, which fell into gradual decline, and the ensuing spirit woman cult for married men. In this latter case, the spiritual image of womanhood was neither maternal nor sexual but rather supplied a second wife who came to senior men as a spiritual bride, maintained her virginity, and aided men with health, fertility, and wealth. As such, the spirit woman brought "all the benefits of a second wife to families without generating sexual jealousy" (Wiessner, this volume). As Wiessner suggests, the overall historical emphasis in Engan spirit woman cults shifts over time from *mote*, primarily for boys, to *sangai*, primarily for bachelors, to the adult spirit woman cult, which is primarily for adult men. This change reflects a difference not only in male roles but in the capacities of femaleness as well—from a focus on images of spiritual motherhood to those of a sexually alluring first wife and then to a spiritual second wife as domestic helpmate.

More generally, the chapters of the present volume, even as they document only a tiny fraction of male cults and initiations in Melanesia, nonetheless reflect a wide range of spiritual emphases that foreground different phases of women's sexual and reproductive experience in male rites. In various societies, these male rites include an emphasis on:

- pregnancy and birth (Ankave initiation)
- "afterbirth" and decontainment (Kamea initiation)
- breastfeeding (Sambia initiation)
- weaning and motherhood generally (Enga *mote* cult, Ömie *ujawe* cult)

- maidenly sexuality and first marriage (Enga *sangai/sandalu* cult; Ipili *omatisia* cult)
- woman as second wife and domestic helper (Engan spirit woman cult).

Certainly these emphases are not discrete; crosscutting features combine female relations and capacities in many of these cults. But it is striking how these rituals collectively portray the depth and importance of the female life cycle in a panoply of different male cults and initiations. These symbolic and cosmological emphases relate obviously to the active role that women play as social actors in the cult activities themselves. Gilbert Herdt's chapter effectively illustrates how, in a single society, women take on a number of important social and cultural positions in initiation rites. In addition to being the ultimate audience of the boys' ritual transformation, Sambia women enact and symbolize key generative and reproductive aspects of ritual transformation. They also act as female ritual "guardians" of the boys, and they give them decorative items. At other times in the rites, Sambia women protest the harsh treatment of boy initiands by orchestrating acts of open defiance and ritual rebellion. Finally, women themselves take on the moral pedagogy of teaching and scolding the boys, assuming a morally authoritative voice that men otherwise seldom allow them. In all these respects, Sambia women play an active part in male initiation rites and, in the process, enact their own liminality and life cycle transformation from individual caregivers to older women who collectively support the moral probity of the community. Herdt notes that his own previous writings on Sambia initiation implicitly backgrounded these features of female participation and transformation, even though it remains true, as he also emphasizes, that women are barred from the secret activities of the rites and play a diminishing role in the initiation sequence after its first stage.

Herdt's account, along with the others in this volume, fundamentally recasts what was previously considered to be a general belief in female pollution that polarized men and women in Melanesian male cults and initiations. As against this, the chapters suggest that women's management of pollution is an important, productive, and in some ways prestigious dimension of womanhood that is highlighted in the success of their child-raising and in the success of the initiation rites, including the successful and nondestructive participation of women in cult proceedings themselves. This point emerges with particular strength in Biersack's account of the Ipili *omatisia* cult. The kind of relational work that women undertake as part of male cults underscores how the potentially adverse relation between female and male bodily substances is effectively managed by women themselves to be ultimately beneficial and productive rather than inimical to the growth and health of men—and women.

Initiation for Whom?

Women's relationship to male novices, bachelors, and adult men in Melanesian rituals and cults begs a crucial question: Who, indeed, is being "initiated"? Given that the initiation of women was for many years backgrounded in Melanesian anthropology (e.g, Allen 1967; contrast Lutkehaus and Roscoe 1995), we may ask if women's life transformations have also been underemphasized in those initiation cults that have been anthropologically designated as male. Is it ultimately only male youths who are initiated in so-called "male cults"? Here we are pushed to examine assumptions encoded in notions of "male cult" and "male initiation." These concepts easily assume the autonomy and separability of individuals and that individualized sex-role identity is the defining feature of adult personhood. That these are more than semantic issues is illustrated in the biases of my own previous perception concerning initiation rituals among Gebusi.

Gebusi Initiation: Male or Female?

For more than a year during 1980–81, the Gebusi who we resided with at Yibihilu staged a complete set of rites and festivities that constituted what I, at the time, considered to be an archetypal male initiation (Knauft 2004, chap. 6). These activities included, in rough order

- rites in the men's exclusive section of the longhouse at which the teenage initiands had their ears pierced
- male narratives (*gisagum*) that foregrounded the debilitating effects and catastrophic consequences of uninitiated men having sex with women
- homosexual insemination of male initiands (aged about fourteen-nineteen) by the older grade of young men during the course of spirit seances, feasts, and during a prolonged period of male exclusion and self-sufficiency in the forest, during which men hunted game and processed and cooked their own sago
- feasts and ritual dances to celebrate various stages of food accumulation— accompanied by sequenced presentation of special costume elements to the male initiands
- decorative body painting and display of male initiands in yellow-striped "transitional" costumes at major feasts
- the tying of heavy, wet bark wigs to the scalps of the yellow-clad male initiands, who were forced to wear these painful wigs while doing domestic tasks in subservience to adult men
- the establishment of lifelong relations of "initiate sponsor" (*tor*) between initiands and those in the community who constructed and gave them decorative items for their climactic red bird-of-paradise initiation costuming

- harangues of the male initiands by senior men, who sternly enjoined them to never have sex with other men's wives, never steal from gardens, and be helpful to allies, initiate sponsors, and extended relatives
- generous hospitality by initiands to a large number of intercommunity male visitors, who were hosted with liberal gifts of tobacco smoke, drinking water, and, especially, cooked starch and meat.
- decoration of the male initiands in their final red bird-of-paradise costumes, supervised by their male initiate sponsors in the forest
- transmission to the initiands of men's secret and often bawdy metaphors and terminology associated with sexuality
- a culminating set of intercommunity feasts during which the pigs of the host community were killed and cooked for distribution on behalf of the male initiands
- public presentation of the male initiates to women, children, and an assembled intercommunity audience during several days of lavish feasting, at which the initiates themselves, despite being the center of constant attention, obeyed strict taboos against speaking, sleeping, and eating or drinking more than tiny amounts of food or water.

My perception of male preeminence at the various stages of this initiation sequence was complemented by the observations and remarks of my wife and fellow fieldworker, Eileen Cantrell Knauft, concerning the role of women in various phases of the ceremonial preparations and activities. At the time, however, the role of women seemed to me decidedly peripheral—a "shadow effect" of the general spirit of male camaraderie, male display, male costuming, and intense male sociality that was refracted, as if secondarily, onto women. This general but unexamined perception stayed with me for many years. It persisted, indeed, until I began to reexamine my fieldnotes and to consult Eileen's extensive photographs for a presentation on the significance of women in Gebusi male ritual for a panel organized on this topic in 1998 by Bonnemère and Herdt at the ASAO meetings in Pensacola, Florida.[6] It quickly became clear to me that my initial perception had been myopic. Gebusi women had been involved at numerous levels in the so-called male initiation. Their involvement included not just extensive labor in sago-gathering and pig-raising for the initiation feasts, but an important role in making parts of the initiation costumes. In this capacity, women as well as men were proclaimed to be "sponsors" (tor) of the initiates. Though I had taken only passing note of it at the time, photographs and my conversations with Eileen reminded me that two young unmarried women of the same teenage cohort as the six male initiands had also been painted in yellow striping in the transitional costume phase of the initiation—a clear analogue to the costuming of the male initiands. Extremely similar to them in appearance, these women danced alongside the male novices when visitors entered the host village.[7]

Yet more striking, selected unmarried women were later painted and decorated in a manner highly similar to the male initiates' climactic red bird-of-paradise costuming. This costuming was replete with forehead-to-toe red ochre body paint, a black eye-band outlined in white, a large red bird-of-paradise headdress, and numerous other accouterments. Not all costume elements were identical between the young women and their male counterparts. The male decoration was slightly more elaborate; it included a greater number of woven chestbands, a shell slab (*gor*) worn over the sternum, a bark girdle/waistband, a cassowary bone dagger, and elaborately carved bows and arrows. The costuming and display of the male initiands was also accompanied by more social energy and attention—shouting, celebration, *wa*-cries, and general social festivity—than those of the women. But the young women's costumes were splendid in their own right and were very much like those of the young men in general appearance. The decorated young women were also the subject of male flirtation and of excited positive commentary by men and women. Having focused my attention on the men, however, I had asked few questions about how women had been decorated or how they had been received by their female kin and friends.

Only the male initiands lined up to receive bows and arrows and other gifts during the initiation's climactic night-long celebration, at which these young men were also subject to final harangues. At dawn, however, young initiates and their similarly decorated female counterparts lined up collectively in the central space outside the main longhouse. They each linked their baby fingers to the male or female initiand standing on either side of them. There, in a uniform line, the six male initiands and two young women bobbed up and down in a unison dance-step. Still in a linked line, they then stopped and were collectively approached and formally exhorted by an active older woman in the village to take care of the village's younger cohort of children. She then called out to each of them, male and female, the name of a child in the community that he or she should befriend and help to adulthood in the years ahead. This final act of nominating the next age-grade of male and female initiands concluded the formal proceedings of the Gebusi initiation.

In the aftermath of the ceremonies, the festivities continued for several more nights. At these, the newly initiated men danced for the first time with drums and with the traditional dance headdress spray of egret feathers, which was arrayed atop the rest of their red bird-of-paradise initiation costume. The similarly costumed young women—minus drums and egret features, but holding small phallic-shaped rattles—also danced, sometimes in one-on-one pairs with the male initiates. This was the only occasion in traditional Gebusi society at which women danced in the longhouse—and in tandem with specific men. Together, the young women and men danced in the long corridor of the longhouse that is normally the male-exclusive sleeping section. This dancing was the most highly charged and festively erotic occasion of Gebusi public life during our two years of fieldwork, and it was accompanied by a great outpouring of sexual joking and male-female flirtation. After several more days, by which time when even the closest visiting relatives had left, daily life in the village drifted slowly back to normal.

Though I had initially cast all these events as a "male initiation," it is obvious in retrospect that they celebrated the fertility, growth, and readiness-for-marriage of young women as well as men (cf. Whitehead 1986). It could of course be countered that the events focused predominant ritual and ceremonial attention on the young men. It was the young men who were the exclusive focus of attention in many of the preparatory rites, it was they who received male secrets, and it was in their name that the pigs of the village were killed and distributed. Their initiate-sponsor relations were much more extensive and intensive than those of young women, and the sponsors supplied the young men many more gifts and decorations for their costumes, which were more elaborate and publicly foregrounded than those of the women. The young men had been inseminated by the older cohort of men to facilitate their masculine growth, while, as Eileen substantiated, there were no parallel sexual or growth-enhancing activities for young women. Finally, the costumed participation of young women in the final ceremonies was neither obligatory nor uniform; some young women opted to be decorated and stand with the initiates while others did not. This choice appears to have been made on an individual and relatively spontaneous basis, depending on the women's desire—or embarrassment—to be presented alongside their male counterparts for public viewing.

Notwithstanding its wider masculine inclusion and greater emphasis on male ceremonialism, the Gebusi initiation included women not just as supporters but as central performers, especially in its final public displays. The allure of the decorated young women alongside the initiates was much commented on, as was their dancing in the longhouse. Though not as elaborately decorated as the young men, the female initiands received costume elements and "sponsorship" relations with women in the community. They were clearly linked as a collectivity with the male initiates at both the penultimate and final events of the initiation. The formal presentation of the young women in almost identical costuming with the young men, physically linked to them during the initiation's final rite, clearly celebrated the growth, vitality, and marriageability of young women as well the young men. This conclusion is underscored by the Gebusi term for the initiation itself. What I had been calling "male initiation" was actually *wa kawala*, which translates literally as "child become big." Though the unmarked referent of *wa* is more commonly a male child, it refers more generically to male and female children collectively.[8]

In short, a significant case could be made—on a number of grounds—that the Gebusi rites are a simultaneous initiation, in different ways, of both young women and young men. Certainly the occasion was a significant rite of passage for young Gebusi women as well as bachelors. Each initiate wore on his or her body the costume elements given by a range of relatives. As the largest event of indigenous Gebusi society, the initiation brought Gebusi from diverse settlements together on an unprecedented scale. Ultimately, the rites symbolized and celebrated the growth and vitality of Gebusi society as a whole, including the maturation and adulthood of both young women and young men.

Though I did not at the time actively deny the significance of Gebusi women in the initiation, neither did I did fully appreciate or foreground their importance. In retrospect, my selective understanding had several sources. As a young male anthropologist, my spontaneous focus of interest and association was with young Gebusi men. Their activities and the festivities that surrounded them swept me up—just as they did the other men and male visitors. Furthermore, the intellectual process of understanding the ritual sequence led me as if naturally to consider Gebusi rites comparatively against the male initiations and bachelor cults I knew from the ethnographic literature on Melanesia that was available at the time. In the process, I left aside the fascinating possibility that a Gebusi initiation that included extreme masculine bonding and homosexual insemination served simultaneously to initiate young women of a similar age-grade (see similarly for the Marind-Anim of south New Guinea; van Baal 1966).

Women in the Ritual Future

A bittersweet feature of the present volume, I think, is that our increased awareness of women's importance in Melanesian "male" cults and initiations emerges at the same time that our ability to document them in their earlier guises is increasingly compromised. In most areas of Melanesia, cult and initiation practices that were robust during the early colonial period have either become moribund or been dramatically transformed. Given the masculinist bias in earlier documentation, it is easy for the role that women have taken in these rituals to be effaced in our understanding. By contrast, one is reminded of Annette Weiner's opening to *Women of Value, Men of Renown* (1976), in which she describes her amazement not only at Trobriand women's ritual exchanges but at the almost complete neglect of these activities in Malinowski's otherwise exhaustive ethnography of Trobriand society and culture.

Beyond retrospective neglect, we also face the possibility that remembered accounts of Melanesian ritual may further downplay the significance of women. As Bonnemère notes in her Introduction, women's ritual engagements are often difficult to recover through subsequent inquiry. In the minds of many Melanesian informants—in addition to lingering ethnographer bias—the ritual activities of women are not as worth recounting as those of men. This is a problem that Rohatynskyj's contribution to this volume confronts. This gendered bias articulates with gendered structure of narrative memory and the reinforced sense during the colonial era that the activities and accounts of men constituted the most important dimensions of local history. And yet, the contribution of Wiessner in the present volume attunes us to the possibilities that ethnohistorical research can nevertheless afford.

Complementing the significance of women in the ritual past of Melanesia is their changing role in the self-conscious traditions of the Melanesian present. In significant parts of Melanesia, there appears to be an increasing sense that "traditionalizing" images of women as bare-breasted, beautifully decorated, and sexually evocative are either anachronistic or immoral. This perception dovetails in many areas with increasing emphasis on Christian morality and contemporary female propriety. More generally, aspirations for a more economically successful and locally modern style of life easily articulate with emphasis on male economic agency, on the one hand, and the importance of women as markers of morality and propriety, on the other (see Knauft 1999, chap. 5).

Among Gebusi in 1998, only a few remote villages still practiced initiations. But among those that did, features of "male initiation" had largely subsumed the ritual role traditionally taken by young Gebusi women. Young women were too embarrassed to appear bare-breasted or to dance in traditional costuming. Instead, they blended with the audience and attired themselves in whatever combination of bras, blouses, and Western-style dresses they could obtain. By contrast, the young male initiands were festooned in costumes identical to those of 1981. Nor did the young women line up with the male initiands in the final celebrations or presentations. That female dancing that did occur was undertaken by older senior women, whose tepid performances amounted to a folkloric icon of previous customs. In 1981, dancing by old women would have been considered the antithesis rather than the presentation of female sexuality. As part of these changes, the sexual joking of the climactic celebrations was muted, particularly between men and women.[9] In general, the onus of modern sexual propriety in the public display of contemporary Gebusi initiations weighs more heavily on young women than on young men. This change has directly influenced the style and degree of young women's ritual participation. Indeed, in the absence of first-hand information from 1981, I would have had little sense in 1998 that young women had traditionally participated in their own rite of initiatory passage (see Knauft 2002a, 2002b, chap. 8). Given the general trajectories of gendered change and cultural development in contemporary Melanesia (Knauft 1997b), it is likely that analogous patterns are present across a range of Melanesian societies.

Though the so-called traditional role of women and men is being transformed in the public cultural displays of contemporary Melanesia, this does not necessarily mean that femaleness or the presence of women is becoming less important in a larger sense. Nowadays, what is ethnographically "unseen" in the study of Melanesian ritual is the relationship of femaleness to modern rites of passage that mark the social transition to adulthood for many Melanesian men. These modern rites of passage include the search for wage labor, periods of out-migration to cities or town, and separation from one's home community during periods of advanced schooling or training. In many cases, these rites of modernity also include periods of intense male camaraderie and conflict punctuated by alcoholic binges, gambling, sexual experimentation with prostitutes, or the criminal activity of being a raskol. Though in some cases these periods of disjunction from village life become permanent for men, in many others they are a life-cycle stage of early adulthood that later ushers in the process of becoming an adult or senior man back in a small town or village.

Such patterns are highly variable, and it is important to avoid disparaging stereotypes of young men's behavior in Melanesia—just as it is for young men in the underclass of Western societies. The larger point is that the contemporary transition to adulthood in Melanesia can be looked at with fresh lenses that include rather than neglect the public presentation of relations between men and women as well as the articulation between more traditional and more contemporary notions of masculinity and femininity. In the same way that women figured importantly in traditional male initiations, even when they were "excluded," so, too, the image of femaleness and the presence of women are centrally important in rites of social transition to adulthood as currently experienced by Melanesian men and women under conditions of wage labor and economic migration.

As notions of development and economic striving are often associated preeminently with men and masculinity in Melanesia, values of morality and sexual propriety are often culturally emphasized for women (see Knauft 1997b). This gendered association often draws Melanesian women to the contemporary ritual of Christian churches.[10] Though men are often if not typically the leaders of Melanesian Christian churches, women form a major part if not a significant majority of most congregations—in partial contrast to their exclusion from many traditional cult practices that were associated with men and masculinity. As a missionary from the southern highlands once told me, "Men have business (bisnis), but women have church (lotu)." In some cases, a dominant emphasis on Christian adherence among women and on bisnis enterprise among men can be alternative ways for women and men to be initiated into a modern Melanesian world, with a dominant emphasis on spirituality, on one hand, and on economic acquisition, on the other. Such developments draw upon prior notions of Melanesian relationality and life-cycle transition but inflect them in decidedly new ways and with new parameters of dominance and inequity.

In analytic terms, a concern with Melanesian forms of relationality can articulate with contemporary features of gendered sociality that engage activities and institutions associated with church, market, business, criminality, government, and so on. The chapters of the current volume pave the way for this understanding by revealing the key and longstanding significance of women and of femaleness in Melanesian male cults and initiations. One does not have to dig too deeply, at least in my own case, to see how received academic assumptions about male cults and initiations have short-shrifted our received understandings in just this respect.

Notes

Introduction. The Presence of Women in New Guinea Secret Male Rituals: From Ritual Space to Ritual Process

I would like to express my gratitude to the anonymous reviewer appointed by first the University of Michigan Press and then the University of Pennsylvania Press, who made very valuable comments at two stages in the course of the revision of this introduction. I would also like to warmly thank Chris Ballard, Bruce Knauft, Polly Wiessner, Margaret Jolly, and Nora Scott for helping me at various stages during the elaboration and writing of this introductory essay. Last of all, the Centre de Recherche et de Documentation sur l'Océanie (CNRS—Université de Provence—EHESS) has kindly paid for the translation of this introduction.

1. See Beidelman (1997: 143) and La Fontaine (1985: 124) for Africa; Hugh-Jones (1979: 77, 96) for Amazonia; Myers (1986: 151–52) and Engelhart (1998) for Australia.

2. In his book on Oceanic art, Nicholas Thomas gives a similar explanation of the neglect, in studies on Oceanic artworks, of the objects produced by women (1995: 115–16).

3. Note that the same is true of female rituals, since the first comparative work devoted specifically to ceremonies organized for girls in New Guinea appeared only recently (Lutkehaus and Roscoe 1995), reflecting the predominance of a representation in which the cultural importance of a ceremony is measured by the collective investment it entails (xiv).

4. Here is what Sørum has to say about women's participation in Bedamini male initiations: "From a sociological point of view, our task must be to delimit the relationship between the novices and the women who participate, and to explicate the role of women in male initiation in terms of their own action." Then he goes on by briefly listing the key points of female participation and noting which category of women (M, MZ, FBw, MBD) is concerned in which activity (1982: 59).

5. In a comparative paper on fertility cultism in New Guinea, Whitehead also addresses the issue of "the degree to which women—in real life not just in concept—participate in the ritual construction and manipulation of fertility" (1986a: 85). But the examples she gives of such participation come from south-coastal fertility cults rather than so-called secret male cults.

6. This ambivalence is not peculiar to menstrual blood: semen is considered by some groups to be both a substance that nourishes the fetus and a potential vehicle for female sorcery (Bonnemère 1990: 108–9).

7. With the notable exception of Harriet Whitehead's 1986 articles, which can be seen as a continuation of the thesis set out by Michael Allen in his book twenty years earlier.

8. Note that these symbolic associations are not always formulated by the participants (Lewis 1980: 106; Tuzin 1980: 236), since the meaning of the ritual actions and objects rarely attains the conscious level in most informants (see, e.g., Bonnemère 2002: 208–10).

9. For a discussion of the contrasting systems of representations of personhood in the West and in Melanesia, see LiPuma (1998).

10. In *The Making of Great Men*, Maurice Godelier undertakes a de facto comparison of the societies practicing different rituals (male initiations and spirit cults), but he does this from the standpoint of forms of male power and inequality (1986, chap. 8) rather than from that of male ritual. In a later article (1991), he devotes more space to the subject, analyzing in particular the Duna *palena* cult.

11. Still, Donald Tuzin describes Ilahita Arapesh women taking part in collective dances (1980: 227–30) and considers them to be indispensable as spectators: "Women are rigidly excluded from membership per se; however, it must be said that, in addition to producing and preparing food for the cult feasts and providing men with the leisure time needed to pursue cult activities, women perform the residual but essential roles of outsider and spectator—without which a good deal of what goes on within the cult would be meaningless" (26). In his article on the role of women in the male cults of the Soromaja of West Papua, Oosterwal expresses the same idea when he says: "It is the women who through their exclusion, fulfill the role of the true believers and who thereby make the rituals real" (1976: 333).

We find another example of the presence of women in some male ritual activities among the Asmat of West Papua (formerly Irian Jaya). There, women played an essential role in the rite of the "sacred children," performed in the context of various rituals intended to reestablish good relations between previously hostile groups. During the ceremony, "one side took the initiative to have some members of the other side ritually reborn as members of the (most important) men's house involved in the conflict" (Jaarsma 1993: 27). The "future mother" and her younger sisters stood with their legs apart in front of the birthing house built for the occasion, and "the 'children' now crawled belly-down through the legs of the women from within the birth dwelling. Upon leaving the dwelling, two old men established their sex and announced the new-born to the village" (Jaarsma 1993: 27 using Zegwaard 1955).

Last, early ethnographic work conducted in West Papua documents the use of female sexual substances in fertility rites performed during what were tantamount to veritable "orgies" (see Knauft 1993: 51–55; Lemonnier 1993b: 132, 151 n. 12; Oosterwal 1976: 325–26).

12. This situation also prevents us from raising the important question whether all categories of women—and men—have similar perspectives on the rituals and their objectives. From my own experience, I would say that this is the case, but one cannot be sure for other ethnographical settings. In any case, given the abandonment of male rituals, it is now probably too late to expect answers to such a question, which certainly would have enriched the analysis of women's participation in male rituals undertaken in this volume.

13. In any case, we all know that ethnographic studies, even ones including direct observation of rituals, depend on the good will of the informants; furthermore, the information gathered can never be claimed to be exhaustive. So whatever the conditions in which the different materials were collected, comparison of central elements in Anga and Ömie rituals remains possible.

14. Such an interpretation is far from being restricted to New Guinea; it has also, for example, been put forward to account for the unfolding of the male rituals among the Gisu of western Uganda (Heald 1999: 57–58).

15. Author's emphasis. Note that I do not here go into the complexities of Marilyn Strathern's argument but merely refer to some of her basic propositions.

16. Herdt's contribution eloquently demonstrates that some men could indeed be "proxies," or even represent female characters (Bateson 1958: 75–76), just as women can take on male attributes (A. Weiner 1982: 59).

17. This is different from the Baruya and Sambia situations, where the ritual performed for girls when they reach puberty is perfectly distinct from the male initiations (see Lemonnier, this volume).

18. I won't go into the discussion of the reasons why they cannot do so, but it probably has to do with local systems of ideas about female pollution.

19. It is interesting in this respect to recall that the flute is used in teaching fellatio (Herdt 1981: 233), a nurturing act that can be assimilated to symbolic breastfeeding (Herdt 1981: 234–35; Bonnemère, this volume).

Chapter 1. Sambia Women's Positionality and Men's Rituals

1. For background, see Bonnemère, Introduction, this volume, Mead (1935), Keesing (1982), Read (1954), M. Strathern (1988, reviewed in Gillison 1993: 10ff, especially her discussion of women's myth as a "public currency"), Herdt and Poole (1982), Herdt (1982).

2. See Herdt (1999a) for a critical appraisal and appreciation of Godelier's work on this subject.

3. I am limited to what I can do in this chapter; I will not be able to explore how women create for themselves a coherent understanding of these events, that is, their narration of the events. However, I will explore the distinction between what can be said in public and what is regarded as sanctioned secrecy on the part of the men, the difference between ritual practices that are seen and unseen (ritual insemination, hidden from women), versus the ceremonial activities and decorations of women in public.

4. I thus mean by positionality what Victor Turner (1967a) called "positionality" (the occurrence of the symbol in events) and "structure" (the form and traits of the symbol) in the meaning of a sign-symbol in the structure of ritual events, as opposed to its exegetic and structural dimensions.

5. Incest rules apply here, as in heterosexual relationships: all sex is forbidden vis-à-vis all kinsmen (matrilateral and patrilateral), as well as with one's agemates and ritual sponsor, but affines, like one's brother-in-law, are appropriate homosexual partners (see Layard 1959). Older bachelors may never serve as fellators (except in the unusual case of their being prematurely initiated, and therefore immature, in which case they may suck the penises of older youth), nor may younger ones be fellated by their seniors.

6. Proverbially men say that women are "agemates" of cassowaries (see Herdt 1981, chap. 5), as elsewhere in New Guinea females are mythological cassowaries in origin.

7. Among these desired goods are vegetal salt (*ntalu*), signified by a cordyline leaf; eel, signified by native spinach leaves (eaten with eel); possum, signified by *chembukeinyu* (New Guinea impatiens), a major presentation in the marriage ceremony; and today canned fish, signified by the label from a can of mackerel.

8. Because many of these women are potentially marriageable affines (*nenyalt-miangu*), personal pronouns must be substituted to conform to the name taboo for them.

9. These events are beautifully captured in the 1994 BBC film *Guardians of the Flutes*,

where the boys are filmed with their mothers and subsequent narratives capture the flavor of people's subjectivity at the time.

Chapter 2. Embodiments of Detachment: Engendering Agency in the Highlands of Papua New Guinea

I would like to acknowledge the help of many people who have read drafts of this paper in its former incarnations. These include Roy Wagner, Susan McKinnon, Fred Damon, Margaret Huber, Joel Robbins, Bruce Koplin, Margo Smith, Rebecca Popenoe, Peter Metcalf, Paul Letkemann, Pascale Bonnemère, Andrew Strathern, Michael Lambek, Eric Silverman, and Lori Beaman. All have provided me with useful commentary that has helped to clarify my interpretations of the data presented in this text. Any deficiencies in interpretation, of course, remain my own.

Fieldwork among the Kamea was undertaken between August 1989 and February 1992. I gratefully acknowledge the Social Sciences and Humanities Research Council of Canada and the Wenner-Gren Foundation for Anthropological Research, whose financial support made this work possible.

1. See Bonnemère's Introduction to this volume for an elucidating account of how this model of "sexual antagonism" has influenced anthropological accounts of male initiation in Papua New Guinea.

2. The term "Kamea" is an administrative designation only and goes wholly unrecognized by the local people themselves. Government officers use the term to refer to those speakers of the Kapau language who reside in Gulf Province and are administered from the district office at Kaintiba. Another 23,000 Kapau-speakers reside across the provincial border in Morobe Province.

3. More recently, several other ethnographic studies have also been undertaken of Anga peoples. Jadran Mimica (1981, 1988) conducted research with Yagwoia-speakers during the late 1970s, while Pascale Bonnemère (1996, 1998b, 2001) and Pierre Lemonnier (1991) studied Ankave peoples during the 1980s. For further information on Anga peoples, see also Blackwood (1939a, b, 1940, 1978), Fischer (1968), Simpson (1953), Sinclair (1966), McCarthy (1964).

4. See Bonnemère (1996, 1998b) for a more detailed comparative discussion of Anga peoples.

5. As throughout much of Papua New Guinea, this was brought about as a consequence of colonial rule.

6. The same holds true of Ankave-speakers, suggesting that an important contrast exists between the ritual practices of northern and southern Angans.

7. The warfare function has lapsed since the government brought an end to fighting in the 1960s. I shall return to this point at the end of the chapter.

8. Here I follow the lead of Collier and Yanagisako (1987) who have argued that gender and kinship cannot be treated as separate analytical domains. As we shall see, grasping Kamea notions of relatedness is a necessary step in understanding how they imagine the elicitation of gendered agency.

9. A fairly common occurrence, given that polygyny is frequent.

10. One man likened the smell of these animals to human feces.

11. Here, I follow Lambek (1992: 248), who writes: "If the semantic content of the taboo elaborates who or what one is not, it is the practice of the taboo that substantiates who one is."

12. Indeed, the tabooed food items should not even be cooked together in the same

container as other food in that the smell of the interdicted game would spoil what was otherwise acceptable food.

13. Prior to being initiated, a young boy is said to be "female-like" (see Herdt 1981, 1987b; Godelier 1986). Indeed, he continues to wear the style of grass skirt that is characteristic of women. As we shall see, it is only through participation in the men's cult that a masculinized form of being is created. At initiation, the previously conjoined identity of the mother and son is disarticulated, thereby marking the point at which gender is created (see M. Strathern 1993).

14. This represents an interesting contrast to the eating behavior of Ankave women as described by Bonnemère (1998b). Among the Ankave, pregnant women are encouraged to eat certain food items (including the fruit of the pandanus tree) on the assumption that such items will contribute to the formation of blood (maternal substance) within the child's body. For the Kamea, by contrast, pregnancy is not imagined as a nourishing-and-sharing of substance between the expectant mother and fetus. Kamea women do not share substance with their offspring. The dietary restrictions that a Kamea woman undertakes during pregnancy are not believed to contribute to the growth or well-being of her fetus. Instead, they are intended to affect the process of childbirth—the ease with which a child can be "de-contained."

15. Menstrual blood and birth fluids are seen to be particularly dangerous to men.

16. See Bamford forthcoming.

17. Elsewhere, I discuss the social and symbolic significance of this tree in greater detail. See, for example, Bamford (1997, 1998b).

18. This taboo applies to all women, not simply the mothers of boys.

19. By this, the Kamea mean that the sore would not heal—it would remain perpetually infected. Eventually, the skin of the nasal septum would rot completely away.

20. Men may or may not have an accurate perception here. Certainly, no woman ever admitted to me that she had handled the bullroarers. At the same time, however, this may be a "publicly acknowledged" secret—known by all but admitted by none.

21. Initiates will have heard the bullroarers cry before, but this is the first time when they will be publicly presented to them.

22. It is significant that the *mautwa* are seen as being the epitome of masculine identity—they signify male virility, potency, strength, and reproductive potential. The slang word for penis is *mautwa*, which is seen to stand as an antonym for the term *panga*, or vagina.

23. Space prevents me from pursuing this point in depth, but it is significant that young girls acquire their "containing" capabilities in a process that emerges in tandem with the engenderment of young boys. We have seen that boys must adhere to numerous food taboos—particularly those concerning the consumption of "smelly" game—prior to being initiated. It is significant that these same items of interdicted game are fed to young girls in copious quantities while they are growing up. The Kamea practice infant betrothal. Second-degree cross-cousins (on either the mother's or father's side) are the preferred category of spouse. An important constituent of Kamea bridewealth prestations is game that has been collected on land belonging to the groom and his family. These items are presented directly to the mother of the bride, who is expected to feed them to her daughter in plentiful amounts. Hence, a distinction emerges early on between the eating patterns of "one-blood" siblings. Items that are taboo to a boy are fed to his sister in abundant quantities. By consuming this foodstuff (quite literally being grown on it) a girl's body comes to contain items that have been produced on the land of her husband-to-be, just as she will later contain her husband's semen and finally, any offspring that the marriage produces. A woman's capacity to act as a "container" is drawn out through these payments. Bridewealth becomes the compelling force that

genderizes the female half of the "one-blood" tie. For those readers who are interested, this point is taken up in greater detail elsewhere. See Bamford (1996, 1997, 1998a, b).

24. When I first arrived at Titamnga, I repeatedly queried my consultants concerning the origin of substances, such as blood, within the body. For the most part, this line of inquiry generated (pardon the pun) substantial confusion. A few people speculated that while the child developed within a woman's womb, its sole source of blood was its mother. An equal number of persons, however, suggested that blood resulted from the unification of male and female substances in utero ("I acquired my blood from both my mother and my father"). By far the majority of people with whom I spoke, however, opined that the question I was asking was nonsensical from the outset. The "blood" of a baby is said to be completely different from that of an adult. Children are born with "yellow" blood—their blood does not turn "red" until they begin to ingest solid foods like sweet potatoes, pumpkin, pig, and the like. A mother's milk, I was told, only helps satisfy hunger: it does not result in the production of substance within the body. Significantly, then, the Kamea, unlike many other Melanesians, do not operate with a "blood"/"bones" ideology—the idea that both parents contribute equally but differently to the creation of a child—resulting in different kinds of social relationships that have to be negotiated after birth.

25. This includes the taboo against "smelly" game.

26. Elsewhere, I take up the question of how female gender is elicited. See Bamford (1997, 1998b) for further details.

27. I hasten to reiterate that the situation would have been different prior to the prohibition of warfare. Until the 1960s and the founding of the government station at Kaintiba, all boys were initiated regardless of whether their mother lived or not. As we have seen, promoting strength was seen to be necessary in creating an effective warrior.

Chapter 3. When Women Enter the Picture: Looking at Anga Initiations from the Mothers' Angle

I would like to thank all the participants in the two ASAO sessions on "Women in Male Rituals of New Guinea" (at Pensacola in 1998 and Hilo in 1999) during which earlier versions of the present work were presented, as well as Chris Ballard, Michael Houseman, Bernard Juillerat, Marika Moisseeff, Marilyn Strathern, and Harvey Whitehouse for their readings of a previous and much different draft. Special thanks go to Pierre Lemonnier who made helpful comments on the more recent version. Any shortcomings are of course my own.

I would also like to thank the Maison des Sciences de l'Homme, the Ministère des Affaires Etrangères, the National Geographic Society, the Fondation Fyssen, and the CNRS (GDR116 and CREDO), which have all enabled me to carry out fieldwork among the Ankave-Anga since 1987. Research would not have been possible without the warm welcome and help of the Papua New Guinea Medical Research.

1. See the Introduction for some details of male rituals.

2. Although the Pax Australiana was established among the Angans in the 1960s or 1970s, according to the groups concerned, the warrior ethos is still very present in the discourse and practices of the Ankave (and in those of the three northern Anga groups mentioned previously, at least in the 1970s and 1980s when the bulk of the anthropological work was done).

3. The analysis of Ankave male initiations is still in progress; in the present chapter, only the women's involvement is emphasized.

4. The following analysis is based on the rich material gathered among the Ankave by Pierre Lemonnier between 1987 and 1998, as well as on my own observations among the women of this group during the 1994 initiations. Here we should add that agents of Christianity have variably entered the Anga area. While people from Menyamya have been subjected to Lutheran influence since the 1960s, no pastor or evangelist has ever spent more than eighteen months in the Mbwei valley. What we can quite reasonably say is that the Baruya rituals witnessed by Maurice Godelier at the end of the 1960s and the Sambia ones attended by Gilbert Herdt in the mid-1970s are both comparable to what Pierre Lemonnier and I saw twenty years later among the Ankave.

5. If I have chosen to reveal practices rather than conceal them, it is mainly because of the oldest Ankaves' concern that their culture be described as precisely and exhaustively as possible in these times of great potential changes. This being said, I would like the reader to be aware of the secrecy that surrounds some of the ritual actions analyzed here and to respect it.

6. For the role played by the women during these rituals, see Herdt, this volume. The analysis of the ritual acts are based upon data that have been published in earlier work.

7. This information is to be taken with caution. Herdt told me that the body of a woman who has just given birth is cleansed with leaves and herbs, among which possibly may be common nettles. Among the Baruya, Sambia neighbors who in many respects are culturally similar to them, I saw women rubbed with nettles several hours after giving birth.

8. Herdt formulates the same idea in different terms: "Fellatio is likened to maternal breast-feeding" (1981: 234); as does Bruce Knauft: "the use of semen from the adult penis as a 'life force' to grow boys into adulthood is a strong analogue—often explicitly stated in (RH) societies—to the growth of infants through the suckling of mother's breastmilk" (1987: 176).

9. This statement should not be seen as contradictory to the Sambia beliefs about female pollution. A body can simultaneously have powerful self-growing capacities and produce substances inimical to someone else.

10. Male "envy" of feminine sexual physiology is an expression that was first used by Bruno Bettelheim in his analysis of puberty rites (1962 [1954]).

11. In his 1971 paper, Hiatt makes the same remark: "when they [men] secretly 'reproduce' youths as men, thus ritually severing the bond between sons and mothers, they do so on a predominantly female generative model" (1971: 80). Donald Tuzin adds that "this procreative 'message' [of Tambaran ceremonialism] refers to something older than either culture [Abelam, Iatmul or Arapesh], anterior to their respective visual and narrative styles, and deeply rooted in the psyche" (1995: 293). Others "claim for pseudo-procreative theory a certain respect for human cognition and its embeddedness in our mammalian heritage" (Shapiro 1996: 12).

12. Besides Godelier's long comments in Ian Dunlop (1992: 8–13), the ethnographic data I use here were communicated to me by Richard Lloyd, a linguist and missionary with the Summer Institute of Linguistics, who has spent nearly thirty years among the Baruya, as well as by Anick Coudart and Pierre Lemonnier, to whom Nunguye Kandavatche and his wife gave crucial information about the behaviors required of the novices' mothers. I warmly thank them all.

13. This is done to keep the sticks, which are full of pollution and dirt, from touching the ground, and more generally to protect the boys from this potential danger.

14. Needless to say, part of the psychological bond between a boy and his mother re-

mains forever, and in that sense there cannot be a total severing of their relations. What I am talking about here are the local representations of what must be made of the mother-son bond for the boys to become adult men.

15. See Hiatt (1971: 88) for Australian Aboriginal peoples.

16. Translated by the author of this chapter.

17. In Tonga too, there exist, according to Françoise Douaire-Marsaudon, different models of human reproduction, one of which she calls *parthenogenetic* (1998: 182).

Chapter 4. *Ujawe*: The Ritual Transformation of Sons and Mothers

I would like to thank all the participants of the "Women in Male Rituals of New Guinea" Session, held at the Annual Meetings of the Association for Social Anthropology in Oceania in Hilo, Hawai'i, in February 1999, for their thought-provoking discussion of many of the issues that bear on this chapter. I especially thank Pascale Bonnemère, Sandra Bamford, Pamela Stewart, and Andrew Strathern for their helpful comments.

Chapter 5. The Bachelors and Their Spirit Wife: Interpreting the *Omatisia* ritual of Porgera and Paiela

I have been inquiring into the *omatisia* ritual for many years. My original fieldwork in the Paiela valley was conducted under a National Science Foundation dissertation grant (1974–78). I resumed fieldwork in Paiela and began fieldwork in the Porgera valley in 1993, with Wenner-Gren Foundation funding. Wenner-Gren as well as Fulbright supported my research in 1995, ending in February 1996. I thank all these institutions and agencies for their support. I also thank Pascale Bonnemère for editorial assistance and Frances Ingemann for access to her Ipili dictionary and for her comments and suggestions. My Paiela hosts—and in particular Luke (né Pakena), Kauwambo, Kongolome, Mata, and Simion (né Toyo)—have been wonderfully forthcoming in our conversations about *omatisia*. Kualata and Koipanda shared with me their knowledge of Porgeran *omatisia* practices. I thank all of them for their information, stimulation, patience, and companionship.

1. Across the span of Ipili (Porgera and Paiela) and Enga clans, the names of the ritual cultigens vary. According to Schwab, east of Birip, among the Laiapu Enga, the word for the plants was *sandalu* (also *tentaru, sadaru*) while west of Birip, among the Mae of the central Enga area, the word was *sanggai* (also *saggai, changai,* and *chainggai*) (1995: 29). In Wiessner and Tumu's spelling, the word is *sangai* (1998). Another word that occurs in the literature is *lepe* (Gibbs 1988, Schwab 1995) or *ita yoko*, bog iris (*Acorus calamus*) (Schwab 1995: 33). Schwab quotes one B. Pori, who, in his "The Sangai and the Bachelor," wrote: "The distinguishing feature between a Sangai Lepe and an ordinary swamp calamus is the colourful stripes in an ordinary cumulus leaf but a special feature in the Sangai Lepe is the special attractiveness of a yellow colour which may force you to blink your eyes and makes them foggy when you see it directly" (1995: 33; see Pori 1978: 76–95). In Porgera the word *sialangai* is used to refer to a striped-leaf plant, one that fits the above description for the *sangai lepe*. Other words for the cultigens that I have heard in the Paiela valley are *kandolopa* (Ingemann 1997: 26) and *pole*—"sweet-flag (Araceae, Acorus)" (Ingemann 1997: 60). In Paiela, adolescent girls had their own plants, which were called *sialangai*. Some of my Porgera informants mentioned planting

two kinds of cultigens, the dark-leafed *omatisia* and the striped-leafed *sialangai*. One woman told me that she cultivated both the *omatisia* and the *sialangai* when she was an adolescent, although in my experience *sialangai* is used more frequently than *omatisia* in women's descriptions of the magical procedures they followed when they were girls. The woman who described planting both cultigens said that the *omatisia* represented the hair while the green-and-yellow-striped leaf *sialangai* represented skin. They were planted as the girl's breasts began to swell to promote her physical maturation. Around the plants a ring of red-leafed cordyline was placed to conceal them and to notify passersby to look away. As with ordinary plants, the girl weeded the plants regularly as she said a spell ("I weed the *sialangai* . . . / The sweet potato garden"). After she finished weeding, she might break off some leaves and place them in her netbag or rub them directly over her skin, reciting a spell that drew an analogy between her own personal growth and the growth of the plants.

Omatisia is the name of the bog iris plant (the plant that I have been shown has a solid, dark green color) that the boys in both the Porgera and Paiela valleys who participated in the ritual cultivated in the hope of growing and beautifying themselves. In the Porgera valley at least, some clans may have cultivated a second plant, one that had a striped rather than a solid-color leaf and that was called *sialangai* (*sialungai* is ginger and is the synonym of *pole*; Ingemann 1997: 63). Adolescent girls, meanwhile, at least in the Paiela valley, grew *sialangai* to nurture their own pubescent transformations (Biersack 1998a).

It should be noted that, due to some misadventures, I have yet to determine the scientific term for *omatisia*. Here I use the term Meggitt uses, bog iris, since his "bog iris" as described appears to be the Ipili *omatisia*. In my first article on the *omatisia* ritual (1982), I identified it as ginger, which is clearly wrong. The use of bamboo tubes is widely reported in the rituals in the Paiela-Porgera area and beyond. According to Schwab's description of eastern Enga rituals: "There are actually two items within the Sandalu ritual: bamboo tubes (*sandalu/sangai penge*) containing fluid, and a plant (*lepe* or *ita yoko*: bog iris: *Acorus calamus*) . . . According to some informants, only the Laiapu have both items, although I got contradicting answers to this. Lacey [in his 1975 thesis] says that the middle zone of Enga from Wapenamanda along the Lai Valley and into part of the Ambum River have the *penge* and *lepe wai*. West and south of the mid-Ambum and around Irelya, they may also have the *penge*, but it plays a minor role compared with that of the *lepe wai*" (1995: 33)

2. The word Ipili is used by linguists to refer to the language spoken in the Porgera and Paiela valleys; Paiela use the word to refer to the people living in the Porgera valley. I use the word here to refer to the indigenous people of the Porgera and Paiela valleys, and with reference to the common language *and* culture that these people share.

3. Among the Duna, in regard to the *palena nane* or boy's growth ritual, Pamela Stewart and Andrew Strathern report: "The ritual expert becomes the spouse to the Female Spirit and does not take a human wife during the time that the Female Spirit remains with him as his help-mate and companion. He instructs the boys during the ritual time when they are enclosed in the *palena anda* (growth house enclosure) in the ways to make them grow. The ritual expert has gained this knowledge from the Female Spirit herself " (Stewart and Strathern 1998: 16). Wiessner and Tumu also identify the female spirit as the spouse of the ritual participants (1998).

4. Father Philip Gibbs, the first to report the presence of a female spirit in the Ipili *omatisia* ritual, was similarly perplexed by the presence and efficacy of the female spirit. As he put it, although a theme of the *umarisia* (in his spelling) ritual was the polluting nature of women and the need to purify young men, the ritual brought young men "into intimate contact with female blood," for it was female blood that was believed to

give men strength and helped men grow in the ritual context (1975: 4). Wiessner and Tumu have noted a similar paradox in regard to the Enga *sanggai*. Even though there were efforts to "purge" initiates' "bodies and senses of all that was considered impure—prior contact with women, female fluids such as breastmilk and menstrual blood" (Wiessner and Tumu 1998: 218), the ritual countenanced "the symbolic marriage of the bachelors to the spirit woman" (Wiessner and Tumu 1998: 217). Of course, other highland ethnographers have reported the presence of a female spirit in the midst of a male cult that is ostensibly gynophobic (M. Strathern 1970; Stewart and Strathern 1998; Stürzenhofecker 1995; Wiessner 1999; see Bonnemère's Introduction).

5. *Kinambuli* refers to married people, male and female, who have failed to produce offspring and to superannuated bachelors and bacheloresses who are also infertile. In the *omatisia* context, *kinambuli* referred to a bachelor who was presumed to be a virgin and who had no children. This is more generally true of Ipili rituals. Those who "carry the knowledge" of the ritual are typically male *kinambulis*. In contrast to adult males and females, those *akali* and *wanda* of the middle zone, *kinambuli* had no standing outside the ritual process, an aspect of Ipili culture that is important in assessing the relevance of Meggitt's analysis, with its emphasis on male fear, to our understanding of the *omatisia* ritual.

6. Much of the Enga reporting on the ritual implies that the water in the tube is "sacred." It is associated with the blood of the female spirit and is introduced into the tubes as sacred water. In all the accounts of the ritual that I have collected, the water seeps into the tubes from the lake itself. Since the swamp is associated with the female spirit, I do not rule out that it may be considered special, even "sacred" water. However, in learning about another ritual, the *mata kamo* ritual of the 1940s, I was specifically told that the water that participants consumed was special "sky water" (*tawe ipa*; Biersack 1996), a term that has not been used in describing water in the bamboo tubes in my conversations about the *omatisia* ritual. Nor have I been given to understand that the water in the bamboo tubes is the lake water and that it enters the tube without the intervention of any agent. Ultimately, for reasons I shall outline at the close, the water is actually a metonym of the mundane rather than celestial world and must be interpreted as such. The spirit woman dwells in a swamp. Interpreting that fact is crucial to interpreting the ritual itself. As the myths I will recount toward the close indicate, the water in the tubes and other ritual paraphernalia may be construed as stemming from the female spirit's body.

7. This detail is reported by Wiessner and Tumu as well: in the central Enga context, in interacting with the bamboo containers, "the bachelors act out the duties of marriage, bringing bespelled *lioko* leaves (*Evodia* sp.) and placing them in the containers, just as a married Enga man brings *lioko* leaves to his wife on the fifth day of her menstrual period. If her period is over, she chews them and spits them out, marking the end of menstrual prohibitions" (1998: 227).

8. Conception is believed to happen only if intercourse occurs with sufficient frequency that the sperm binds the menstrual blood, keeping it from coming outside. Although Paiela are aware of the fact that out-of-wedlock conception can and does occur, given the clandestine and episodic nature of adulterous unions, extramarital intercourse is not expected to result in pregnancy—only marital intercourse is. In local belief, then, reproduction is normatively conjugal.

9. There is, of course, a considerable literature on *ritual* sacrifice, defined by Valeri as "any ritual action that includes the consecration of an 'offering' to a deity'" (1985: 37). The word is widely used outside a ritual setting, however, to refer to "the surrender or destruction of something prized or desirable for the sake of something considered as having a higher or more pressing claim" (*Random House Dictionary*). In this case, sacrifice

does not refer narrowly to a prestation to a deity in return for a variety of quid pro quo but, more broadly, specifies a loss sustained in exchange for something else. By this definition, all exchange involves sacrifice. However, in my usage of the word *sacrifice* I retain the sense of a prestation specifically *of life*, and the quid pro quo is equally specific—a life for a life or an exchange of lives. The setting for the "sacrificial principle" is not a ritual setting but, rather, the life cycle itself and the lineage of lives within which any one life cycle unfolds (Biersack 2001). Among Ipili speakers, in short, filiation rests upon an exchange of life for life, a mode of reciprocity that has sacrifice at its heart.

10. The identification of the female spirit as a "sky woman" appears widespread. According to Polly Wiessner and Akü Tumu, "Origin myths from central Enga and the Porgera valley (Gibbs 1975) depict the woman as one of the mythical sky beings to whom human origins are traced in Enga cosmology, who are believed to protect people so long as they obey certain standards of conduct. . . . Huli oral traditions collected by Stephen Frankel (1986: 99–100) and Laurence Goldman (1983: 325–26) also attribute the origin of bachelors' cults to a spirit woman with supernatural powers but do not specify her relationship to Huli deities or ancestors" (1998: 221). According to Philip Gibbs's account of the origin of *omatisia*, based largely, although not exclusively, on Porgera research, the spirit woman "was the last of the sky beings to go to the sky" (1975: 85). (In the stories that I have collected, she refuses to go to the sky even though, as a sky person, she has the privilege of doing so; see below). Among the Kawelka, the female spirit, *amb kor*, "was closely linked to Sky-Folk (*Tei-Wamb*)" (Stewart and Strathern 1998: 8; see also A. Strathern 1970: 573, fig. 2).

11. There are several accounts of the origin of the *omatisia* ritual or *omatisia*-like rituals that parallel, in important particulars, the accounts I offer here. Gibbs's account of the origin of the ritual, presumably reflecting stories he heard in the Porgera valley but possibly also drawing on materials collected in the Paiela valley, reflects some of the detail that I have collected, and it indicates that the water in the tube was thought to be the spirit woman's blood: "The spirit woman was shot in the breast by a Hewa man. She bled and blood fell into the small lake. She went to the sky but said that she would send her son to plant bog iris plants" (1975: 85). He reported that "One of the older bachelors has a large bamboo tube filled with the 'blood' (tundua, *tunduka?*)" of the *omatisia* woman. "This blood has been taken from the lake where her blood fell after the Hewa man shot her. A small amount of the 'blood' is poured into each tube. Then all the boys put a plug of makua leaves in the top of the tubes and [sing a song] where the woman is said to be menstruating. They then put the tubes in the water near their bog iris plants. The bamboo tubes would tend to float in the water but they are tied to a stake so that the tops are about an inch above the surface. This operation is called umaritsia pene [on the contrary, *umaritsia pene* should refer to the bamboo tubes or *uiyapa pene*]. When the bachelors return the following year they will look into the tubes. If the fluid inside has risen almost to the level of the water outside, then all is well. If there is only a little fluid inside, then there is something wrong. The water is not 'growing' and neither will the boy" (Gibbs 1975: 87).

The story that John Schwab, writing about the Laiapu Enga, recounts is this: "Some men from the Milyopo-Kandepe-Wandi carried a woman, unnamed, on a 'bed.' Getting tired they put her down. She told them: I have legs, I can walk. Suddenly they did not see or hear her any more. Looking around they saw some blood on the ground. They cut a special bamboo (*taro*), gathered the blood in it, and called out: "Oke, Oke': I don't know where she went. This is the beginning of the Sandalu" (Shwab 1995: 29).

According to Wiessner and Tumu, "Our studies revealed only three 'centers' with Sangai origin myths for the Enga or their immediate neighbors—among the Mai and Yandapo dialect speakers of central Enga, the Ipili of Porgera valley (Gibbs 1975), and the Huli of the Tari area (Goldman 1983, Frankel 1986). . . . That there are no Sangai origin traditions among the Layapo of eastern Enga was confirmed by our investigations and by those of Roderic Lacey (1975) and Fr. John Schwab (1995: 3). . . . Although these areas are widely separated in space and their inhabitants speak different dialects or languages, bachelor' cults from all three have the same essential beliefs and practices, and share certain themes in their origin myths. A young bachelor encounters a beautiful woman who seduces him and, through her power as a supernatural being, transforms him into an attractive, socially competent, mature man. He then unintentionally betrays her or does her harm, resulting in her death. Upon or after her death, he is instructed either to fill a bamboo container . . . with her blood or to pluck the bog iris plant (*lepe*) on her grave to pass on with the appropriate spells—or to do both—so that young men in future generations can be similarly transformed" (1998a: 220–21).

Wiessner has written: "The Spirit Woman is shot by a shunned, aggressive bachelor. When another bachelor who had been transformed by the Spirit Woman and not shunned finds her, as she lies dying, [s]he instructs him to cut some bamboo containers and arrange them in two clusters of four one male and the other female, separated by a cluster of two, one male and one female. When this is done she tells him to pull out the arrow and fill the containers with her blood, plug them with clay and leaves, and bury them in a swampy area. Then she instructs him to bury her and return later to harvest *lepe* plants from her grave, one which will grow by her head and the other by her feet" (1998: 15; this volume).

According to Maria Dlugosz's account, the Engan story of one ugly bachelor named Lelyakali and his encounter with a beautiful woman who could help him become handsome has been reported by several (Dlugosz 1995; Gibbs 1988). In summary, the story is this: There was once a small and ugly bachelor. He tried to attend the *sangai*, but was beaten off by other participants, presumably because he was so ugly. An elder of his clan instructed him as to how to find another *sangai* group, and he set off. He did as he was told and came upon a beautiful woman. The woman seduced him. After they had made love, the woman asked him if he wished to join his handsome brothers, and when he said yes, she led him to where other young, but handsome, men were. The woman then took him to her house and dressed him in ceremonial costume. As he stepped forward, he was transformed into a beautiful man. The beautiful woman named him Lelyakali. He attended a singing. "He walked across the ceremonial ground, and some of the young women were kneeling down in admiration, hoping to be touched by the cordyline leaves that he was wearing. When he started to dance with the other dancers, people would not take their eyes off him. The way he danced made the whole area shake and he was really splendid" (Dlugosz 1995: 12). Another ugly bachelor was there in the crowd, and Lelyakali told him how he had achieved his good looks. This second ugly bachelor went to look for the beautiful woman. When he found her, she asked him who he was and why he had come, and he responded, "*I have come for the sangai*" (Dlugosz 1995: 12). The beautiful woman tried to seduce him, but he pushed her away. She tried repeatedly to seduce him, and one night he shot her and she fell down with an arrow in her side. Lelyakali suspected something had happened to the beautiful woman, and he went to look for her. He came upon her as she was dying. Before she died, she told him to go to the forest and find bamboo. When he returned with the bamboo, she told him to pull the arrow out of her side, collect her blood in the tubes, and plant the tubes in swampy water. "Then she said: '*Three days after you have buried me, return and you will see two plants growing here on my grave. One will grow on the side of my head and the other by my legs. I want you to take the plants and plant them where you buried the bamboo containers. You may think that you are wasting your time, but what you are doing now, will be very im-*

portant for you and for your descendants. The plants will produce many suckers. You should take them and distribute them to the boys whom you will bring to the sangai'." After she died, Lelyakali buried her. He returned to her grave three days later and found two *lepe* plants growing on her grave, one black and one red (Dlugosz 1995: 13–14).

For the Mount Hagen area, Andrew Strathern has reported a myth that resonates with the ones I have recounted, a myth that accounts for the origin of the *amb kor* cult. In the story, a young bachelor came upon a beautiful girl. He watched her rub her vagina against a banana tree, and when he inserted a shell fragment and an axe blade in the stem and she rubbed herself again against the stem, she cut herself and "made a vagina." Her sisters came later, and all except the youngest repeated this act, making vaginas for themselves. All the sisters who had vaginas were then married off, but the youngest sister remained a virgin. The bachelor eventually created the *amb kor* cult, "sacrificing to the 'youngest sister, ' who did not become a human wife as the other sisters did. . . . Further versions of the myth which are more explicit . . . stress the importance of the idea that the spirit is a virgin woman, with closed-up genitals" (1970: 575). The story distinguishes the ritual wife from real wives in terms of presence of genitalia and fertility. "She comes to men as a kind of wife—this is how men speak of her—but bears instead of children, the cult rituals which protect men against their real wives" (575).

12. *"Lepe* will not die out, it will always grow its new shoots. There is a saying in Mae Enga expressing a belief in continuity of clan: Akali lepe wai dokonya baa tata doko kumao etelyamopa mendai mende lenge tao mee singi. This means: even if most of the men of a clan will die, at least one will remain to continue life of the clan, just like the new shoots springing of the lepe plant. Thus, the people hold a believe [sic] that if a family has only one or two sons and both of them die, they believe that out of lepe a son will be born and the clan will not die out. This belief is passed on and expressed in the Enga art" (Dlugosz 1995: 28).

13. Dlugosz offers a similar interpretation in her summary of her study of Enga myths. In interpreting the story of the origin of *lepe* (see note 11 above), she refers to the " 'paradox' of the Sky-Woman's violent death becoming the life giving death" and concludes that in Enga thinking *"life comes through death"* (1995: 35). There are some aspects of her interpretation that I find extraneous, at least in the Ipili context, but this perception that life has essentially sacrificial foundations in indigenous thought is a shared one. Her purpose is to explore the parallels between indigenous thinking and Christian doctrine, something I have also done, albeit with a very different motivation, in my paper "Sacrifice and Regeneration" (1998b).

Chapter 6. Cults, Closures, Collaborations

We wish to thank all those who participated in the discussions during the ASAO sessions which centered on this topic. Special thanks go to Pascale Bonnemère for organizing the sessions and bringing the contributors together so as to engage the role of women in what has been known as "male cults."

1. See Bamford (1997, 1998a), Barlow (1995), Bonnemère (1996), Jolly (1994), Juillerat (1996), Kelly (1993), Knauft (1993, 1999), Lemonnier (1990), Lipset (1997), Lutkehaus and Roscoe (1995), Mimica (1988), Sillitoe (1979, 1985), M. Strathern (1988), Tuzin (1997), and for a further selection of references, Stewart and Strathern (1999a).

2. Ballard explains that " *'Iba'*, the term for water, forms the root for a lexicon of

fertile fluid terms such as *ibane* ('grease, fat'), *wi ibane* ('penis-grease, ' semen), *andu ibane* ('breast-grease,' breast milk), *dindi ibane* ('soil-grease') and *ira ibane* ('tree-grease,' sap). In their fertile state these fluids introduce moisture or grease to people and to the land" (Ballard 1998: 75). Duna ideas about "water" (*ipa*) are comparable to these Huli notions. Water in the form of rain and lakes is particularly linked with the female spirit for the Duna. They also make a distinction between water and "grease" (*nggwani*) in some contexts.

3. The tree oil motif and the reference to the spirit's eye here are reminiscent of the Hagen *wöp* cult.

4. As is well attested in the literature, the cassowary in general provides an image that can be seen as either male or female and thus can stand both for difference and for mutual substitutability of these categories, again showing their interdependency (see Strathern and Stewart 2000b with references, and compare Tuzin 1997).

5. This is also the first basis for Herdt's notion of "male parthenogenesis" in initiation rituals.

6. In a recent reconsideration of the data now available on those cults that center on male initiation in Melanesia, Allen has reordered his earlier (1967) typological scheme into a contrast between blood-letting rites, associated with exogamous marriage and bridewealth, and semen-ingesting rites, associated with sister-exchange and cross-cousin marriage. In the former, he argues, men are concerned to keep control of the productive domain, in the latter to control the reproductive domain. This new classification might be said to apply to the Eastern Highlands of Papua New Guinea (blood-letting) and the Anga-speakers (semen-ingesting) respectively (Allen 1998). Notable here is the absence of those societies of the Western and Southern Highlands, which we argue primarily evince the workings of our Collaborative Model, although these did fall within the purview of Allen's original (1967) study. Notable also, however, is the fact that Allen observes that males took on female-gendered roles in both types of initiations. For example, he remarks on the report by Herdt (1981: 235) that "the men quite explicitly compared the oral consumption of semen from men's penises by novices with the drinking of breast milk by babies" (Allen 1998: 192). Information of this kind suggests that we indeed could profitably rethink the meaning of such analogies enshrined at the heart of male initiation practices.

Chapter 7. The Variability of Women's "Involvement" in Anga Male Initiations

This chapter draws on published accounts by Blackwood (1978), Fischer (1968), Godelier (1986, 1999), Herdt (1981, 1987b), Mimica (1981, 1991), Bonnemère (1993, 1996, 1998a), Bamford (1997), on Australian archives patrol reports, on my own observation of Baruya and Ankave initiations (twice among the Baruya, 1979 and 1985, four times among the Ankave, 1994, 1997, and 1998), and on the narratives I collected among the Kapau, Langimar, Menye, and Watchakes in 1980. Since 1978, my research has been funded primarily by the French Centre National de la Recherche Scientifique. The PNG Institute of Medical Research (Goroka) provided my family and me with both moral and material support every time I was in the country.

1. From gardening or salt-making techniques to healing or social representations of illness, Anga societies exhibit immense differences that more often than not can be interpreted in terms of systems of transformation. For syntheses on these particular mat-

ters, see Lemonnier (1982, 1984b, 1992). For a general view of Anga cultures, see Lemonnier (1998a).

During the 1999 ASAO meeting, the discussant of my paper—Polly Wiessner—very rightly proposed that a single historical event may have engendered different local interpretations and triggered different cosmological themes or ritual configurations in several Anga groups. This may well have been the case, but unfortunately, Anga oral history does not say anything about the changes that, for anthropologists, obviously took place over the long history of these groups. We are reduced, for lack of data, to considering local ritual systems as the result of a historical and structural transformation whose impetus and process are probably lost for ever.

2. This "découverte des grands hommes" described by Herdt (1987b: 155) for the Sambia and Godelier (1986: 100) for the Baruya is also part of the Ankave, Menye, and Watchakes rituals (but not of the Kapau ones, I was told).

3. The reference to the containing of fear is also explicit in the narrative of the Menye male initiations I obtained in Menyamya in 1980.

4. The first stages concern the transformation of the boys into adult men. Further stages concern the initiates' own adult life: marriage, fatherhood, etc. It is not surprising that their mothers are involved only in the first stages (Herdt, this volume), because only those ceremonies reenact the human birth and growth processes. The Baruya and Ankave explicitly explain the presence of the mothers during the first stages of the ritual by reference to the pain the mother experienced when pregnant and when giving birth to the novice (Bonnemère, this volume).

5. Bamford (this volume) recalls van Gennep's general interpretation of initiation rites, but does not take a position on this particular point. At any rate, Blackwood's description of the marita ceremony among the Kapau parallels the Ankave second-stage initiation and therefore fits with Bonnemère's hypothesis about Anga male initiations being modeled on human birth.

6. Dunlop (1992: 5–19). When no reference is given to Godelier's or Lory's work, the Baruya data presented come from my own observations. I witnessed this scene during the 1979 *muka* (first-stage) ceremony in Wonenara.

7. The patrol reports by Hurrell (1950–51) and Hastings (1961–62: 3) give by far the most detailed account of Anga initiations ("nose-piercing ceremony" and "marita ceremony" in both cases) witnessed by Australian administrators. Simpson's description in *Adam with Arrows* (1954: 102–11) is based on Hurrell's report of the "Pewi-Anga" initiations, near Naniwe. Naniwe is actually a Menye-speaking group, but Hurrell's description does not at all correspond to what my own Menye informants told me in 1980. On the other hand, it fits exactly with both Blackwood's data on the Kapau rituals (Blackwood 1978: 123–33) and the information I collected in Aseki in 1980. Hastings's description of "Inland Tauri River Kukukuku" ceremonies concern Kapau groups as well, as far as the kinship terminology and, above all, the shape of the houses are concerned. Menye initiations are described briefly by Bjerre (1956: 91–97). His account concurs with what I was told in Menyamya and with the unpublished data collected by the SIL couple in the area (Pat and Carl Whitehead) and very kindly communicated to me, but which are not for quotation.

8. For instance, I could easily demonstrate that, although both are sacred objects the possession and use of which define the greatest of all Anga great men, a Baruya *kwaimatnie* and an Ankave *oxemexe'* present as many differences as they do similarities.

9. With possible intermediary cases: the Menye are supposed to rub semen on the initiates (Mimica 1981: 60); they also have a separate stage centered on the eating and rubbing of red pandanus juice.

10. I must add that the absence of boy-inseminating practices among southern Angans is not a guess. Of course, we have no proof of that absence, except that (a) in any case, it could not have had the same extension as among the northern Angans, where the men's house is a key institution connected with boy-inseminating practices (Mimica 1981: 60); and (b) there is just no room for semen in a society like the Ankave (for instance): what is consistent throughout their symbolic system is the use of blood/pandanus juice; (c) there has never been any suggestion of boy-inseminating practices among these southern peoples; and (d) for 19 1/2 years now, my informants in the area have told me a lot of "secrets" that often made them shiver, perspire, whisper, and look desperately around to see if anyone was listening. But no Ankave ever gave me the slightest hint that boy-inseminating practices might have existed. (I must add that they are unaware that the far-away "Padeye," that is, Baruya, have them.)

11. I have no "proof" that the Watchakes practiced boy-insemination. However, the secrecy of the playing of the flutes, the large number of initiation stages (five, piercing then a multistage ritual, as among the Baruya), and the long residence in a men's house makes me think so. Mimica (1981: 60) has no doubt about the existence of boy-insemination among the Ampale (Watchakes).

12. In the case of the Menye—whose ethnography is the least documented—it would be interesting to know how their complementary use of blood and semen works (this last fluid is rubbed on the novice's body, according to Mimica's Iqwaye informants). This is an open question. Actually I doubt that anyone knows much about Menye ideas on procreation.

13. Here, too, the Iqwaye, who use flutes publicly but keep the bullroarers a secret and have boy-inseminating practices, would be an intermediary case.

14. My own notes indicate that the Menye children go back to their parents' house after a four months' confinement in the bush, and that they may talk freely to their mothers. In addition to Bamford's description (this volume), Simpson (1954: 105, after Hurrel 1950–51: 15), Hastings (1961–62: 4), and my own notes clearly indicate that coming back to village and family life was the rule among the Kapau-Kamea.

15. For the occasion, the initiate changed his nose and head ornaments and there was an offering of food to the "mother's brother" who pierced his nose.

16. Fischer (1968: 128) indicates that a Yagwoia mother must remain standing while a boy has his nose pierced. There is no information on a possible seclusion of the mother. I have very little information on the Watchakes, except that the mothers of the initiates are regularly said to bring food for the initiates during the first two stages.

17. Among the Baruya and Sambia, one of the most important acts performed by the mothers, after the seclusion of the boys has begun, has to do with the change of the initiates' name (Nunguye Kandavatche, personal communication; Herdt 1987b: 157–58; see also Dunlop 1992: 10–12).

18. So that a real gestation does not take place while a "symbolic" one is going on, according to my own interpretation.

19. The information I collected among the Watchakes describes a situation entirely comparable to that of the Sambia and Baruya. A girl who menstruates for the first time is individually lectured in a way that explicitly refers to her lower status as a woman: "You cannot walk for nothing as men do, you are a woman" (and therefore must carry something). Nose-piercing was done on little girls (6–8 years), who were collectively secluded for a week or so. They also received new body decorations and took part in a ritual similar to that of Baruya mothers' "killing" the names of their sons, probably indicating a change in their social identity (unfortunately, I have no information on a possible change of name). When a girl menstruated for the first time, she was secluded in

her parents' house, next to a big fire, severely beaten, and given new items of clothing, which replicates the Baruya collective ritual for young women.

20. We lack information for the Iqwaye-Jagwoia. Fischer (1968: 132) mentions that women used to have their noses pierced, which does not mean that there were female initiations among the Yagwoia. Mimica (1981: 52–53) writes that there are no female initiations among the Iqwaye (whose language and culture are almost exactly the same as those of the Yagwoia), and he mentions the existence of a ceremony for the birth of a woman's first child but gives no more information.

21. It is remarkable that, when asked why parts of the ritual are kept secret from the women, the Ankave say merely that this important part of their culture cannot be shown to the women, who are supposed to marry out. The fear is simply that they might communicate these secrets to the enemies. The idea that some male secrets could be shared by women does not trigger furor or horror in Ankave men.

22. This beating prior to anointing is practiced among the Ankave and Menye (my observations), and also among the Kapau (Hastings 1961–62: 5; Simpson 1954: 106), and Yagwoia (Fischer 1968: 137–38).

23. For instance, when the boys, led by their mothers' brothers, approach the secret (and sacred?) enclosure where their septum is going to be pierced, they are told that the men who sit at the top of a sort of "ladder" and whirl the bullroarers are big birds that they are going to hunt. As Blackwood herself remarked, this somehow parallels the origin myth of that stage of the initiations she collected among the Langimar or Kapau, in which a little boy was hunting birds when a spirit having the appearance of his mother's brother pierced his septum and made him a strong warrior (Blackwood 1940: 221–22).

24. Other "grids" of analysis are possible (and necessary). To mention just one, it is clear that the Ankave initiations could (and should) be read "also" in terms of the classical brief encounter of the initiates with a state of death or dead people prior to being reborn (e.g. Panoff 1998). Besides explicit mention of that process ("The *oxemexe'* kills the boy," "Follow that dead man!"), the entire succession of cold/hot, dirty/clean states could be analyzed that way. At a higher level, male initiations in New Guinea could be studied conjointly with hunting rituals (e.g., Schieffelin 1976, 1982) and other journeys to the spirit world.

25. It is difficult to quantify shouting and blows, but the observer is struck by the harmonious climate among the Ankave. It is true as well that suicide, which accounts for up to 10 percent of female deaths among the Baruya, is totally absent among the Ankave (Bonnemère 1992).

Chapter 8. Of Human and Spirit Women: From Mother to Seductress to Second Wife

1. Concepts of contamination were reciprocal. For instance, the power of a male gaze was believed to be able to harm an infant during its first days of life, and the power of male ancestors could deform a fetus in the womb should women attend cults for the ancestors to partake of food prepared for the sacred rites.

2. I have compared issues inciting conflict mentioned in women's life stories with conflicts that occurred over a six-month period in the Enga community of Kundis, Ambum valley, 1986 (unpublished). Subjects of dispute were similar, except that cash had become a major point of contention between husband and wife in the past few decades.

3. The term "phratry," as used by Meggitt (1965a), is perhaps the most accurate anthropological term for *tata andake* of Enga, political units composed of aggregates of clans united by an origin tradition and genealogy that links members to a common ancestor. As discussed elsewhere (Wiessner and Tumu 1998), we have chosen "tribe," a less precise notion, in order to use a term familiar to the Enga themselves.

4. This description is based on a tabulation of male and female activities mentioned in historical traditions for this period (Wiessner and Tumu 1998)

5. For a married woman to participate publicly in exchange would probably have been unacceptable, because she would usurp her husband's role. For a widow to do so seemed not to violate rules governing division of labor, since she was without a spouse.

6. In a sense, it was the institutionalized inequality between males and females that made achieved inequalities between males possible. Because women were removed from politics, during times of conflict they simply removed themselves, their children, and their pigs from the scene. When the conflict was resolved, the future generation returned home unharmed, and exchange ties based on female ties could be resumed immediately to provide wealth for reparations and other payments. Had women and children been equals and subject to violence, this would not have been the case.

7. Enga opinions differ on the question whether the ancestors are composed only of deceased males or of both males and females.

8. First-generation male immigrants often returned to their natal clans for cult performances.

9. Girls did perform rites to speed or enhance growth and beauty, though these were not regarded as essential for girls to mature. Both men and women were thought to lose vitality with the expenditure of fluids related to reproduction—sperm and breast milk respectively. Men could counteract the loss of sperm through appropriate rites, but there were no rites to reverse aging brought about through loss of breast milk. However, sacrifices of motherhood were acknowledged and compensated materially through payments to maternal kin.

10. While ritual experts could explain the meaning of all other rites with greater clarity, they did not know the significance of certain aspects of the *mote*.

11. The sacred stones used in Enga ritual were frequently mortars and pestles made by former inhabitants of Enga, perhaps their distant forebears, pestles representing male ancestors and mortars female ones. The *yupini* figure appears to have been imported from the Sepik region (Wiessner and Tumu 1998).

12. Few if any traces of the *mote* have appeared in contemporary religious movements.

13. Unlike the spirit or sky women in the *mote*, who are identified as the morning and evening stars, there were no clues in any of the *sangai* origin traditions that we collected that would help locate the *sangai* spirit woman more precisely in the world of the sky people.

14. Consumption of pandanus is a widely used image associated with sexual relations in Enga.

15. Enga believe that transfer of sacred words and objects must be made in exchange for wealth, else their power will be lost to the donor.

16. The *sangai* was not exclusively for clan or subclan members; in certain cases young men attended performances of clans or subclans where they had close kinship ties, for example, the clan of mother's brother.

17. The fluid was buried in sealed containers in a swamp and only opened for examination or transferral into new containers.

18. The life histories of several big men of eastern and central Enga indicate that

young men with strong ambitions in exchange attended fewer *sangai* performances and married earlier to launch on their careers. By contrast, men who became senior bachelors in the *sangai* and married later were less likely to become big men. However, the sample size is not representative enough to determine if this was a common trend throughout Enga or if it varied by area.

19. Intentionality in importing and performing both *sangai* and Female Spirit cults at this point in history is openly stated in Enga oral accounts and consistent with Enga religious attitudes; few Enga would consider spiritual life as something apart from pragmatic economic and political initiatives. This is not to say that much experimentation did not take place within cult performances nor that cults performances had unintended consequences, however, big men were those who knew how to channel such unforeseen consequences to their own benefit.

Chapter 9. Relating to Women: Female Presence in Melanesian "Male Cults"

1. See Read (1952), Langness (1967, 1974), Meggitt (1964, 1976), Allen (1967), Keesing (1982), Modjeska (1982), Josephides (1985), Godelier (1986), Herdt and Poole (1982).

2. For example, Nicholson (1990), di Leonardo (1991), Moore (1994); see discussion in Knauft (1996, chap. 7).

3. See Knauft (1985, chap. 11, 1986, 1989). It may be noted that Gebusi women could easily hear spirit séances through the sago-leaf wall that separated their sleeping section from that of the men. However, this division accentuated and underscored their inability to respond to or emulate the persona of the spirit woman in daily practice. Men themselves were not averse to foisting themselves on Gebusi women privately when they got the chance; it was the woman's responsibility to stay in the company of other women and repel these advances (see Cantrell 1998).

4. As Cantrell (1998) has emphasized, this disapproval was strongest for married women—structurally analogous to the spirit woman herself—and less so for never-married women, who were afforded significantly more tolerance by men and women alike.

5. The exclusion of female-associated influences was underscored by repeated warnings to me by my male Gebusi friends, for example, that the fish-poisoning would be a failure if I had had sexual intercourse with my wife at any time during the preceding week.

6. This panel was a precursor to conference papers subsequently collected in the present edited volume.

7. These women were not merely acting in their capacity as sisters or close kin of the novices.

8. For instance, the term *wa dep* or "true child" is a common idiom for a senior man. Though the unmarked term *wa* is more often used to refer to male children—at least by men—it refers more generally a child of either sex, which may then be distinguished as "male child" (*arl wa*) or "female child" (*ulia wa*).

9. Sexual joking and camaraderie among men was also reduced. Concerning the diminution of sexual relations among Gebusi men, see Knauft (in press).

10. One might here recall the remarks of Wiessner (this volume) concerning the relationship between indigenous female spirit cults and the cult of the Virgin Mary among contemporary Enga.

Bibliography

Allen, Michael R. 1967. *Male Cults and Secret Initiations in Melanesia*. Melbourne: Melbourne University Press.

———. 1998. Male Cults Revisited: The Politics of Blood Versus Semen. *Oceania* 68: 189–99.

Ballard, Chris. 1998. The Sun by Night. In *Fluid Ontologies: Myth, Ritual, and Philosophy in the Highlands of Papua New Guinea*, ed. Laurence R. Goldman and Chris Ballard, 67–85. Westport, Conn.: Bergin and Garvey.

———, ed. 1999. Special Focus on Myth and History in the New Guinea Highlands. *Canberra Anthropology* 22 (1): 1–87.

Bamberger, Joan. 1974. The Myth of Matriarchy: Why Men Rule in Primitive Society. In *Woman, Culture, and Society*, ed. Michelle Z. Rosaldo and Louise Lamphere, 263–80. Stanford, Calif.: Stanford University Press.

Bamford, Sandra C. 1997. The Containment of Gender: Embodied Sociality Among a South Angan People. Ph.D. dissertation, University of Virginia.

———. 1998a. To Eat for Another: Taboo and the Elicitation of Bodily Form Among the Kamea of Papua New Guinea. In *Bodies and Persons: Comparative Perspectives from Africa and Melanesia*, ed. Michael Lambek and Andrew Strathern, 158–71. Cambridge: Cambridge University Press.

———. 1998b. Humanized Landscapes, Embodied Worlds: Land Use and the Construction of Intergenerational Sociality Among the Kamea of Papua New Guinea. In *Identity, Nature, and Culture: Sociality and the Environment in Melanesia*, ed. Sandra C. Bamford, 28–54. *Social Analysis* 42 (3) (special issue).

———. forthcoming. Unholy Noses. In *Embodying Modernity and Postmodernity: Ritual, Praxis, and Social Change in Melanesia*, ed. Sandra C. Bamford, Durham, N.C.: Carolina Academic Press.

Barlow, Kathleen. 1995. Achieving Womanhood and the Achievements of Women in Murik: Cult Initiation, Gender Complementarity and the Prestige of Women. In *Gender Rituals: Female Initiation in Melanesia*, ed. Nancy C. Lutkehaus and Paul B. Roscoe, 121–42. New York: Routledge.

Barth, Frederik. 1987. *Cosmologies in the Making: A Generative Approach to Cultural Variation in Inner New Guinea*. Cambridge: Cambridge University Press.

Bateson, Gregory. 1958. *Naven: The Culture of the Iatmul People of New Guinea as Revealed Through a Study of the "Naven" Ceremonial*. 1936. 2nd edition. Stanford, Calif.: Stanford University Press.

Beidelman, T. O. 1997. *The Cool Knife: Imagery of gender, Sexuality, and Moral Education in Kaguru Initiation Ritual*. Washington, D.C.: Smithsonian Institution Press.

Bettelheim, Bruno. 1962 (1954). *Symbolic Wounds: Puberty Rites and the Envious Male*. Glencoe, Ill.: Free Press. Reprint New York: Collier.

Biersack, Aletta. 1982. Ginger Gardens for the Ginger Woman: Rights and Passages in a Melanesian Society. *Man* 17: 239–58.

————. 1987. Moonlight: Negative Images of Transcendence in Paiela Pollution. *Oceania* 57: 178–94.

————. 1995a. Heterosexual Meanings: Society, Economy, and Gender Among Ipilis. In *Papuan Borderlands: Huli, Duna, and Ipili Perspectives on the Papua New Guinea Highlands*, ed. Aletta Biersack, 229–61. Ann Arbor: University of Michigan Press.

————, ed. 1995b. *Papuan Borderlands: Huli, Duna, and Ipili Perspectives on the Papua New Guinea Highlands*. Ann Arbor: University of Michigan Press.

————. 1996. Word Made Flesh: Religion, the Economy, and the Body in the Papua New Guinea Highlands. *History of Religions* 36: 85–111.

————. 1998a. Horticulture and Hierarchy: The Youthful Beautification of the Body in the Paiela and Porgera Valleys. In *Adolescence in the Pacific Island Societies*, ed. Gilbert H. Herdt and Stephen Leavitt, 71–91. ASAO Monograph Series. Pittsburgh: University of Pittsburgh Press.

————. 1998b. Sacrifice and Regeneration Among Ipilis: The View from Tipinini. In *Fluid Ontologies: Myth, Ritual, and Philosophy in the Highlands of Papua New Guinea*, ed. Laurence R. Goldman and Chris Ballard, 43–66. Westport, Conn.: Bergin and Garvey.

————. 1999. The Mount Kare Python and His Gold: Totemism and Ecology in the New Guinea Highlands. In *Ecologies for Tomorrow: Reading Rappaport Today*, ed. Aletta Biersack, 68–87. *American Anthropologist* 101 (1) (special issue). A Contemporary Issues Forum.

————. 2001. Reproducing Inequality: The Gender Politics of Male Cults in Melanesia and Amazonia. In *Gender in Amazonia and Melanesia: An Exploration of the Comparative Method*, ed. Thomas A. Gregor and Donald Tuzin, 69–90. Berkeley: University of California Press.

Bjerre, Jens. 1956. *The Last Cannibals*. New York: William Morrow.

Blackwood, Beatrice. 1939a. Life on the Upper Watut, New Guinea. *Geographical Journal* 94 (1): 11–28.

————. 1939b. Folk Stories of a Stone Age People in New Guinea. *Folklore* 1 (3): 209–42.

————. 1940. Use of Plants Among the Kukukuku of South East Central New Guinea. *Proceedings of the Sixth Pacific Science Conference 1939*, 4: 111–26. Berkeley, California.

————. 1978 (1950). *The Kukukuku of the Upper Watut*. Edited from her published articles and unpublished fieldnotes with an introduction by C. R. Hallpike. Pitt Rivers Museum Monograph Series 2. Oxford: University of Oxford.

Bloch, Maurice. 1992. *Prey into Hunter: The Politics of Religious Experience*. Cambridge: Cambridge University Press.

Bloch, Maurice and Jonathan Parry, eds. 1982. *Death and the Regeneration of Life*. Cambridge: Cambridge University Press.

Bonnemère, Pascale. 1990. Considérations relatives aux représentations des substances corporelles en Nouvelle-Guinée. *L'Homme* 30 (2): 101–20.

————. 1992. Suicide et homicide: Deux modalités vindicatoires en Nouvelle-Guinée. *Stanford French Review* 16: 19–43.

————. 1993. Maternal Nurturing Substance and Paternal Spirit: The Making of a Southern Anga Sociality. *Oceania* 64: 159–86.

————. 1994. Le pandanus rouge dans tous ses états: L'univers social et symbolique d'un arbre fruitier chez les Ankave-Anga, *Annales Fyssen* 9: 21–32.

————. 1996. *Le pandanus rouge: Corps, différence des sexes et parenté chez les Ankave-Anga (Pa-*

pouasie Nouvelle-Guinée). Paris: CNRS / Éditions de la Maison des Sciences de l'Homme.

————. 1998a. Quand les hommes répliquent une gestation: Une analyse des représentations et des rites de la croissance et de la maturation chez les Ankave-Anga (Papouasie Nouvelle-Guinée). In *La production du corps: Approches anthropologiques et historiques*, ed. Maurice Godelier and Michel Panoff. Paris: Éditions des Archives contemporaines. 81–113.

————. 1998b. Trees and People: Some Vital Links. Tree Products and Other Agents in the Life Cycle of the Ankave-Anga of Papua New Guinea. In *The Social Life of Trees: Anthropological Perspectives on Tree Symbolism*, ed. Laura Rival, 113–31. Oxford: Berg.

————. 2001. Two Forms of Masculinized Rebirth: The Melanesian Body and the Amazonian Cosmos. In *Gender in Amazonia and Melanesia: An Exploration of the Comparative Method*, ed. Thomas A. Gregor and Donald Tuzin, 17–44. Berkeley: University of California Press.

————. 2002. L'anthropologie du genre en Nouvelle-Guinée: Entre analyse sociologique et psychologie du développement, *L'Homme* 161: 205–24.

Brennan, Paul W. 1977. *Let Sleeping Snakes Lie: Central Enga Religious Belief and Ritual*. Adelaide: Australian Association for the Study of Religions.

Buchbinder, Georgeda and Roy A. Rappaport. 1976. Fertility and Death Among Maring. In *Man and Woman in the New Guinea Highlands*, ed. Paula Brown and Georgeda Buchbinder, 13–35. Special Publication 8. Washington, D.C.: American Anthropological Association.

Burton, R. V. and John W. M. Whiting. 1961. The Absent Father and Cross-Sex Identity. *Merrill-Palmer Quarterly of Behavior and Development* 7: 85–95.

Cantrell, Eileen M. 1998. Woman the Sexual, a Question of When: A Study of Gebusi Adolescence. In *Adolescence in Pacific Island Societies*, ed. Gilbert H. Herdt and Stephen C. Leavitt, 92–120. ASAO Monograph 16. Pittsburgh: University of Pittsburgh Press.

Chodorow, Nancy J. 1974. Family Structure and Feminine Personality. In *Woman, Culture, and Society*, ed. Michelle Z. Rosaldo and Louise Lamphere, 43–66. Stanford, Calif.: Stanford University Press.

Clark, Jeffrey. 1999. Cause and Afek: Primal Women, Bachelor Cults and the Female Spirit. *Canberra Anthropology* 22 (1): 6–33.

Collier, Jane F. and Sylvia J. Yanagisako. 1987. Toward a Unified Analysis of Gender and Kinship. In *Gender and Kinship: Essays Toward a Unified Analysis*, ed. Jane F. Collier and Sylvia J. Yanagisako, 14–50. Stanford, Calif.: Stanford University Press.

Descola, Philippe. 1992. Societies of Nature and the Nature of Society. In *Conceptualizing Society*, ed. Adam Kuper, 107–26. London: Routledge.

Devereux, Georges. 1982. *Femme et mythe*. Paris: Flammarion.

di Leonardo, Micaela, ed. 1991. *Gender at the Crossroads of Knowledge: Feminist Anthropology in the Postmodern Era*. Berkeley: University of California Press.

Dlugosz, Maria. 1995. Mae Enga Myths and Christ's Message: Fullness of Life in Mae Enga Mythology and Christ the Life (Jn 10:10). Doctoral dissertation, Facultate Missiologiuae Pontificiae Universitatis Gregorianae, Rome.

Dosedla, H. C. 1984. Kultfiguren aus Flechtwerk im zentralen Hochland von PNG (Papua-Neuguinea). *Abhandlungen und Berichte des Staatlichen Museums für Völkerkunde Dresden* 41: 86–100.

Douaire-Marsaudon, Françoise. 1998. *Les premiers fruits: Parenté, identité sexuelle, et pouvoirs en Polynésie occidentale (Tonga, Wallis, et Futuna)*. Paris: CNRS / Éditions de la Maison des Sciences de l'Homme.

Douglas, Mary. 1966. *Purity and Danger: An Analysis of Concepts of Pollution and Taboo.* London: Routledge and Kegan Paul.

Dunlop, Ian, ed. 1992. *Baruya Muka Archival. Documentation and Translation.* Vol. 4 (part 7). Lindfield, NSW: Film Australia.

Ellen, Roy. 1996. Introduction. In *Redefining Nature: Ecology, Culture, and Domestication*, ed. Roy Ellen and Katsuyoshi Fukui, 1–36. Oxford: Berg.

————. 1998. Comparative Natures in Melanesia: An External Perspective. In *Identity, Nature, and Culture: Sociality and Environment in Melanesia*, ed. Sandra Bamford, 143–58. *Social Analysis* 42 (3) (special issue).

Elliston, Deborah A. 1995. Erotic Anthropology: Ritualized Homosexuality in Melanesia and Beyond. *American Ethnologist* 22 (4): 848–67.

Engelhart, Monica. 1998. *Extending the Tracks: A Cross-Reductionistic Approach to Australian Aboriginal Male Initiation Rites.* Stockholm: Almqvist and Wiksell.

Feil, Daryl K. 1984. *Ways of Exchange: The Enga Tee of Papua New Guinea.* St. Lucia: University of Queensland Press.

————. 1987. *The Evolution of Highland Papua New Guinea Societies.* Cambridge: Cambridge University Press.

Fischer, Hans. 1968. *Die Negwa: Eine Papua-Gruppe im Wandel.* Munich: Klaus Renner.

Frankel, Stephen. 1986. *The Huli Response to Illness.* Cambridge: Cambridge University Press.

Geertz, Clifford. 1973. *The Interpretation of Cultures.* New York: Basic Books.

Gell, Alfred. 1975. *Metamorphosis of the Cassowaries: Umeda Society, Language, and Ritual.* London: Athlone Press.

————. 1998. *Art and Agency.* Oxford: Oxford University Press.

Gibbs, Philip. 1975. Ipili Religion Past and Present. Diploma thesis, University of Sydney.

————. 1978. The *Kepele* Ritual of the Western Highlands of Papua New Guinea. *Anthropos* 73 (3–4): 434–48.

————. 1988. Lepe: An Exercise in Horticultural Theology. *Catalyst* 18: 215–34.

Gillison, Gillian. 1980. Images of Nature in Gimi Thought. In *Nature, Culture, and Gender*, ed. Carol P. MacCormack and Marilyn Strathern, 143–73. Cambridge: Cambridge University Press.

————. 1993. *Between Culture and Fantasy: A New Guinea Highlands Mythology.* Chicago: University of Chicago Press.

Glasse, Robert M. 1968. *Huli of Papua: A Cognatic Descent System.* Paris: Mouton.

Godelier, Maurice. 1982. Social Hierarchies Among the Baruya of New Guinea. In *Inequality in New Guinea Highlands Societies*, ed. Andrew Strathern, 3–34. New York: Cambridge University Press.

————. 1986. *The Making of Great Men: Male Domination and Power Among the New Guinea Baruya.* Cambridge: Cambridge University Press. Trans. from *La production des Grands Hommes.* Paris: Fayard, 1982.

————. 1991. An Unfinished Attempt at Reconstructing the Social Processes Which May Have Prompted the Transformation of Great-Men Societies into Big-Men Societies. In *Big Men and Great Men: Personifications of Power in Melanesia*, ed. Maurice Godelier and Marilyn Strathern, 275–304. Cambridge: Cambridge University Press.

————. 1992. Corps, parenté, pouvoir(s) chez les Baruya de Nouvelle-Guinée. *Journal de la Société des Océanistes* 94: 3–24.

————. 1999. *The Enigma of the Gift.* Chicago: University of Chicago Press. Trans. from *L'énigme du don.* Paris: Fayard, 1996.

Goldman, Laurence A. 1983. *Talk Never Dies: The Language of Huli Disputes*. London: Tavistock.

Goldman, Laurence A. and Chris Ballard, eds. 1998. *Fluid Ontologies: Myth, Ritual, and Philosophy in the Highlands of Papua New Guinea*. Westport, Conn.: Bergin and Garvey.

Gray, Brenda. 1973. The Logic of Yandapu Enga Puberty Rites and the Separation of the Sexes. M.A. thesis, University of Sydney.

Gregor, Thomas A. 1985. *Anxious Pleasures: The Sexual Lives of an Amazonian People*. Chicago: University of Chicago Press.

Guddemi, Philip. 1993. We Came from This: Knowledge, Memory, Painting and "Play" in the Initiation Rituals of the Sawiyano of Papua New Guinea. Ph.D. dissertation, University of Michigan.

Hage, Per. 1981. On Male Initiation and Dual Organisation in New Guinea. *Man* 16 (2): 268–75.

Harvey, David. 1989. *The Condition of Postmodernity: An Enquiry into the Origins of Cultural Change*. Cambridge: Blackwell.

Hastings, L. J. 1961–62. Morobe Province Patrol Reports, Menyamya Patrol Report 4.

Hauser-Schäublin, Brigitta. 1995. Puberty Rites, Women's Naven, and Initiation: Women's Rituals of Transition in Abelam and Iatmul Culture. In *Gender Rituals: Female Initiation in Melanesia*, ed. Nancy C. Lutkehaus and Paul B. Roscoe, 33–53. New York: Routledge.

Hays, Terence E. and Patricia Hays. 1982. Opposition and Complementarity of the Sexes in Ndumba Initiations. In *Rituals of Manhood: Male Initiation in New Guinea*, ed. Gilbert H. Herdt, 201–38. Berkeley: University of California Press.

Heald, Suzette. 1999. *Manhood and Morality: Sex, Violence and Ritual in Gisu Society*. London: Routledge.

Healey, Alan. 1981. *Angan Languages Are Different*. Language data, Asian-Pacific Series 12. Huntington Beach, Calif.: Summer Institute of Linguistics.

Herdt, Gilbert H. 1981. *Guardians of the Flutes: Idioms of Masculinity*. Chicago: University of Chicago Press.

———, ed. 1982a. *Rituals of Manhood: Male Initiation in Papua New Guinea*. Berkeley: University of California Press.

———. 1982b. Sambia Nose-Bleeding Rites and Male Proximity to Females. *Ethos* 10 (3): 189–231. Reprinted in Herdt, *Sambia Sexual Culture: Essays from the Field*. Chicago: University of Chicago Press, 1999.

———, ed. 1984a. *Ritualized Homosexuality in Melanesia*. Berkeley: University of California Press.

———. 1984b. Ritualized Homosexual Behavior in the Male Cults of Melanesia, 1862–1983: An Introduction. In *Ritualized Homosexuality in Melanesia*, ed. Gilbert H. Herdt, 1–81. Berkeley: University of California Press.

———. 1984c. Semen Transactions in Sambia Culture. In *Ritualized Homosexuality in Melanesia*, ed. Gilbert H. Herdt, 167–210. Berkeley: University of California Press.

———. 1987a. Transitional Objects in Sambia Initiation. *Ethos* 15: 40–57.

———. 1987b. *The Sambia: Ritual and Gender in New Guinea*. New York: Holt, Rinehart, and Winston.

———. 1989. Father Presence and Ritual Homosexuality: Paternal Deprivation and Masculine Development in Melanesia Reconsidered. *Ethos* 17 (3): 326–70.

———. 1992. Sexual Repression, Social Control, and Gender Hierarchy in Sambia Culture. In *Gender Hierarchies*, ed. Barbara D. Miller, 121–35. New York: Cambridge University Press.

———. 1999a. Rituels de sexuation et pouvoirs du corps en Nouvelle-Guinée: Essai comparatif en hommage à Maurice Godelier. In *La production du social: Autour de Maurice Godelier*, ed. Philippe Descola, Jacques Hamel, and Pierre Lemonnier, 345–68. Paris: Fayard.

———. 1999b. *Sambia Sexual Culture: Essays from the Field.* Chicago: University of Chicago Press.

———. 2003. *Secrecy and Cultural Reality: Utopian Ideologies of the New Guinea Men's House.* Ann Arbor: University of Michigan Press.

Herdt, Gilbert H. and Fitz John P. Poole. 1982. Sexual Antagonism: The Intellectual History of a Concept in New Guinea Anthropology. In *Sexual Antagonism, Gender, and Social Change in Papua New Guinea*, ed. Fitz John P. Poole and Gilbert H. Herdt, 3–28. *Social Analysis* (special issue) 12: 52–65.

Herdt, Gilbert H. and Robert J. Stoller. 1990. *Intimate Communications: Erotics and the Study of Culture.* New York: Columbia University Press.

Hiatt, Lesley R. 1971. Secret Pseudo-Procreation Rites Among the Australian Aborigines. In *Anthropology in Oceania*, ed. Lesley R. Hiatt and Chandra Jayawardena, 77–88. London: Angus and Robertson.

Hogbin, Ian. 1970. *The Island of Menstruating Men.* Scranton, Pa.: Chandler.

Hugh-Jones, Stephen. 1979. *The Palm and the Pleiades: Initiation and Cosmology in Northwest Amazonia.* Cambridge: Cambridge University Press.

Hurrell, A. L. 1950–51. Morobe District Patrol Reports, Menyamya Report 4.

Ingemann, Frances. 1997. Ipili Dictionary. Typescript.

Ingold, Tim. 1996. Hunting and Gathering as Ways of Perceiving the Environment. In *Redefining Nature: Ecology, Culture, and Domestication*, ed. Roy Ellen and Katsuyoshi Fukui, 117–55. Oxford: Berg.

Jaarsma, Sjoerd R. 1993. Women's Roles in Ritual: (Re)Constructing Gender Images in the Dutch Ethnography of the Southern New Guinea Lowlands (1950–1965). *Canberra Anthropology* 16 (1): 15–35.

Jeudy-Ballini, Monique. 1999. Dédommager le désir: Le prix de l'émotion en Nouvelle-Bretagne (Papouasie Nouvelle-Guinée). *Terrain* 32: 5–20.

Jolly, Margaret. 1994. *Women of the Place: Kastom, Colonialism, and Gender in Vanuatu.* Chur, Switzerland: Harwood.

Josephides, Lisette. 1985. *The Production of Inequality: Gender and Exchange Among the Kewa.* London: Tavistock.

———. 1991. Metaphors, Metathemes, and the Construction of Sociality: A Critique of the New Melanesian Ethnography. *Man* 26: 145–61.

Juillerat, Bernard. 1993. Des fantasmes originaires aux symboles culturels: Médiations et seuils. *Revue Française de Psychanalyse* 3: 713–31.

———. 1996. *Children of the Blood.* Oxford: Berg. Trans. from *Les enfants du sang: Société, reproduction et imaginaire en Nouvelle-Guinée.* Paris: Éditions de la Maison des Sciences de l'Homme, 1986.

Keesing, Roger M. 1982. Introduction. In *Rituals of Manhood: Male Initiation in Papua New Guinea*, ed. Gilbert H. Herdt, 1–43. Berkeley: University of California Press.

Kelly, Raymond C. 1976. Witchcraft and Sexual Relations: An Exploration in the Social and Semantic Implications of the Structure of Belief. In *Man and Woman in the New Guinea Highlands*, ed. Paula Brown and Georgeda Buchbinder, 36–53. AAA Special Publication 8. Washington, D.C.: American Anthropological Association.

———. 1993. *Constructing Inequality: The Fabrication of a Hierarchy of Virtue Among the Etoro.* Ann Arbor: University of Michigan Press.

Knauft, Bruce M. 1985. *Good Company and Violence: Sorcery and Social Action in a Lowland New Guinea Society.* Berkeley: University of California Press.

————. 1986. Text and Social Practice: Narrative "Longing" and Bisexuality Among the Gebusi of New Guinea. *Ethos* 14: 252–81.

————. 1987. Homosexuality in Melanesia. *Journal of Psychoanalytic Anthropology* 10: 155–91.

————. 1989. Imagery, Pronouncement, and the Aesthetics of Reception in Gebusi Spirit Mediumship. In *The Religious Imagination in New Guinea*, ed. Gilbert H. Herdt and Michele Stephen, 67–98. New Brunswick, N.J.: Rutgers University Press.

————. 1993. *South Coast New Guinea Cultures: History, Comparison, Dialectic*. Cambridge: Cambridge University Press.

————. 1996. *Genealogies for the Present in Cultural Anthropology*. New York: Routledge.

————. 1997a. Theoretical Currents in Late Modern Cultural Anthropology: Toward a Conversation. *Cultural Dynamics* 9: 277–300.

————. 1997b. Gender Identity, Political Economy, and Modernity in Melanesia and Amazonia. *Journal of the Royal Anthropological Institute* 3: 233–59.

————. 1999. *From Primitive to Postcolonial in Melanesia and Anthropology*. Ann Arbor: University of Michigan Press.

————. 2002a. Trials of the Oxymodern: Public Practice at Nomad Station. In *Critically Modern: Alterities, Alternatives, Anthropologies*, ed. Bruce M. Knauft, 105–43. Bloomington: Indiana University Press.

————. 2002b. *Exchanging the Past: A Rainforest World of Before and After*. Chicago: University of Chicago Press.

————. 2004. *The Gebusi: Lives Transformed in a Rainforest World*. New York: McGraw-Hill.

————. In press. What Ever Happened to Ritual Homosexuality?: Modern Sexual Subjects in Melanesia and Elsewhere. *Annual Review of Sex Research*.

Kumbon, Daniel. 1998. *Climbing Mountains*. Sydney: Oxford University Press.

Kyakas, Alome and Polly Wiessner. 1992. *From Inside the Women's House: Enga Women's Lives and Traditions*. Brisbane: Robert Brown.

Lacey, Roderic. 1975. Oral Tradition as History: An Exploration of Oral Sources Among the Enga of the New Guinea Highlands. Ph.D. dissertation, University of Wisconsin.

La Fontaine, Jean S. 1985. *Initiation: Ritual Drama and Secret Knowledge Across the World*. Harmondsworth: Penguin.

Lambek, Michael. 1992. Taboo as Cultural Practice Among Malagasy Speakers. *Man* 27: 245–66.

Langness, Lewis L. 1967. Sexual Antagonism in the New Guinea Highlands: A Bena Bena Example. *Oceania* 37 (3): 161–77.

————. 1974. Ritual, Power, and Male Dominance. *Ethos* 2: 189–212.

————. 1999. *Men and "Woman" in New Guinea*. Novato, Calif.: Chandler and Sharp.

Lattas, Andrew. 1989. Trickery and Sacrifice: Tambarans and the Appropriation of Female Reproductive Powers in Male Initiation Ceremonies in West New Britain. *Man* 24 (3): 451–69.

Leacock, Eleanor. 1981. *Myths of Male Dominance: Collected Articles on Women Cross-Culturally*. New York: Monthly Review Press.

Lederman, Rena. 1986. *What Gifts Engender: Social Relations and Politics in Mendi, Highland Papua New Guinea*. Cambridge: Cambridge University Press.

Lemonnier, Pierre. 1981. Le commerce inter-tribal des Anga de Nouvelle-Guinée. *Journal de la Société des Océanistes* 37: 39–75.

————. 1982. Les jardins Anga (Nouvelle-Guinée). *Journal d'agriculture traditionnelle et de botanique appliquée* 29 (3–4): 227–45.

————. 1984a. L'écorce battue chez les Anga de Nouvelle-Guinée. *Techniques et culture* 4: 127–75.

————. 1984b. La production de sel végétal chez les Anga (Papouasie-Nouvelle-Guinée). *Journal d'agriculture traditionnelle et de botanique appliquée* 31 (1–2): 71–126.

————. 1990. *Guerres et festins: Paix, échanges, et compétition dans les Highlands de Nouvelle-Guinée*. Paris: Éditions de la Maison des Sciences de l'Homme.

————. 1991. From Great Men to Big Men: Peace, Substitution and Competition in the Highlands of New Guinea. In *Big Men and Great Men: Personifications of Power in Melanesia*, ed. Maurice Godelier and Marilyn Strathern, 7–27. Cambridge: Cambridge University Press.

————. 1992. Couper-coller: Attaques corporelles et cannibalisme chez les Anga de Nouvelle-Guinée. *Terrain* 18: 87–94.

————. 1993a. The Eel and the Ankave-Anga of Papua New Guinea: Material and Symbolic Aspects of Trapping. In *Tropical forests, People, and Food: Biocultural Interactions and Applications to Development*, ed. Claude-Marcel Hladik, Annette Hladik, Olga F. Linares, Hélène Pagezy, A. Semple, and Malcolm Hadley, 673–82. Man and the Biosphere Series 13. Paris: UNESCO and Parthenon.

————. 1993b. Pigs as Ordinary Wealth: Technical Logic, Exchange, and Leadership in New Guinea. In *Technological Choices: Transformation in Material Cultures Since the Neolithic*, ed. Pierre Lemonnier, 126–56. London: Routledge.

————. 1998a. "Mipela wan bilas": Identité et variabilité socioculturelle chez les Anga de Papouasie-Nouvelle-Guinée. In *Le Pacifique-Sud aujourd'hui: Identités et transformations culturelles*, ed. Serge Tcherkézoff and Françoise Douaire-Marsaudon. Paris: CNRS Ethnologie. 197–227.

————. 1998b. Showing the Invisible: Violence and Politics Among the Ankave-Anga (Gulf Province, Papua New Guinea). In *Common Worlds and Single Lives: Constituting Knowledge in Pacific Societies*, ed. Verena Keck, 287–307. Oxford: Berg.

————. 2002. Women and Wealth in New Guinea. In *People and Things: Social Mediations in Oceania*, ed. Monique Jeudy-Ballini and Bernard Juillerat, 103–21. Durham: Carolina Academic Press.

————. n.d. La mémoire de l'os ou les vacances de Monsieur Soleil: À propos de deux objets sacrés anga (Papouasie Nouvelle-Guinée). Typescript.

Lévi-Strauss, Claude. 1963. *Totemism*. Boston: Beacon Press. Trans. from *Le totémisme aujourd'hui*. Paris: PUF, 1962.

————. 1986. *The Savage Mind*. Chicago: University of Chicago Press. Trans. from *La pensée sauvage*. Paris: Plon 1962.

Lewis, Gilbert. 1980. *Day of Shining Red: An Essay on Understanding Ritual*. Cambridge: Cambridge University Press.

Lidz, Ruth W. and Theodore Lidz. 1977. Male Menstruation: A Ritual Alternative to the Oedipal Transition, *International Journal of Psycho-Analysis* 58: 17–31.

Lindenbaum, Shirley. 1972. Sorcerers, Ghosts, and Polluting Women: An Analysis of Religious Belief and Population Control. *Ethnology* 11: 241–53.

————. 1984. Variations on a Sociosexual Theme in Melanesia. In *Ritualized Homosexuality in Melanesia*, ed. Gilbert H. Herdt, 337–61. Berkeley: University of California Press.

————. 1987. The Mystification of Female Labors. In *Gender and Kinship: Essays Toward a Unified Analysis*, ed. Jane F. Collier and Sylvia J. Yanagisako, 221–43. Stanford, Calif.: Stanford University Press.

Lipset, David. 1997. *Mangrove Man: Dialogics of Culture in the Sepik Estuary*. Cambridge: Cambridge University Press.

LiPuma, Edward. 1998. Modernity and Forms of Personhood in Melanesia. In *Bodies and Persons: Comparative Perspectives from Africa and Melanesia*, ed. Michael Lambek and Andrew Strathern, 53–79. Cambridge: Cambridge University Press.

Lutkehaus, Nancy C. 1995. Feminist Anthropology and Female Initiation in Melanesia. In *Gender Rituals: Female Initiation in Melanesia*, ed. Nancy C. Lutkehaus and Paul B. Roscoe, 3–29. New York: Routledge.

Lutkehaus, Nancy C. and Paul B. Roscoe, eds. 1995. *Gender Rituals: Female Initiation in Melanesia*. New York: Routledge.

Malcolm, Lawrence A. 1968. Determination of the Growth Curve of the Kukukuku People of New Guinea from Dental Eruption in Children and Adult Height. *Archaeology and Physical Anthropology in Oceania* 4: 72–78.

McCarthy, J. K. 1964. *Patrol into Yesterday: My New Guinea Years*. London: Angus and Robertson.

Mead, Margaret. 1935. *Sex and Temperament in Three Primitive Societies*. New York: Dutton.

———. 1938. *The Mountain Arapesh*. Vol. 1, *An Importing Culture*. Anthropological Papers 36, Part 3. New York: American Museum of Natural History.

———. 1949. *Male and Female: A Study of the Sexes in a Changing World*. New York: Morrow.

Meggitt, Mervyn J. 1964. Male-Female Relationships in the Highlands of Australian New Guinea. In *New Guinea: The Central Highlands*, ed. James B. Watson. *American Anthropologist* 66 (4): 204–24 (special issue).

———. 1965a. *The Lineage System of the Mae-Enga of New Guinea*. New York: Barnes and Noble.

———. 1965b. The Mae Enga of the Western Highlands. In *Gods, Ghosts and Men in Melanesia*, ed. Peter Lawrence and Mervyn J. Meggitt, 105–31. Melbourne: Oxford University Press.

———. 1972. System and Sub-System: The "Te" Exchange Cycle Among the Mae Enga. *Human Ecology* 1: 111–23.

———. 1974. "Pigs Are Our Hearts!" The Te Exchange Cycle Among the Mae Enga of New Guinea. *Oceania* 44: 165–203.

———. 1976. A Duplicity of Demons: Sexual and Familial Roles Expressed in Western Enga Stories. In *Man and Woman in the New Guinea Highlands*, ed. Paula Brown and Georgeda Buchbinder, 63–85. Washington, D.C.: American Anthropological Association.

———. 1977. *Blood Is Their Argument: Warfare Among the Mae Enga Tribesmen of the New Guinea Highlands*. Palo Alto, Calif: Mayfield.

Meigs, Anna S. 1984. *Food, Sex and Pollution: A New Guinea Religion*. New Brunswick, N.J.: Rutgers University Press.

Merlan, Francesca and Alan Rumsey. 1991. *Ku Waru: Language and Segmentary Politics in the Western Nebilyer Valley, Papua New Guinea*. Cambridge: Cambridge University Press.

Milton, Kay. 1958. Male Bias in Anthropology. *Man* 14 (1): 40–54.

Mimica, Jadran. 1981. Omalyce: An Ethnography of the Iqwaye View of the Cosmos. Ph.D. dissertation, Australian National University.

———. 1988. *Intimations of Infinity: The Cultural Meanings of the Iqwaye Counting and Number System*. Oxford: Berg.

———. 1991a. The Incest Passions: An Outline of the Logic of the Iqwaye Social Organization (Part 1). *Oceania* 62 (1): 34–58.

———. 1991b. The Incest Passions: An Outline of the Logic of the Iqwaye Social Organization (Part 2). *Oceania* 62 (2): 81–113.

Modjeska, Charles Nicholas. 1977. Production Among the Duna. Ph.D. dissertation, Australian National University.

———. 1982. Production and Inequality: Perspectives from Central New Guinea. In

Inequality in New Guinea Highlands Societies, ed. Andrew Strathern, 50–108. Cambridge: Cambridge University Press.

Moisseeff, Marika. 1987. Entre maternité et procréation: L'inceste. *Patio Psychanalyse* 7: 121–45.

Moore, Henrietta L. 1988. *Feminism and Anthropology*. Cambridge: Polity Press.

———. 1994. *A Passion for Difference: Essays in Anthropology and Gender*. Bloomington: Indiana University Press.

Myers, Fred R. 1986. *Pintupi Country, Pintupi Self: Sentiment, Place, and Politics Among Western Desert Aborigines*. Berkeley: University of California Press.

Naouri, Aldo. 1994. Un inceste sans passage à l'acte: La relation mère-enfant. In *De l'inceste*, ed Françoise Héritier, Boris Cyrulnik, and Aldo Naouri, 73–128. Paris: Editions Odile Jacob.

Newman, Philip L. 1965. *Knowing the Gururumba*. New York: Holt, Rinehart and Winston.

Newman, Philip L. and David J. Boyd. 1982. The Making of Men: Ritual and Meaning in Awa Male Initiation. In *Rituals of Manhood: Male Initiation in Papua New Guinea*, ed. Gilbert H. Herdt, 239–86. Berkeley: University of California Press.

Nicholson, Linda J., ed. 1990. *Feminism/Postmodernism*. London: Routledge.

Nunguye Kandavatche, K. 1997. Personal Communication.

Oosterwal, Gottfried. 1976. The Role of Women in the Male Cults of the Soromaja in New Guinea. In *The Realm of the Extra-Human: Agents and Audiences*, ed. Agehananda Bharati, 323–34. The Hague: Mouton.

Ortner, Sherry and Harriet Whitehead. 1981. *Sexual Meanings: The Cultural Construction of Gender and Sexuality*. Cambridge: Cambridge University Press.

Panoff, Michel. 1998. L'âme double chez les Maenge (Nouvelle-Bretagne). In *La production du corps: Approches anthropologiques et historiques*, ed. Maurice Godelier and Michel Panoff, 39–61. Paris: Editions des Archives contemporaines.

Pori, B. 1978. The Sangai and the Bachelor. *Oral History* 6/5, 2: 76–95.

Read, Kenneth E. 1952. Nama Cult of the Central Highlands, New Guinea. *Oceania* 23: 1–25.

———. 1954. Cultures of the Central Highlands, New Guinea. *Southwestern Journal of Anthropology* 10 (1): 1–43.

———. 1965. *The High Valley*. London: Allen and Unwin.

Reay, Marie. 1992. An Innocent in the Garden of Eden. In *Ethnographic Presents: Pioneering Anthropologists in the Papua New Guinea Highlands*, ed. Terence E. Hays, 137–66. Berkeley: University of California Press.

Reiter, Rayna Rapp. 1975. *Toward an Anthropology of Women*. New York: Monthly Review Press.

Rival, Laura. 1998. Trees, from Symbols of Life and Regeneration to Political Artefacts. In *The Social Life of Trees: Anthropological Perspectives on Tree Symbolism*, ed. Laura Rival, 1–36. Oxford: Berg.

Rohatynskyj, Marta. 1978. Sex Affiliation Among the Ömie of Papua New Guinea. PhD dissertation, University of Toronto.

———. 1990. The Larger Context of Ömie Sex Affiliation. *Man* 25: 434–53.

———. 1997. Culture, Secrets, and Ömie History: A Consideration of the Politics of Cultural Identity. *American Ethnologist* 24 (2): 438–56.

———. 1998. Solicited and Unsolicited History: The Transformation in Ömie Self-Presentation. *Oceania* 69 (2): 81–93.

Rosaldo, Michelle Z. and Louise L. Lamphere, eds. 1974. *Women, Culture, and Society*. Stanford, Calif.: Stanford University Press.

Roscoe, Paul B. 1990. Male Initiation Among the Yangoru Boiken. In *Sepik Heritage:*

Tradition and Change in Papua New Guinea, ed. Nancy Lutkehaus et al., 402–13. Bathurst, NSW: Crawford House Press.

Roscoe, Paul B. 1995. "Initiation" in Cross-Cultural Perspective. In *Gender Rituals: Female Initiation in Melanesia*, ed. Nancy C. Lutkehaus and Paul B. Roscoe, 219–38. New York: Routledge.

Salisbury, Richard F. 1965. The Siane of the Eastern Highlands. In *Gods, Ghosts and Men in Melanesia: Some Religions of Australian New Guinea and the New Hebrides*, ed. Peter Lawrence and Mervyn J. Meggitt, 50–77. Melbourne: Oxford University Press.

Sanday, Peggy R. 1981. *Female Power and Male Dominance: On the Origins of Sexual Inequality*. Cambridge: Cambridge University Press.

Schieffelin, Edward L. 1976. *The Sorrow of the Lonely and the Burning of the Dancers*. New York: St. Martin's Press.

————. 1977. The Unseen Influence: Tranced Mediums as Historical Innovators. *Journal de la Société des Océanistes* 33: 168–78.

————. 1982. The *Bau A*. A Ceremonial Hunting Lodge. In *Rituals of Manhood: Male Initiation in Papua New Guinea*, ed. Gilbert H. Herdt. Berkeley: University of California Press. 155–200.

Schwab, John. 1995. The Sandalu Bachelor Ritual Among the Laiapu Enga (Papua New Guinea). *Anthropos* 90: 27–47.

Schwimmer, Erik. 1984. Male Couples in New Guinea. In *Ritualized Homosexuality in Melanesia*, ed. Gilbert H. Herdt, 292–317. Berkeley: University of California Press.

Shapiro, Warren. 1996. Introduction. In *Denying Biology: Essays on Gender and Pseudo-Procreation*, ed. Warren Shapiro and Uli Linke, 1–25. Lanham, Md.: University Press of America.

Sillitoe, Paul. 1979. *Give and Take: Exchange in Wola Society*. Canberra: Australian National University Press.

————. 1985. Divide and No-One Rules: The Implications of Sexual Division of Labor in the New Guinea Highlands. *Man* 20: 494–522.

Simpson, Colin. 1953. *Adam with Arrows: Inside New Guinea*. Sydney: Angus and Robertson.

Sinclair, James. 1966. *Behind the Ranges*. London: Cambridge University Press.

Sørum, Arve. 1980. In Search of the Lost Soul: Bedamini Spirit Seances and Curing Rites. *Oceania* 50: 273–96.

————. 1982. The Seeds of Power: Patterns in Bedamini Male Initiation. *Social Analysis* 10: 42–62.

Spiro, Melford E. 1968. Virgin Birth, Parthenogenesis and Physiological Paternity: An Essay in Cultural Interpretation. *Man* 3 (2): 242–61.

Stewart, Pamela J. 1998. Ritual Trackways and Sacred Paths of Fertility. In *Perspectives on the Bird's Head of Irian Jaya, Indonesia: Proceedings of the Conference, Leiden 13–17 October 1997*, ed. Jelle Miedema, Cecilia Ode, and Rien Dam, 275–89. Amsterdam: Rodopi.

Stewart, Pamela J. and Andrew Strathern. 1997. Sorcery and Sickness: Spatial and Temporal Movements in Papua New Guinea and Australia. *Centre for Pacific Studies Discussion Papers Series* 1: 1–27. School of Anthropology and Archaeology, James Cook University of North Queensland.

————. 1998. Female Spirit Cults in Highlands New Guinea: Gendered Collaboration and Division. Okari Research Group Working Paper 7. Department of Anthropology, University of Pittsburgh.

————. 1999a. Female Spirit Cults as a Window on Gender Relations in the Highlands of Papua New Guinea. *Journal of the Royal Anthropological Institute* 5 (3): 345–60.

————. 1999b. "Feasting on My Enemy": Images of Violence and Change in the New Guinea Highlands. *Ethnohistory* 46 (4): 645–69.

————. 1999c. "East Meets West": Comparisons of Indonesian and Melanesian Ethnographic Themes. *International Institute for Asian Studies Newsletter* 18: 28.

————. 2001. *Humors and Substances: Ideas of the Body in New Guinea*. Westport, Conn.: Bergen and Garvey, Greenwood.

————. 2002. *Remaking the World: Myth, Mining, and Ritual Change Among the Duna*. Washington, D.C.: Smithsonian Institution Press.

Strathern, Andrew J. 1970a. Male Initiation in New Guinea Highlands Societies. *Ethnology* 9 (4): 373–79.

————. 1970b. The Female and Male Spirit Cults in Mount Hagen. *Man* 5 (4): 571–85.

————. 1979. Men's House, Women's House: The Efficacy of Opposition, Reversal, and Pairing in the Melpa *Amb Kor* cult. *Journal of the Polynesian Society* 88: 37–51.

————, ed. 1982. *Inequality in New Guinea Highland Societies*. Cambridge: Cambridge University Press.

————. 1996. *Body Thoughts*. Ann Arbor: University of Michigan Press.

Strathern, Andrew J. and Pamela J. Stewart. 1997. The Efficacy-Entertainment Braid Revisited: From Ritual to Commerce in Papua New Guinea. *Journal of Ritual Studies* 11 (1): 61–70.

————. 1998a. Embodiment and Communication: Two Frames for the Analysis of Ritual. *Social Anthropology* 6 (2): 237–51.

————. 1998b. Melpa and Nuer Ideas of Life and Death: The Rebirth of a Comparison. *In Bodies and Persons: Comparative Perspectives from Africa and Melanesia*, ed. Michael Lambek and Andrew Strathern, 232–51. Cambridge: Cambridge University Press.

————. 1999a. *"The Spirit Is Coming!" A Photographic-Textual Exposition of the Female Spirit Cult Performance in Mt. Hagen*. Ritual Studies Monograph Series 1. Pittsburgh: Department of Anthropology, University of Pittsburgh.

————. 1999b. *Curing and Healing: Medical Anthropology in Global Perspective*. Durham, N.C.: Carolina Academic Press.

————. 1999c. Water in Place: The Hagen and Duna People of Papua New Guinea. Okari Research Group Prepublication Working Paper 14: 1–19. Paper prepared for a collection edited by Mel Williams in honor of Arthur Tuden.

————. 1999d. Objects, Relationships, and Meanings: Historical Switches in Currencies in Mount Hagen, Papua New Guinea. In *Money and Modernity: State and Local Currencies in Melanesia*, ed. Joel Robbins and David Akin, 164–91. ASAO Monograph Series 17. Pittsburgh: University of Pittsburgh Press.

————. 2000a. *Arrow Talk: Transaction, Transition, and Contradiction in New Guinea Highlands History*. Kent, Ohio: Kent State University Press.

————. 2000b. *The Python's Back: Pathways of Comparison Between Indonesia and Melanesia*. Westport, Conn.: Bergen and Garvey, Greenwood Press.

Strathern, Marilyn. 1972. *Women in Between: Female Roles in a Male World: Mount Hagen, New Guinea*. London: Seminar Press.

————. 1980. No Nature, No Culture: The Hagen Case. In *Nature, Culture, and Gender*, ed. Carol MacCormack and Marilyn Strathern, 174–223. New York: Cambridge University Press.

————. 1981a. Self-Interest and the Social Good: Some Implications of Hagen Gender Imagery. In *Sexual Meanings: The Cultural Construction of Gender and Sexuality*, ed. Sherry B. Ortner and Harriet Whitehead, 166–91. Cambridge: Cambridge University Press.

————. 1981b. Culture in a Netbag: The Manufacture of a Subdiscipline in Anthropology. *Man* 16: 665–88.

————. 1987. An Awkward Relationship: The Case of Feminism and Anthropology. *Signs* 12: 276–92.

————. 1988. *The Gender of the Gift: Problems with Women and Problems with Society in Melanesia.* Berkeley: University of California Press.

————. 1991. *Partial Connections.* ASAO Special Publications 3. Savage, Md.: Rowman and Littlefield.

————. 1993. Making Incomplete. In *Carved Flesh / Cast Selves: Gendered Symbols and Social Practices,* ed. Vigdis Broch-Due, Ingrid Rudie, and Tone Bleie, 41–51. Oxford: Berg.

Strauss, Hermann and Herbert Tischner. 1962. *Die Mi-Kultur der Hagenberg-Stämme.* Hamburg: Cram, de Gruyter.

Stürzenhofecker, Gabriele. 1995. Dialectics of History: Female Witchcraft and Male Dominance in Aluni. In *Papuan Borderlands: Huli, Duna, and Ipili Perspectives on the Papua New Guinea Highlands,* ed. Aletta Biersack, 287–313. Ann Arbor: University of Michigan Press.

Talyaga, Kundapen K. 1982. The Enga Yesterday and Today: A Personal Account. In *Enga Yaaka Lasemana,* vol. 3, *Enga: Foundations for Development,* ed. Bruce Carrad, David A. M. Lea, and Kundapen K. Talyaga, 59–75. Armidale: University of New England.

Thomas, Nicholas. 1995. *Oceanic Art.* London: Thames and Hudson.

Turner, Victor W. 1967a. Betwixt and Between: The Liminal Period in *Rites de passage.* In Turner, *The Forest of Symbols,* 93–111. Ithaca, N.Y.: Cornell University Press.

————. 1967b. *The Forest of Symbols: Aspects of Ndembu Ritual.* Ithaca, N.Y.: Cornell University Press.

Tuzin, Donald F. 1972. Yam Symbolism in the Sepik: An Interpretive Account. *Oceania* 28: 230–54.

————. 1980. *The Voice of the Tambaran: Truth and Illusion in Ilahita Arapesh Religion.* Berkeley: University of California Press.

————. 1995. Art and Procreative Illusion in the Sepik: Comparing the Abelam and the Arapesh. *Oceania* 65 (4): 289–303.

————. 1997. *The Cassowary's Revenge: The Life and Death of Masculinity in a New Guinea Society.* Chicago: University of Chicago Press.

Valeri, Valerio. 1985. *Kinship and Sacrifice: Ritual and Society in Ancient Hawaii.* Chicago: University of Chicago Press.

van Baal, Jan. 1966. *Dema: Description and Analysis of Marind-Anim Culture.* The Hague: Nijhoff.

van Gennep, Arnold. 1960. *The Rites of Passage.* Chicago: University of Chicago Press. Trans. from *Les rites de passage.* Paris: Picard, 1909.

————. 1981 (1909). *Les rites de passage.* Paris: Picard.

Vicedom, Georg F. and Herbert Tischner. 1943–48. *Die Mbowamb.* 3 vols. Hamburg: Friederichsen, de Gruyter.

Waddell, Eric. 1972. *The Mound Builders: Agricultural Practices, Environment and Society in the Central Highlands of New Guinea.* Seattle: University of Washington Press.

Wagner, Roy. 1972. *Habu: The Innovation of Meaning in Daribi Religion.* Chicago: University of Chicago Press.

————. 1974. Are There Social Groups in the New Guinea Highlands? In *Frontiers of Anthropology: An Introduction to Anthropological Thinking,* ed. Murray Leaf, 95–122. New York: Van Nostrand.

————. 1975. *The Invention of Culture.* Chicago: University of Chicago Press.

————. 1977. Analogic Kinship: A Daribi Example. *American Ethnologist* 4 (4): 623–42.

Watson, James B. 1967. Tairora: The Politics of Despotism in a Small Society. *Anthropological Forum* 2: 53–104.

————. 1983. *Tairora Culture: Contingency and Pragmatism*. Seattle: University of Washington Press.

Weiner, Annette B. 1976. *Women of Value, Men of Renown: New Perspectives in Trobriand Exchange*. Austin: University of Texas Press.

————. 1980. Reproduction: A Replacement for Reciprocity. *American Ethnologist* 7: 71–85.

————. 1982. Sexuality Among the Anthropologists, Reproduction Among the Informants. In *Sexual Antagonism, Gender, and Social Change in Papua New Guinea*, ed. Fitz John Porter Poole and Gilbert H. Herdt. *Social Analysis* (special issue) 12: 52–65.

————. 1992. *Inalienable Possessions: The Paradox of Keeping-While-Giving*. Berkeley: University of California Press.

Whitehead, Harriet. 1986a. The Varieties of Fertility Cultism in New Guinea, Part I. *American Ethnologist* 13 (1): 80–99.

————. 1986b. The Varieties of Fertility Cultism in New Guinea, Part II. *American Ethnologist* 13 (2): 271–89.

Whiting, John W. M., Robert Kluckhohn, and Albert Anthony. 1961. The Function of Male Initiation Ceremonies at Puberty. In *Readings in Social Psychology*, ed. Eleanor E. Maccoby, Theodore M. Newcomb, and Eugene H. Hartley, 359–70. New York: Holt.

Wiessner, Polly. 1999. Of Human and Spirit Women: From Mother to Lover to Second Wife. Paper given at the annual meeting of the Association of Social Anthropologists of Oceania, Hilo, Hawai'i, February.

————. 2001. Of Feasting and Value: Enga Feasts in a Historical Perspective. In *Feasts: Archaeological and ethnographic Perspectives in Food, Politics and Power*, ed. Michael Dietler and Brian Hayden, 115–43. Washington: Smithsonian Institution Press.

Wiessner, Polly and Akii Tumu. 1998. *Historical Vines: Enga Networks of Exchange, Ritual, and Warfare in Papua New Guinea*. Washington, D.C.: Smithsonian Institution Press.

Williams, Francis E. 1925. Plant Emblems Among the Orokaiva. *Journal of the Royal Anthropological Institute* 55: 405–24.

————. 1932. Sex Affiliation and Its Implications. *Journal of the Royal Anthropological Institute* 63: 51–81.

————. 1944. Mission Influence Amongst the Keveri of South-East Papua. *Oceania* 15: 89–141.

Wohlt, Paul B. 1978. Ecology, Agriculture and Social Organization: The Dynamics of Group Composition in the Highlands of New Guinea. Ph.D. dissertation, University of Minnesota.

Zegwaard, Gerard A. 1955. Primitieve verbroederings ceremonieën. *Nederlands Nieuw Guinea* 3 (5): 4–5; 3 (7): 10–11.

Contributors

Sandra C. Bamford teaches in the Department of Anthropology, University of Toronto. Her work has focused on issues relating to gender, kinship, ritual, embodiment, and indigenous conceptions of the landscapes. In addition to publishing in these areas her most recent research examines the spread of Western environmentalist agendas into the Pacific and their implications for emerging forms of political agency.

Aletta Biersack does research among the Ipili-speakers of the Paiela and Porgera valleys. In addition to writing many journal articles and book chapters, she is the editor of *Clio in Oceania: Toward a Historical Anthropology*, *Papuan Borderlands: Huli, Duna, and Ipili Perspectives on the Papua New Guinea Highlands*; and "Ecologies for Tomorrow: Reading Rappaport Today." which appeared in the *American Anthropologist*. Among other writing projects, she is presently finishing *Imagining Political Ecology*, coedited with James Greenberg.

Pascale Bonnemère, a member of the CREDO (Centre de Recherche et de Documentation sur l'Océanie) team based in Marseilles, holds a research position at the Centre National de la Recherche Scientifique (CNRS), and also teaches at the University of Provence and the École des Hautes Études en Sciences Sociales. She is engaged in long-term fieldwork among the Ankave-Anga of Papua New Guinea. Her main subjects of interest are life cycle exchanges and rituals, personhood, and gender, on which she has published articles and the monograph, *Le pandanus rouge: Corps, differences des sexes et parenté chez les Ankave-Anga*.

Gilbert Herdt, a cultural anthropologist, is Director of Human Sexuality Studies and Professor of Human Sexuality and Anthropology and now Director of the National Sexuality Resource Center, a Ford Foundation funded project, at San Francisco State University. He earned a Ph.D. at Australian National University in 1978 in anthropology for a study of the Sambia of Papua New Guinea. He has conducted 13 field trips, for a total of more than three years fieldwork among the Sambia between 1974 and 1993. Among his honors, he has been awarded a Fulbright scholarship to Australia, an Individual NIMH Postdoctoral Fellowship at UCLA, and a Guggenheim Fellowship. He has taught at Stanford University, the University of Chicago (where he was a professor and chair of the Committee on Human Development), and occasionally at the University of Amsterdam. He has authored many books and papers, including *Guardians of the Flutes: Idioms of Masculinity*; *Same-Sex, Different Cultures: Gays and Lesbians Across Cultures*; *Sambia Sex Culture: Essays from the Field*; and *Secrecy and Cultural Reality: Utopian Ideologies of the New Guinea Men's House*.

Bruce M. Knauft is Samuel C. Dobbs Professor of Anthropology at Emory University. Author of seven books and numerous journal articles and chapters, his research focuses on the political economy of subjectivity, change, and crisis. His recent books include *Exchanging the Past: A Rainforest World of Before and After* and an edited collection entitled *Critically Modern: Alternatives, Alterities, Anthropologies*.

Pierre Lemonnier is a Director of research at the Centre de Recherche et de Documentation sur l'Océanie (CREDO, Marseilles) and teaches at the University of Provence. After repeated field research from 1978 to 1982 among the various Anga people of Papua New Guinea, he chose an Ankave valley, to which he regularly returns, for long-term anthropological fieldwork. He has published several books on the anthropology of technical systems, among which *Elements for an Anthropology of Technology*; *Technological Choices: Transformation in Material Cultures Since the Neolithic*; and, on Melanesia, *Guerres et festins: Paix, échanges et compétition dans les Highlands de Nouvelle-Guinée*, as well as numerous articles. He just finished a book on witchcraft, mortuary rituals, and forgetting among the Ankave (*Le Sabbat des lucioles*). His other fields of interest are the interpretation of the Ankave male initiations and the comparative study of Anga cultures.

Marta A. Rohatynskj is Associate Professor in the Department of Sociology and Anthropology at the University of Guelph, Ontario. She has published on her long-term research among the Ömie of Oro Province and is currently researching regional identity systems among peoples of the south coast in East New Britain, Papua New Guinea.

Pamela J. Stewart and Andrew Strathern are a husband and wife research team in the Department of Anthropology at the University of Pittsburg. They have published widely on their research in the Pacific, Europe, and Asia. Their recent co-authored books include *Witchcraft, Sorcery, Rumors, and Gossip*; *Remaking the World: Myth, Mining, and Ritual Change Among the Duna of Papua New Guinea*; and *Arrow Talk: Transaction, Transition, and Contradiction in New Guinea Highlands*

History. Stewart and Strathern serve as series editors for the "Ethnographic Studies in Medical Anthropology Series" with Carolina Academic Press. Stewert and Strathern's webpage, listing further publications and other scholarly activities, is http://www.pitt.edu/~strather/.

Andrew Strathern and Pamela J. Stewart are a husband and wife research team in the Department of Anthropology at the University of Pittsburg. They have published widely on their research in the Pacific, Europe, and Asia. Their recent co-authored books include *Minorities and Memories: Survivals and Extinctions in Scotland and Western Europe*; *Violence: Theory and Ethnography*; and *Gender, Song, and Sensibility: Folktales and Folksongs in the Highlands of New Guinea*. Strathern and Stewart coedit the *Journal of Ritual Studies* and they are series editors for the "Ritual Studies Monograph Series" with Carolina Academic Press. Stewart and Strathern's webpage, listing further publications and other scholarly activities, is http://www.pitt.edu/~strather/.

Polly Wiessner is a Research Professor at the University of Utah. She is carrying out long-term fieldwork among the !Kung Bushmen of the Kalahari Desert on demography, subsistence, and exchange and among the Enga of Papua New Guinea on precolonial ethnohistory. She has published numerous articles on the Bushmen and two books together with Enga authors, *Historical Vines: Enga Networks of Exchange, Ritual, and Warfare in Papua New Guinea* (with Akii Tumu) and *From Inside the Women's House: Enga Women's Lives and Traditions* (with Alome Kyakas).

Index

Acknowledgments

The collective reflection that has resulted in the present volume enjoyed the support of many individuals and institutions without which a publishable document would never have seen the light of day. I would like to begin by thanking those who took part in the workshops I organized on two occasions, first with Gilbert Herdt in 1998 and then by myself the following year. I hope the outcome will not disappoint them. Gilbert Herdt deserves special mention because I am not sure that, without his encouragement and support, I would have found the confidence to take on such a project. I would also like to thank the members of the bureau of the Association for Social Anthropology in Oceania for their warm welcome and their highly efficient logistical support, with a special thought for Jan Rensel and Michele Dominy. My trips to Pensacola and to Hilo were paid for respectively by the French Centre National de la Recherche Scientifique and the Ministry of Foreign Affairs. The Centre de Recherche et de Documentation sur l'Océanie (CREDO) funded the translation of the Introduction as well as the copy editing of the entire volume. A special thank-you to Nora Scott, and not only because she is a talented translator.

I am very grateful to Bruce Knauft for agreeing to write the closing chapter of this volume and for assisting me all the way. I greatly appreciated Polly Wiessner's helpful and friendly presence in Hilo. And I am also indebted to Paul Roscoe, who, having coedited a book on a closely related subject, kindly shared his experience with me.

Among the participants in the Pensacola and Hilo workshops, I do not want to forget those who do not actually appear in this volume, either because they did not express the desire to do so or because they were discussants. Maurice Godelier and Dan Jorgensen officially ensured this role for the 1998 workshop, and their comments not only were a great help in getting on with our articles, but also provided impetus for the collective reflection.

That same year, Gillian Gillison, Eric Silverman, and Holly Wardlow presented contributions whose innovative problematics made an important contribution. In 1999, Margaret Jolly played a remarkable role as an enlightened, improvised discussant; it was as I was transcribing the discussion tapes that I realized her crucial input, for which I am retrospectively most grateful. I would also like to thank Chris Ballard, who provided me with bibliographical information and read my introduction, thus enabling me make a number of improvements. The anonymous comments of two referees were also of great help in fine tuning the theoretical aspect of the Introduction.